T0159126

LITTLE PAPERS ARE JOURNALISM TOO

Kathleen Hoffman

authorHOUSE®

AuthorHouse™
1663 Liberty Drive
Bloomington, IN 47403
www.authorhouse.com
Phone: 1 (800) 839-8640

Published by AuthorHouse 09/18/2018

ISBN: 978-1-5462-5707-3 (sc)
ISBN: 978-1-5462-5706-6 (e)

Library of Congress Control Number: 2018910057

Print information available on the last page.

CONTENTS

CHAPTER ONE
That Brief December Day

The December day was more than half a century ago, questionable chronological territory for someone whose memory is suspect, but it's whole and vivid in my aging mind—the blowing bits of paper, the swirling dust. That's because it was one of those milestones, a time when I knew it was the first day of the rest of my life and all the rest, new beginning, unlimited horizons, the great unknown.

Actually, it had advanced quite a few hours into the first day of that new life when I reported to begin what I saw as my calling: my first newspaper job. It was 2:40 p.m., twenty minutes before the official starting time of the workday, and the horizons showed unmistakable signs of limits.

Was it really a good sign that I was awaiting the theoretically momentous beginning of major changes and developments, standing by myself on a dingy side street in Culpeper, Virginia (population in the neighborhood of 2,500), outside a tightly locked-up and rather shabby-looking building? A building that had once been a Safeway store? And was it necessary for quite so much debris to be kicked up by the wind? Or more specifically, for there to be that much debris to kick up?

Across the big plate-glass window of the building, in dark letters not easily read against scruffy, dark-green shades that were pulled down and sagging, it said CULPEPER STAR-EXPONENT. As of that day, Sunday, December 11, 1966, I was a reporter for the *Star-Exponent*, the person who would be expected to spend an unknown amount of time and energy learning about and understanding a small Virginia town, its identity, its political underpinnings, its place in the world and where it was going and maybe why – and then write about it so readers would learn with me. Who knew whether I could do this, or even why I thought it was a worthwhile thing to do?

I'd had in mind being a journalist since I was a sophomore at Albemarle County High School near Charlottesville, and a teacher asked our class what we planned to do. I really hadn't much idea, but when Teresa Crenshaw said firmly that she was going to be a journalist I figured it was good enough for me. Teresa was absolutely a "cool kid," in the current sense of the term, plus she was sensible. So, following her lead—although not until a seemingly endless six years later, after high school and four years at a liberal-arts college, a couple of months of unsuccessful applications to bigger papers and four months of an aghast reaction to the only job I could get, at a federal defense supply center—I was finally ready to give it a shot.

Actually, when I think about it, I was doing surprisingly well so far on what could loosely be called my career path. My parents, a union pipe fitter and a secretary, had always planned that my older brother, David, should go to college, and he did, and went on to get a master's degree and become an electrical engineer. He was in fact the first person on either side of our family to go to college, and I was the second. But that was only after a high school guidance counselor pointed out to my parents that even though I was a girl, I would benefit from a higher education. My mother had always assumed that if I went to college it would be on my way to becoming a nun, but as disappointing as it was for her . . .

Anyway, I was going to be a journalist, although thus far I had generally been shy and reserved. And also never mind that the day before, while I was returning to the home where I grew up near Charlottesville after moving a Volkswagen load of belongings to a tiny rented house in Culpeper, I had passed a car on fire in front of, oddly enough, the current Safeway building on Main Street. There was help on the scene, firemen and cops, lots going on, but I sort of ducked and kept on my way. I wasn't a reporter yet, I told myself. But I think that was the only fire I was to drive away from in the next seventeen years. I did come to enjoy the adrenaline rush of a fire—the heroics, the excitement, even the fear.

Which brings me very quickly to my attitude toward news. In my job, I really was a set of eyes and ears for others, and I didn't often react on a personal level to what was happening, good or bad. Part of my detachment, no doubt, was the insensitivity of youth, and part was a determination to do what I was supposed to do even when it was boring or frightening or even grisly—which it sometimes was. I was on hand for each meeting of the Culpeper County Board of Supervisors, every noteworthy traffic accident, and even a horrible incident in the darkness during which cattle were flung off a railway trestle by a speeding train, and my feelings were seldom involved in any of it.

At any rate, from early on I didn't think about how I could be the person being taken out of the wrecked car by the rescue squad, and I didn't feel much disagreement with or support for any given member of the board of supervisors (generally speaking.) Culpeper's governing bodies, the supervisors who made county decisions and the separate town council, were fairly unified in those years and hesitated to disagree in public, so generally there was little contention to be covered.

The cattle deaths that I wrote about didn't seem particularly real to me, or bring tears. Now an animal death or injury does me in. Just now and then, it would be nice to still approach the world the way I did in those days, but that will never happen again. Now that I am more than seventy years old, to me each tragedy is explosively real, each death equates to all deaths, and I not only know there is pain involved but feel it inescapably.

The detachment even increased as I adjusted to the work, but there wasn't much calm disinterest on that December day. It was pretty much all about me. I had moved into the thick of all things Culpeper, and had spent the night before in my newly rented digs on Main Street. It was 606 North Main, a tiny building that I was told had been the carriage house for Greenlawn, the home of the some of the Greens of widespread past and present rural newspaper fame. This was during a time when one or two people would establish a local paper, staff it with family, and keep it in that family for generations. There wasn't a lot of profit; needless to say, no conglomerates were waiting back then to seize those thin weekly papers and combine them in ever-growing mergers. The Greens did have several weeklies in area counties, and had owned one

3

of the current daily's predecessors, the *Exponent*, started in 1881 by Angus McDonald Green. A newspaper mostly meant visibility, a local voice and a way to influence thinking. Really, it was a form of power for not much investment.

My landlady was Ann Green Graves, who had put in her own time writing and editing on the *Exponent*, but who was now retired and married to a very old and very marvelous veterinarian. The big house had been subdivided into a number of apartments, and it and the little brick building where I lived absolutely reverberated with history; it was said that a Green son had at one time inhabited the erstwhile carriage house, and was a mainstay of one of the papers. When the weekly cycle rolled around, he and/or Ann or someone had always managed to get it done.

My dwelling had an upstairs and a downstairs, a kitchen, and two bathrooms. I felt strongly that it was an appropriate spot for me, and that I was carrying on a tradition when I headed up the street to the office. My location did require me to sleep next to a wall that was only feet away from a busy shop that did car repairs and body work, but the noise never bothered me at all, even when I slept in after a late night.

The Green house was just a few blocks from the *Star-Exponent* office, but I drove my less-than-reliable VW to work that first day so I would be poised to go out and cover something. My introduction to the news biz felt pretty intimidating as I stood in my neat, professional, but not very warm dress outside the building. When my new boss, Bill Diehl, showed up about ten minutes past three (official working hours on the five-days-a-week paper were 3 p.m. to midnight, Sunday through Thursday), he made a perfunctory excuse for his lateness, opened the door, and showed me my desk. It wasn't in an office or a cubicle; it was half of an ancient partners desk, with him maybe six feet away on the opposite side. The setup streamlined our communication, I found, as he could easily toss rejected offerings back for me to redo, with a disparaging word or two mumbled around the ever-present cigarette or badly chewed cigar.

On that Sunday the other reporter, a tall, somewhat somber man who might have been thirty-five or fifty, it was hard to tell then or remember now, meandered in even later than Bill had, and set out with me to show me his rounds. George Whaley had been there for a couple of years, but he and his wife had a new baby and new financial demands, so he was moving on to Baltimore for a better-paying job. I was to take his place.

I trailed after him that Sunday to the very small police station and the sheriff's office located in an ancient brick building across the lawn from what really was a glorious white-pillared courthouse. Weekdays, the rounds would include various courts and the town office. Also on George's regular beat were any Culpeper Town Council meetings that were scheduled, a daily telephone call to the state police for traffic accidents, and a check of fire calls that had been made that day by the all-volunteer department.

When we came back I was no longer noticing the blowing trash, the dark blinds, or even the scratched-up partners desk. I was busy thinking about walking into an actual county jail office every day, trying to get information out of a town police station where everyone seemed more or less incapable of speech beyond a grunt or two of greeting, and then coming back to sit across from Bill Diehl and type it up on a manual typewriter. I could do it, I told myself firmly, but it was a lot of pressure for someone who was an undeniable introvert.

Bill Diehl—like Mary Tyler Moore with "Mr. Grant," I would never call him anything but "Mr. Diehl"—was sort of Santa-shaped, smoked like a madman, and was easily sent into paroxysms of overwrought but temporary anger, leading to coughing fits from the aforementioned cigars. But despite a quickly flaring temper and a searing gift for sarcasm, he was a set of paradoxes that added up to a nice man. He had five children with his very Catholic wife, Dorothy, and spoke of each child with a caressing fondness that indicated each was his favorite (I never did figure out which one actually was). As far as I could tell, he had had very little in the way of extra funds for his whole working life supporting that large family, and he was as eager as the next newspaperman to be taken out to a free lunch by someone with ulterior motives.

Still, when he died many years later he left his legally blind wife apparently pretty secure. He was a soft touch for children and animals, sometimes writing about the family cat, Kitty-Boots, without embarrassment, and he was an unabashed sexist who nonetheless almost invariably treated me as an equal.

He had come to the *SE* in 1964 from the *Orlando Sentinel* in Florida. Before that he had operated radio stations in Florida and North Carolina. But most of his career had been with the papers in Norfolk, where he started while still in high school. He was a newsman, and the goal of his life was to uncover "a hell of a story" wherever it appeared, and tell it.

Undoubtedly he loved his profession; he also permitted no mistake to go unremarked on and promptly corrected, worked constantly and hard, and was an excellent teacher. Our pattern was set the first night— he would pull stories off the clicking Associated Press machine, write a head size in a penciled scrawl (say, 3/18/2, which meant a three-column head in 18-point type, with two lines). I would type up a suggested offering, say, "Vietcong Overrun U.S. Forces but Don't Get Far," clip it to the copy, and send it back to him. If he didn't like it, he'd say something brief, like "More specific on 'far,'" scrunch up his beetled and already graying eyebrows, and toss it back. I'd rewrite it, repeat the handoff, and hope it wouldn't return again.

When he was satisfied he would send it back to the typesetters, then and for many years to come the very accurate and hardworking duo of Mary Payne and Margaret Long; they would type the story into a phototypesetter that would spit it out in a long column, and then set the headline in the required point size.

The *Star-Exponent* was only a few years past having used "hot type," set on a Linotype machine, and the new equipment was still prone to malfunctioning. Hyphenation was suspect, lines could be uneven, odd letters could jump above or below the rest of the sentence. The typeset copy came out on heavy, slick paper. An adhesive was applied to the back, and the copy was cut into strips and pasted down on a full-size page setup. The phototype machines were not good at kerning—varying the space between lines, or compacting or stretching a line so it would fit—and if the headline wasn't quite the right size, it had to be redone. The process stayed that way for most budget-conscious operations until I left newspapers, in 1992, to find that, OMG, you could do *all* of that by computer and that was in fact the way most papers were operating.

It wasn't fast, but it worked, and under Bill Diehl's leadership the paper was a tightly run ship, with everyone feeling very responsible for their part in the product. What was produced looks even more remarkable to me now, a half century later, than it did then—the daily paper was a reflection of the town and its place in the state and the nation. It was a mishmash of what was happening down the street, sixty miles away in Washington, D.C., and in Southeast Asia. Crowded into it were things to inform, amuse, mystify, and make people think and even hope.

The paper was owned by Walter B. Potter, a man with a past full of accomplishments well beyond little Culpeper. He had spent five years as civilian aide to the secretary of the army in World War II, and ended as a major. During the war he spent two and a half years overseas as liaison officer with the British 78th Division, and had been awarded a Bronze Star, a Combat Infantry Badge, two invasion arrowheads, and five battle stars. He didn't go around saying this, mind, and I only learned it from biographical information published when he spoke publicly or ran for office.

A graduate of Washington & Lee University, Potter had served as president of the Virginia Press Association and of the National Newspaper Association, and owned a number of small papers. He always wore a suit and tie, and never seemed be in any state that could be described as relaxed.

Potter had bought the *Culpeper Exponent* and the *Virginia Star*, the two local weeklies, and soon combined them into a five-days-a-week daily. At the high point of his newspaper involvement, Potter's remaining and scattered weeklies were incorporated as the Southwest Virginia Newspaper Corporation. They included the *Richlands News-Press* and the *Clinch Valley News*, but not the *Star-Exponent*. He took the provision of honest news, which was apparently very much his calling too, quite seriously, but rarely interfered with the daily running of things. He was an upright man who, as far as I could see, always came down on the moral and ethical side of things. But he was distant and demonstrated a personality that matched his military bearing.

He and his wife, Kay, had two sons. Walt Jr. was already producing the occasional story while he was still in high school, and Robert, an airplane enthusiast, contributed aerial photos for a big early story on a flood. Walt Jr. was to make his own considerable mark; a graduate of Vanderbilt University with a master's degree in journalism from the University of Missouri, he worked as a reporter and editor at various papers, and was publisher of the *Independent-Messenger* in Emporia, Virginia, a paper co-founded by his grandfather, A. M. Potter.

In later years he contributed quite a bit of money to journalistic causes, and worked on a project with the Reynolds Journalism Institute in Missouri to explore the future of community newspapers. He even established the Missouri School of Journalism's Walter B. Potter Fund for Innovation in Local Journalism.

Kay Potter was very willing to go to boring women's events, and wrote them up willingly, thoroughly, literately, and on time. All in all, I was pretty proud to work for the Potters.

During my first night of working on this small town's "first rough draft of history," I did one story from scratch. In the bottom right-hand corner of the front page that appeared Dec. 12, 1966, there it was, and still is in the bound volumes, although without a byline. Bylines, I quickly learned, were granted if the story was breaking news, or had required some effort to get, or was simply pretty important.

This one was none of those things. "Field's Exploits Reviewed" was the headline, and it was ten paragraphs beginning with "The heroic activities of Colonel John Field of Culpeper are an inspiring part of the colonial story of the area," the Rev. George West Diehl told the Culpeper Historical Society yesterday in the Northern Piedmont Electric Cooperative auditorium. Who, what, when, where, and why—I knew that much from the single journalism course I had in college. But the lead (and yes, I know now that it's spelled "lede," but I learned that pretty late, and I like "lead" better anyway) in retrospect reminds me strongly and embarrassingly of a section introduction I wrote for our high school yearbook.

According to Reverend Diehl and hence my story, Field was born in Culpeper in 1720, and died in battle with the Shawnee Indians in 1774. He was a leader not only on the battlefield but also in the House of Burgesses. Reverend Diehl was a member of various historical and genealogical societies, and was on the school board in Rockbridge

County. He was also a relative of editor Bill Diehl. I never heard of Colonel Field or Reverend Diehl again, thus experiencing without delay the transitory nature of newspaper work.

I'm a newspaper person to the core, despite having sold out for a decent income in the early '90s, and when I went back to the *Star-Exponent* building, then housing mostly operations, to look over the old issues so long after they were printed, and took notes on that first week and that first year, I was pretty much flummoxed by the lack of a focus for the story I thought I'd like to tell. It was just about impossible to pick out a prevailing theme.

I thought maybe I could write about the community presence and integral importance of the paper; I could home in on the social changes, including the evolution of attitudes toward gender and race, that were developing even though I had little clue about them then, in the midst of them; I could concentrate on the really big stories that were ongoing, the aftermath of the Kennedy assassination, the student riots, Lurleen Wallace and Jimmy Hoffa and President Lyndon Johnson (poor man, shown with the cartoon rock of Vietnam tied around his neck); or maybe I could write about my own growing familiarity with the seamy and small-change side of downtown life that involved cheap wine from the 7-Eleven and readily available and varied weaponry. Or, oh yes, I could center my thoughts on how the more things change the more they do indeed stay pretty much the same, because people don't learn very fast.

It was all too much to shape into anything coherent, because it encompassed life and society—a community grappling with what it wanted to be, and how it and its citizens fit into the times, and the relative importance of weddings, tragedies, graduations, and even the economy. The funny thing is, I'm not sure I had any consistent sense of where the nation or Culpeper was then, or what I felt and thought about it. My job was to be a conduit, and that is what I learned and what I became.

In the present day climate of dueling accusations of fake news and apparent corruption on all sides, my conviction is that newspapers do indeed have ethics. Reporters and editors for the most part aren't rich, they don't have jets or gold faucets, but what they have is a perhaps outsized belief in the importance of what they do and a conviction that they should do it honestly and properly. I know I did.

Diehl, in spite of the aforementioned sarcastic bent, quick temper, and horrible cigars, was a man of high and consistent journalistic ethics, and I was a willing pupil. Never did we discuss what and how much I should write, or whether I should withhold anything. If I knew something newsworthy, something the public needed to know or simply wanted to, I would write it and he would approve and print it.

I've decided to begin this account by describing my assimilation into the news world as it was then, with a description of the papers that were the product of my first few years, then move on to what I have found most surprising about my review of those times, the very different society that I lived and worked in fifty years ago. To start, here is a summary of the first issue of that first paper I worked for—really, for the full flavor, most of the week's issues.

CHAPTER TWO
My First Issue

My first was a Monday paper, meaning it was a bit sparse, since we pretty much printed everything as we found it out, a twenty-four-hour news cycle being what passed for instant information then. We had only from 3 p.m. until late evening on generally quiet Sundays to come up with anything local; after the weekend, advertising was also a bit lacking, and the "news hole"—the blank space available, according to a set layout of pages made possible by the advertising that had been sold—was correspondingly scant. But this particular issue had quite a bit of interesting information in areas where there was no hurry, articles no doubt carried over from the week before with an eye to making the day's effort not seem dead in the water.

On the front page was a large photo of an Angus bull, very blocky and short-legged, since this was well before the lean-meat trend. With him was his owner, Lewis L. Strauss, former chair of the Atomic Energy Commission and friend of Dwight D. Eisenhower. This is an excellent illustration of a theme than ran through newspapering as practiced in Culpeper: it was a very small town, but odd people and fairly significant happenings kept turning up there. That was partly because the town was only about sixty miles from Washington, and things of national import kept spilling over, and partly just because it seemed to attract oddness.

Anyway, Strauss was accepting a grand-champion trophy on the bull's behalf, while the bull hulked calmly and didn't seem to care one way or the other who got the limelight. The front page included a story about Mrs. John F. Kennedy suing to stop publication of the William Manchester book on the president's death. She wanted to keep out of print the "highly personal and poignant recollections" that she by then regretted pouring out to Manchester; recollections that among other things were "likely to increase tensions between Lyndon B. Johnson and the Kennedy clan." Well, right.

More local news was inside. There was a huge photo of Mrs. Erskine Bankhead and Mrs. Brent Sandidge making felt birds to be used in decorating a Christmas tree, Scandinavian style. This was on the Society and Women page, and that was kind of what women of significance did then to be noticed—they made holiday ornaments and had husbands who were known because they were ministers or school superintendents or bankers. The women didn't have names of their very own, as far as the reader could tell, but were identified by their husbands' names.

Other items deemed suitable for Society and Women were a column, The Extension Agent Speaks, written by the agricultural agent, at that time the truly wonderful Roy Heltzel, and lists of hospital births and bridge winners. There was an item about the Home Demonstration Club, something that was already inexorably moving past its time.

On another page appeared syndicated writer James J. Kilpatrick's column, A Conservative View, on that day for some reason or other written about Rhodesia. Kilpatrick, who had spent most of his career at the *Richmond News Leader*, was another example of a Culpeper connection, since he then lived in neighboring Rappahannock County. This was before he became a familiar presence on the "Point-Counterpoint" segment of *60 Minutes*, arguing the conservative side with obvious relish. Another story explained that the present military draft law would soon expire but was sure to be renewed, and still another crowded-in item noted that former president Eisenhower ("Ike" fit into a one-column head very nicely) was having his gall bladder removed.

The headlines were all up style, meaning most words were capitalized. Again, to meet the demands of the primitive typesetting machines, they had to be sized to fit the space available, carefully counted as they were typed out on manual typewriters according to a formula that assigned two points to each M and half a point to an I. I wrote many, many heads in those early years, and if the count was wrong or the head was dumb it was of course tossed back to me.

A notice in that Monday issue revealed that subscription rates by mail were $10 a year in Virginia, $12 elsewhere. A one-time classified ad was five cents a word. Comics were printed so they were big enough to be read by seventy-year-olds, rather than squished into tiny spaces, and included *Alley Oop* and *Bugs Bunny.* There were no graphics, unless you count a rudimentary sample ballot, and there was no color. Monday's TV listings showed four channels, with *The Donna Reed Show* and *Father Knows Best* among the programs.

On the sports page, the main head was "Redskins Scalp Cowboys" (insert another OMG here for staggering political incorrectness), and there was a big picture of a UCLA sophomore who was "fabulous" and "aiming for a streak." Lew Alcindor was to have quite a bit more than a streak. And as always, the racing lineup and the previous night's results from the Thoroughbred track at Charles Town, W.Va. West Virginia, appeared.

Staples of the *SE* that were missing that day but included the next, Tuesday, were Boston (Virginia, of course—it was up the road toward Rappahannock) Area News, written by Alice Dorsey, as well as Woodville News Notes and Culpeper Area News. They were accounts of who visited whom, who was ill, whose child was home from college, and perhaps who was having a baby shower. And by gosh there were more women making Christmas decorations, since it was, after all, December.

On that theme, an editorial titled "Here Come the Gals" was featured, and had to have been written by Bill, who as I've said had a sexist streak that was inevitable for his time and irrepressible, despite his being apparently a good husband who was pretty cooperative with and even obedient to a wife he respected. By 1970, he wrote in that editorial, half of all the drivers in the U.S. would be women, and women drivers were here to stay. He continued to explain that there is still the occasional cynic "who insists that when a woman sticks out her hand in traffic, it means one thing—that the window is down." Admittedly that loses in translation over time, but back then hand signals for stops and turns lingered on, and one learned them in driver training. And with that background and before everyone's consciousness was raised, it was a pretty good joke.

Bill added a parenthesis meant to calm the "gals": "That's only a quote, ladies, and does NOT necessarily reflect the view of this newspaper."

And this in a paper in which the main story, under the front-page head "Large Turnout Sought for Today's Referendum. Endorsements Continue Pouring In," was written by a woman, Miss Mary Stevens Jones. Mary Stevens invariably used both first and middle names, was unmarried and nearing retirement age, and lived with her also unmarried sister, Miss Mildred Jones. Both were intelligent, educated, and from what was considered Culpeper society. But while Miss Mildred followed the traditional route of teaching English, Mary Stevens was different, by which I mean she was cool.

She was about as genteel as they come, but the proper appearance and behavior were a veneer over a sharp intelligence and a brisk temperament. No one kept Mary Stevens from writing it as she saw it, and she saw with accuracy and perception. She did the women's page and wrote a column called Culpeper's Main and Davis (the title denoting the town's very noticeable center cross streets), but she also covered the school board and most other news that happened before three in the afternoon. Winner of repeated Virginia Press Association awards for columns, feature writing, and news, year after year, she was a power, but a ladylike power.

I didn't want to be her when I grew up, though; I wanted to be Lucy Catherine Bowie, another older woman who had been in the small-town newspaper world apparently from birth. Lucy Catherine was tough and outspoken. She and her brother Bruce had run the *Rappahannock News* for many years, and she was listed as the publisher when it began in 1949. There were old photos around of her in a long, drab dress operating a Linotype machine. Thin, angular, and wry, she was management but not afraid to get her hands dirty with printer's ink; she felt free to do anything and say anything, and while she rarely went in those directions she was not hung up on being ladylike.

Other items of note in the Tuesday paper: Another front-page head read "Great Society in Trouble—Funding Running Short." The first coverage of the fire I had seen at the Safeway on my moving-in day appeared that Tuesday, since no one with the volunteer fire department had been available to talk to on Sunday. I of course learned the tough lesson that I should have stopped. We were playing catch-up with the story, as frequently happened after a weekend, with a lead noting that a five-year-old boy had been admitted to the hospital with burns from the car fire. So it was a big deal—if I had stopped I could have had a full narrative and family names and reactions. No pictures, though, since I didn't have access to the office Polaroid.

There were land transfers, a sticking point when it came to freedom of the press because most people didn't want their major buying and selling to be public. And it seemed that "Miss Tinsley Urges Yule Donations Now," she being the Christmas Seals campaign chair. Shoehorned in was the fact that Ike's surgery was successful, but that Jimmy Hoffa had lost his court appeal and was going to prison.

If anyone was wondering how this compendium of everything a person needed to know on a few sheets of newsprint was financed, there was a big "shop in Culpeper" ad along with smaller paid blocks. One lucky reader could win $25 in merchandise in a drawing by responding to the suggestion and shopping in Culpeper.

And every day, this was done again. One shortish man sat at a partners desk with such help, over the years, as a just-out-of-college girl and/or an obviously alcoholic sports guy hovering, and decided what people needed to read about in the paper the next day. He wanted them to read that the school bond easily passed, that shoplifting costs added to retail prices so maybe the answer was a "housewives strike" to push for stronger policing and enforcement, and that the cost of the Vietnam War was threatening the Great Society.

He had little sway over Mary Stevens's domain, but he had no problem with making big news out of "Mrs. Smoot's Madonna Arrangement Is Cited," which revealed that the lady had had her photo in the *National Gardener*, the magazine of the National Council of State Garden Clubs. And certainly he asked the town's professional photographer to produce the local picture of election judges waiting during the referendum vote, and he identified the lone female judge as Mrs. Jimmy Booth.

CHAPTER THREE

Okay, I Didn't Notice a Lot

That was the mixture, eight or ten pages a day, a kind of bombardment of subjects and ideas, not unlike life and society in general. It kept me busy and occupied; I thought pretty much constantly about the paper, and I had no social life, not that I'd ever had much. I wasn't at all lonely, though; all my extra time was taken up with a wonderful companion, one I had sought for many years.

As a child I had read the Albert Payson Terhune books. *Lad: A Dog* and the other books were a paean to collies, and they were the reason a splendid if somewhat belligerent mixed breed border collie had become my constant companion during my childhood and adolescence. I had wanted another such dog ever since, and during my first year in Culpeper I acquired a beautiful sable and white honest-to-God purebred collie puppy.

I named him John, and proudly registered him as Just John, under the influence of another great childhood book called *Just David*. Since I didn't go to work until 3 p.m. and had no yard work and by choice no housework to do, we went for long walks and spent quality time as he grew from a puppy to a lovely dog.

So I was content and entertained, and perhaps not doing a lot of deep thinking or reacting. At the time, I know, I didn't recognize the gender gap; that was partly because I didn't think it applied to me, and partly, I guess, because my young and untried consciousness was decidedly unraised.

That seems incredibly odd to me now, looking back at old papers, because the treating of women as really different was pervasive in my early days working on that draft of history. Examples go from small to large: A *Bugs Bunny* strip has Petunia Pig boarding driver Bugs's bus, only to find she can't locate her coin purse inside her handbag. Bugs holds the bag while she looks, and ends up loaded down with an armful of stuff from the overflowing purse and an expression of pained but tolerant weariness. Another cartoon has a wife saying to her husband "If we don't get a color TV set this year, people will think there's something WRONG with us!"

The Jayceettes—female Jaycees—were, appropriately, selling fruitcakes as a fund-raiser, and husband-named women were featured in pictures on page after page during that December either doing good or, right, making Christmas decorations. Obituaries were headed "Mrs. Clatterbuck"; men got their initials when they died. In a story headlined "Length of Hair Real Problem," a faculty member at the high school was quoted as saying "I don't think boys should look like girls." The weekend entertainment section had a photo of a glamorous Miss World, who had noticeable thighs and in fact didn't look overly fit. It was a long time ago.

Mary Stevens Jones accepted things as they were too, ignoring the fact that while she occupied the traditional female backseat in our office, in many ways she was more identified in the community with the paper than its newcomer owner was. In the Christmas supplement, a few weeks after I arrived, her traditional and eagerly awaited Christmas poem appeared. As usual it was an entire page, and had taken up her spare time for months. The flavor was that of the society page, although there was the occasional political aside because Mary Stevens paid attention. Here's a small sample of how it read, including a couplet in which Mrs. Bruce Bowie got her own name because of her position:

> For our first Councilwoman Gladys Bowie
> We wish a Christmas that is grand and gooey.
> Peal a joyous Christmas bell
> For Culpeper Circuit Court Judge Harold Purcell.
> Give him an air-conditioned court
> So he'll be cooler than an astronaut.
> For Mr. and Mrs. George Chuckinas
> May the New Year bring more grand-bambinas.

Mary Stevens died on Christmas Day, 1990, at the age of eighty-two. I counted back and realized she was only fifty-eight when I first knew her, although she had seemed truly venerable to me.

This whole women-as-different thing was pervasive beyond reason in those years, which is clear from the evolution since then. At the end of 1966, in the season of religious observance, a head read "Women Priests Distracting." It noted that the Church of England was told by a psychiatrist that men would find female priests a problem that might mess with their piety, and a poll concluded that women found the idea "revolting." That's right, revolting.

Women got quite a bit of print in these early years of my newspaper experience, and the ink runs the proverbial gamut. In that same issue, three women and one man were pictured cutting a cake for the March of Dimes kickoff. The women had only husband names. Elsewhere, Mrs. Adam Clayton Powell, her own given name unmentioned, was said to be on her lawmaker husband's payroll while he was representing New York pretty much dishonorably in the House of Representatives. Never mind that he was depositing her checks to his own account while she was living in Puerto Rico, apparently in a creditable effort to be disassociated from him.

Frequent attention was paid to the miniskirt. A fashion article, "Skirt Vanishes Inch by Inch," noted that its survivor, the long blouse, was "left to cover the seatuation."

A big headline, "Reds Suffer Major Defeat in Central Coast Battle," for a story datelined Saigon, ran next to a wire photo of a flower queen. There was a big sports-page photo of Peggy Fleming, defending her crown in the World Figure Skating Championships. In the classifieds there appeared an ad for "Female help wanted—receptionist, Baby Jim's." Baby Jim's was the only genuine, order-at-the-window fast food place in town that I can recall then, since a Culpeper MacDonald's was well in the future, and presumably the receptionist was to take burger orders.

The Culpeper librarian, another remarkable older woman permitted some authority in a profession approved for females, had a column called What Culpeper Is Reading. Miss Crimora Waite advised that answers to questions about childhood education, oriental rugs, and other matters could be found in the library. Another story said that Mrs. Clarence Mills had become the town's new deputy treasurer. A beacon of financial competence, she was to last in her job (and be promoted) long enough to be referred to as Gloria Mills.

One of my early bylines was for a story about the appearance of state Sen. Henry Howell at the Culpeper Woman's Club. (Diehl, of course, covered his talk at the all-male Lions Club, of which he was a member.) My story was headed "Women Told to Participate" and noted that Howell urged the Woman's Club members to "restore vitality to state and local government" through their own active participation. The senator was also quoted as saying the state was ready to change "the nineteenth-century prejudice" against political activity by women, but women had to initiate that change. I recall being stirred to some unfamiliar thought processes by this event. It sounded like a valid idea, and Howell sounded like the herald of something that could matter.

Interestingly, my story was accompanied by a photo of Mrs. William K. Diehl pouring coffee for Howell at the meeting. She was the club's legislative chair, and she was wearing a hat and smiling. A slender little woman, already coping deftly with failing eyesight, Dorothy was undeniably cute—and I knew she was smart. I was kind of proud of her, too, hat and all, and thought it was all right if she was willing to pour coffee.

A woman who was known in Culpeper without the need of a recognizable husband's name was Liz Plevakis, owner of the Ritz-Hi Hat Restaurant on Main Street. "Aunt Liz" got a full feature by Bill Diehl when she retired. He stressed that her standard greeting for everyone had to be conveyed with an all-caps word; "Hi, HONEY, I'm so glad to see you!" The Ritz tended to draw mostly male customers, since it was a place to see and be seen at business lunches. When George Whaley took me in there during the week I was learning his rounds, I was surprised when he remarked offhandedly "That's the mayor," and introduced T. I. Martin, whose white hair and mustache made him look like a wiry little Col. Harlan Sanders.

Another Page 1 event that paid attention to women was a photo of the ladies' auxiliary of the volunteer fire and rescue squad presenting a check for $3,000 to the squad. "There is no likelihood of members of

Culpeper's Volunteer Fire and Rescue Squad underestimating the power of a woman . . . and surely not women," the cutline read. But while this somewhat tongue-in-cheek approach was being taken toward some real organization and effort in fund-raising, Mary Stevens had the byline on a story of very significant interest to Culpeper citizens, one not to be entrusted to just anyone: "Real Estate Tax to Rise," the headline read. "True value goes to 25%."

A one step forward, two back demonstration of hovering change was in the identification of a photo of student nurses completing a course. The students got their own names, even though they were a class of adults, but the instructor was identified as Mrs. Maurice O'Bannon. Somewhat later in 1967 a headline noted that "Rochester Ropes Taps Mrs. Ball for Board of Directors." Rochester was one of Culpeper's major industries, and inclusion on its board was remarkable for a woman. In the story, Mrs. Ball was in fact identified as Mrs. Harriet N. Ball. Her appointment and her name look like progress, but she is then identified as the widow of the first vice president of Rochester Ropes.

Another local industry opened, and Keller (a furniture maker) got a photo in the paper when its first finished product rolled off the line. Workers pictured included Mrs. Mary Cave, who was wearing jeans, not the skirt and dressy blouse or jacket that women wore in the photos with their flower arrangements or donations.

The editorial page got serious in discussing the gender issue about this time, echoing the power-of-women theme: "Never Underestimate Women; They're Doing It Themselves." There is substance to that editorial, as it noted that the percentage of master's degrees and doctorates obtained by women was falling, and jobs were still limited. "Deplorable underdevelopment of women's talents" was a quote from a national speaker. It's hard to square that with the importance that women claimed with their flower arrangements. Why didn't I notice at the time? I don't know, but I didn't. I was a person trying to learn a job, and being female never seemed to me to be a drawback. I think I did dimly realize that if the *Star-Exponent* were in a bigger locale with a larger readership and a higher pay scale, the reporter job would have been held by a man. In fact, I was there mainly because my hometown paper, the much larger Charlottesville *Daily Progress,* had declined to hire me, even as a proofreader.

Actually, as far as I know I was the paper's first female reporter to work the night shift and cover "hard news" aside from Mary Stevens's financial and meetings stories. Learning the job was to a great extent about getting comfortable with the town police and sheriff's department, and the world of cops was pretty foreign to me. Again, I was twenty-three; some of the officers were young, and they were uniformed men of action. I have to confess that I was not unaware of the testosterone level, and admittedly there may have been some eyelash-batting going on.

Gender does exist—there are ways it matters and ways it doesn't. At any rate, both law-enforcement and political players accepted me slowly but without undue hesitation. I had come to the paper not long after the departure of a very popular young reporter named Gary Ebbels, someone I heard a lot about in the early days. From time to time I felt the vibe "But you, ma'am, are no Gary Ebbels."

Still, at least one person in the sheriff's office was particularly nice to me, and apparently preferred me to ol' Gary. Martha Breeden was a young woman who was married to the jailer and spent quite a bit of time at the front desk as receptionist and dispatcher. I chatted with her frequently, although she always referred me to someone else, usually the young sheriff, Robert E. Peters, for usable information (that is, anything that could be printed). I had a byline on a feature about her in April 1967.

The lead was "Jail matron seems an improbable term to apply to Martha—she is 5'1" and weighs barely over 100 pounds." The story continued, "She regards her impressive list of jobs (dispatcher, cook, secretary to Sheriff Peters) as sideline work. Full-time, she is the busy mother of three small children." There was more, all emphasizing that she was a woman in a somewhat unexpected position: "As a member of a sex at which lawyers aim court appeals for jury sympathy, Martha does not pretend to be unaffected by the prisoners who pass through the jail." Details included the fact that she treasured a picture painted by an eighteen-year-old inmate, and at her own expense regularly gave Christmas packages to prisoners.

She proudly escorted me through the family's living quarters upstairs at the jail, including a dainty room for her eight-year-old daughter. What did not appear in the story was a side trip that she took me on to a very modest little house a few blocks away in a quiet neighborhood. It was empty; it belonged to the Breedens and they had lived there before he became the jailer. It represented her aspiration to a quiet and isolated home life, unlikely for her family at that point. I did abandon my reporter's detachment enough to feel very sorry for her, while tremendously admiring her spirit. It was a story very much of its time: look at the woman being womanly while operating out of her comfort zone.

A feature by Mary Stevens that year demonstrated that there were other ways for women to deserve that much space in print. "Miss Gertie" was celebrating her one-hundredth birthday, and the story declared that on that occasion Miss Mary Gertrude Durant would "eclipse all her guests in gaiety and charm." Although her family members were major Rappahannock County landowners, she hadn't spent all her life in that rural area. She was born in Salt Lake City and lived in Washington, D.C., for some years. She had even attended a party at the White House when Teddy Roosevelt was president. The Roosevelt connection was an early demonstration for me, like the photo of Admiral Strauss's bull, of the oddities of being so near the nation's capital. Miss Gertie had no arthritis and used glasses only for reading, the article noted.

Features were not hard to find in Culpeper. I found as I worked my way into the community that people I met in casual contact were often very interesting. Looking back I realize that I wrote more about men than about women, simply because men were more noticeable in the operation of the community.

What should have been a painful example of gender-insight news among the stories picked up every evening from the wire service was the saga of Lurleen Wallace. (In hindsight, I remember no burning indignation at the time, but I certainly feel unhappy with the silly young woman that I was.) Lurleen had replaced her husband, George, as governor of Alabama just to keep George's hand firmly on the tiller, an arrangement that was happily hailed by the same voters who were planning to support George Wallace in the 1968 presidential race.

On July 5 of 1967 a head read "Lurleen Brave as She Goes into the Hospital." The poor woman was always referred to by that somehow slightly ludicrous first name, a forerunner to the use of "Hillary" but without the hint of iron that Hillary Rodham Clinton's name always carried. Lurleen Burns Wallace had cancer, and had surgery for it that was described publicly as at least somewhat successful, although it really was not.

On July 10 the paper noted that "Lurleen Undergoes Surgery Today." There were later progress reports, but little in the way of truth or accuracy until she died in office the next year. It was apparently acceptable then for surgeons to give information directly to husbands, particularly powerful ones, and then make the decision together about what to impart to the fragile female. Wallace was believed by many to have kept her condition secret from his wife, the governor, until it was too late for much to be done and no treatment decisions were left to be made, although he did tell members of his staff. She lived a no doubt agonizing year, leaving behind an official portrait of a somewhat fragile-looking governor in a white evening gown and long white gloves.

CHAPTER FOUR

Gender and Race

P arallel to the beginnings of change in gender bias were the stirrings of racial progress. It is odd to think how truly in their infancy these two social revolutions were at that time, and how little thought there was of tying them together. A Southern newspaper would not have carried an editorial on race, as the *Star-Exponent* did on women, about how members of the politically undervalued group of black voters were underestimating themselves. One of the more thoughtful pieces on the topic of race that ran in the Culpeper paper, somewhat later, was by the very conservative Kilpatrick, who had vociferously backed separate-but-equal and massive resistance to desegregation. It was along exactly the same lines as the talk about women by Senator Howell and that surprising editorial about women needing to help themselves. Kilpo, as the truly famous Kilpatrick was familiarly called, wrote that change had to begin from within the black community, and he pointed out that many from the South had been saying this. "But Southern accents" are not heard nationally, he said, and that was pretty much true even when the White House was home to a much-imitated Southern (really, Texan) accent.

Not surprisingly, the coverage of the racial question was both more limited and more focused on hard news. Just after my arrival at the *Star-Exponent*, a Dec. 30, 1966, headline on a national story noted "Deadline Set for Next Fall on Full School Integration." In the first week of 1967, state political writer John Daffron wrote about voting changes in Virginia. The state was under restrictions levied by the federal Voting Rights Act of 1965 and could not impose registration requirements such as a literacy test without federal approval. Gov. Mills Godwin felt that

Virginia was wrongfully included under the restrictions, but the state would have to wait out a five-year period before any such requirement could be approved.

There were two kinds of black leaders who got attention in those days. There were the flamboyantly embarrassing types like Adam Clayton Powell, mentioned earlier as a gender transgressor for co-opting his wife's paycheck. Described as the "negro Democrat from Harlem," he drew cheers from mostly black crowds despite his unquestionably illegal activities in office, but did not bother to attend the civil rights activities down the street from him in Washington.

Then there was twenty-six-year-old Julian Bond, seated in 1967 in the Georgia legislature. He had been denied a seat a year earlier, but was not challenged this time around. The reason given for his exclusion earlier was that he had endorsed a statement labeling U.S. involvement in Vietnam as aggression and murder, and had called for an alternative to the draft. Closer to home, there was an article headlined "Fredericksburg Negro Honored" when a black minister who was on the city council was named Young Man of the Year. That young man, Lawrence Davies, later served as Fredericksburg's mayor for many years.

Black sports figures were of course in a class of their own, with some of the stars very much admired. Mohammed Ali, then going by the name Cassius Clay, received a lot of attention, mostly bad. In contrast to the affection in which Ali is held now, his early press was uniformly negative, some fairly rabidly so. Cocky and voluble, Ali sparked controversy perhaps as much for being black as for being loud and pesky. A British writer called him "the Champ of Sneer and Snarl" after he said he was not sorry he had taunted Ernie Terrell during a match by demanding "What's my name?" Another headline said that "By Debasing Foes, Clay Debases Himself." The man known then as "Ali Babble" was very unpopular, at least among whites quoted in newspapers.

But Lyndon Johnson was continuing his efforts to create the Great Society, by proposing a Fair Housing Act. Black ministers were jailed here and there, including in Danville, Virginia, for protesting racial inequality, and in early summer there was rioting by blacks in Tampa and Alabama. No huge uprisings ensued, but then LBJ moved decisively to put the first African-American on the Supreme Court. He appointed Thurgood Marshall, saying "I believe it is the right thing to do, the right time to do it, the right man and the right place."

CHAPTER FIVE
We Were the News

I had taken my lone journalism class at liberal-arts bastion Mary Washington College, in Fredericksburg, in my sophomore year. One of the requirements announced by the professor, Michael Houston, was that we subscribe to and read a daily newspaper. I got the *Richmond Times-Dispatch*, which had a conservative editorial policy but nonetheless straightforwardly and conscientiously covered the news. I was fiercely a print person, and never watched much television news even before it went so badly off the rails.

Journalism was a three-days-a-week afternoon class, and it was cancelled on the day John F. Kennedy was assassinated. I'll admit that what stayed with me was not the newspaper coverage but the sight of Walter Cronkite taking off his glasses as he stared at the clock on the verge of tears—a lasting image from TV news. The immediate reaction, not the more considered print coverage, was most striking and real.

Still, once I moved on from a class to the real thing, television news didn't intrude into my big picture. I was living and working in a place where the printed page was the whole picture, since the local radio station didn't have news as such and the nearest TV stations were sixty and a hundred miles away. When I went home in the evenings on my dinner hour, I never turned on my very questionable second-hand black-and-white set. Some years later, I was a bit startled to realize that I hadn't seen the all-too-real coverage of fighting in Vietnam that changed the way the world looked at the war.

In general news consumption beyond the war, though, print was holding its own. Even though it was the era of Cronkite, most people read newspapers eagerly, in addition to watching the 7 p.m. and 11 p.m.

broadcasts. Certainly there was big national news, interesting news, strange news, news worth slipping a coin into a newspaper vending machine, whether it was for the *Post* or the abridged coverage of the *Star-Exponent*. Would Johnson run in 1968? Jack Ruby, close to dying, insisted that there was no conspiracy in the shooting of Lee Harvey Oswald. Two surgeons at the Medical College of Virginia successfully performed dog heart transplants, predicting that the same thing would be done with humans in five years. Barry Goldwater criticized the *New York Times* for being "the mouthpiece for Communist propaganda." A magazine in Germany made cuts that Jackie Kennedy had asked for as it serialized *Death of a President*, and the editor sent a message to her saying contritely "I am sorry to have caused you displeasure."

LBJ "Unveils Biggest Budget and Military Request in History," trumpeted an *SE* headline. Eight people were injured in a local collision, and the wreck was big enough that I got a byline and Goad Studio went out to take a photo. And I had another byline on a story about the town's annexation case, ready to go to court and enlarge Culpeper so that you could no longer count up quickly in your head the blocks from one end to the other.

One front page was largely taken up with "Oil Truck–Train Collision Sets Off Big Blaze," an AP story from the Fauquier County community of The Plains with some local input. Wrecks and other tragic happenings were to me a set of facts, to be gathered from local police or the division headquarters of the Virginia State Police, which was located a few miles out of town. I struck up a familiar phone relationship with the various dispatchers who read me accident reports. One man, a slow-voiced Rappahannock bachelor who charmed me by phone, eventually asked me out. I was considerably less charmed in person, and so indicated during an interval in which he parked his car in a deserted spot and cut the motor off. Awkward phone exchanges over accident reports resulted, and there were no more dates.

I found very little in my work that was boring. Town and county politics, elections, zoning, and all the rest were fascinating to me from the first. It was the very beginning of a slow process of local governments taking control of the land within their jurisdictions, real estate that was the property of a particular person or persons right then but would remain a part of the county and town after those people had died or gone broke or sold out. It was kind of like the V8 vegetable juice rap on the head—oh, right, maybe an owner doesn't have the right to put up a horrible eyesore or begin holding rock concerts in a quiet neighborhood. The basic arguments came down to "This is my land and it was my father's land and our family has been here forever" versus "I moved from [some probably Northern, urban clime] to the country to enjoy the peace and quiet and space." The people who made the latter argument, having been attracted to Culpeper by its low taxes, were generally the first in public hearings to demand free school textbooks or better parks, but that's the American way.

At any rate, these slow and hard-fought changes made good news stories, and again I honed my ability to see all sides and come down on none. A shopping center? Sure, shopping is good, but then green space is good too. The elected leaders who had to grapple with this tried to see the long view, while undoubtedly getting snubbed at church and PTA meetings.

The modern tendency of local papers, owned by big conglomerates most of the time, is to focus on all local, all the time, because that is the prime slot they can fill in the twenty-four-hour news format. But then, while of course people read the *Star-Exponent* avidly to see what their local governments were daring to do, they were also given a neat compendium of whatever else was happening, and in the '60s that was often a lot.

It was all shoehorned into eight or ten pages. Astronaut Gus Grissom was buried at Arlington, following his death with two others in a flash fire during an Apollo 1 test, and an editorial asked that we honor the memory of Grissom, White, and Chaffee "by continuing the work they did not live to complete." A figure in the JFK probe was found dead in bed in New Orleans. That man, the largely forgotten David Ferris, was to have been arrested within days, and suicide was the tentative finding. Ex-army major Clay Shaw was also accused of involvement in the Kennedy assassination. All this was closely followed, a mystery that kept taking strange turns.

And then the larger world of often dire happenings came home, and the international connected with the local: Marine Corps Lance

Cpl. Michael Edward Stewart became the first Culpeper man killed in Vietnam. Bill Diehl, father of three sons, visited the family and wrote an affecting story that included quotes from the young man's last letter home.

As all this was going on around me, I pretty much woke up every day in my converted carriage house at 606 North Main Street, walked my collie, John, did my laundry at the laundromat or got groceries, paid my bills (a losing proposition for someone making $60 a week, but fortunately I had funds left over from my few lucrative months with the federal government), and read books like *War and Peace* that I hadn't gotten around to in college. Then I got myself some sort of lunch in an almost complete absence of fast-food places, and went to work at 3 p.m.

There was a young man who lived in a basement apartment of the Green house and who played catch or tag with John from time to time and was of growing interest to me as well, but I wasn't home evenings and I went to Charlottesville most weekends. I was busy.

My life was given over to my new identity: I was a reporter, with no desire to be an editor or anything else. I wanted to find out the news and tell it to our seven thousand readers as quickly and accurately as possible. The pattern of my days was fairly set. I checked in at the office and then was off to make my rounds. Besides police and fire, generally I'd look in at the office of Town Manager Claude Huffman, a man who was outwardly cordial but not very forthcoming to newspaper folk, and maybe sit in on some court sessions. After the few hours this took, I came back and called the state police office, hoping I wouldn't get the dispatcher I had gone out with, and took notes while someone read me the accident reports for the day. I wrote up what I had, and then often at 7 p.m. I went off to a government meeting of some kind. Otherwise, I might work on a feature I was doing.

There was always something to do, if only writing heads to toss across the desk, or proofreading copy. It wasn't *War and Peace*; it was all done quickly, with an occasional call to check a fact or a pause to look up a word in the dictionary. A set of habits was established that would follow me for a lifetime—mostly of writing with probably undue haste, while taking the steps to avoid embarrassing errors.

But I certainly could have used access to Google, or a law library, or any of the electronic resources now available. But if they had been at hand, I might have wandered off course on Yahoo to see what some celebrity had done, or wasted time checking Facebook, or read what the *Washington Post* had to say on a particular topic. It's mind-boggling to think how single-minded I was in my role as conduit. I gathered news, I wrote it down, Bill Diehl edited it lightly and occasionally asked a question designed to protect both our rears, and then I wrote some headlines, and that was what people read the next day. Most Virginia communities got their news that way, sometimes along with one of the city papers.

Late evenings were also educational as well as undeniably entertaining. In the huge back room of that old Safeway store the press loomed, ready to throw out papers, impressive in its well-oiled and potentially deafening presence. But getting the paper set up for it was done by hand, and editor Bill and the night reporters (all two of us) migrated to the back of the building as the evening wore on. The pasteup person, who changed only every few years, stood behind a tall, slanted counter, with pages in various states of completion lined up down its length. Most of us who worked there, including the pressmen, would watch, kibitz, occasionally make a correction, gossip and mildly libel the town fathers or cops, and generally get to know each other. The only ego in the back at night wielded the scissors and paste roller that put the pages together. No one other than the pasteup guy was allowed to perform the work; I don't know why, since there was certainly no union and no harm to be done. That was, as Cronkite said, "the way it was."

When the copy came from the phototype printers in long columns, it was trimmed with painstaking care and pasted onto newsprint-sized pages that would later be put through a photographic process to make the plates that would go on the press. Stories were sandwiched between tight column markers put in place by the pasteup person using very fine black plastic tape. It took a steady hand to put a straight half-page length of narrow tape in place. Headlines had to be trimmed and pasted separately, and if one was put down askew everyone who picked up one of the thousands of copies the next day would wonder who had been drinking at the *Star-Exponent* the night before.

A small hand roller was run across the completed part of a page to be sure the strips were down flat. Pictures were "sized" earlier in the evening—that is, marked with a percentage for the camera reproduction to reduce or enlarge them to fit their spot as indicated on scrawled 8 ½ by 11 dummy sheets—and the reproduced photos were also carefully trimmed, waxed, and pasted down. Very occasionally a page would be held for updates, and that would make people late in finishing, as a typesetter hurried to get the new copy set and developed. But no one minded; we were all newspaper people, and a bit of inconvenience was to be expected in getting the news as up to date as we could. There were no Google alerts; there was no radio or television in the building. We *were* the news. It was heady stuff.

As non-techno-savvy as I am now, I was in the same position then, and I mostly knew that the finished pasted pages were taken back to the camera and transferred to metal sheets that would be put on the press and convey the ink to the paper. Lord knew how; my interest ended when the copy was on the page and you could see how it would look when people opened it over their morning coffee. Oh, sure, when the press was going full throttle it was as intoxicating to me as to anyone else, but by then it was kicking out paper copies, real newspapers.

If it was happening in Culpeper or close by, we were there, so that through some alchemy of observation, note-taking, and typing on a manual typewriter it would get out to people the very next day in black and while. And, by gosh, in Culpeper it was read all over.

CHAPTER SIX
Turns Out Journalism Is Exciting

I tend to believe that nobody starting out in the newspaper biz has had more exciting stories in their first year or two than I did. Sure, it was a small town, but it had pretty amazing stuff happening if you were twenty-three years old and toting a reporter's notebook. At first I had to constantly remind myself *Okay, not shy, not shy* as I forced my way into the middle of things, but not only did the process turn out to be intoxicating, I found myself feeling sort of invisible. I was the fourth estate, there to record and observe and tell. I wasn't pushy and nosy; I was on a mission.

Which brings me to what I am perfectly willing to describe as a highlight of my life: the assassination and nonburial of American Nazi Party leader George Lincoln Rockwell. It happened in August 1967. Only a year before, I had been bored, bored, bored, surrounded by a morass of horrible paperwork and unmotivated people in my job at the Defense General Supply Center in Richmond. This was not boring.

On the day the assassination took place, I was coming back to Culpeper from Manassas, where I had been visiting a friend from college. My collie companion John, who had spent much of the visit thoughtfully observing the apartment complex swimming pool from a balcony, was in the backseat. I was about to be late to work, because somehow I had gotten onto U.S. Route 1 rather than Route 29, when I heard about it on the radio.

Rockwell, then forty-eight years old, had been shot by a sniper (who turned out to have ties to the Nazi organization his victim led) in a parking lot in Arlington. The party, which still exists at this writing and welcomes people to its website with "Racial Greetings White Brothers and Sisters!" was quite active and well-organized then, just over twenty years after the end of World War II. It made no bones about its connection with German Nazism, but it wasn't widely known.

A writer at the *Post* revisited Rockwell's story almost exactly fifty years later, following the horrible reappearance of swastikas and armbands at the Aug. 12, 2017, demonstrations in Charlottesville that resulted in three deaths and a city in an upheaval of self-examination. *Post* writer Michael E. Miller wrote that Rockwell had hung swastikas on the National Mall in Washington and called for shipping blacks to Africa and sending "communist Jews" to the gas chambers. In recalling the story of the slain party leader, Miller quoted Martin Kerr of the New Order, a successor to the American Nazi Party, as saying that the Charlottesville rally of white supremacists was "infused with Rockwell's ideology."

"He is the grandfather of the white racialist movement as it exists today," Kerr is quoted as saying. "To see these many hundreds of racially conscious white men on the streets of Charlottesville, I'm sure he would have been pleased." Rockwell was even given credit by some for coining the term "White Power."

Fifty years ago almost nobody in Culpeper knew about these things. Still, the situation heated up when news reports announced plans to bury Rockwell, who was widely shown in a then-recent portrait holding a pipe and looking like a kind of noble Hugh Hefner, in Culpeper National Cemetery because he had served in the military.

Even though I was only about thirty miles from the Nazi headquarters when the shooting took place, and later saw the fanaticism that the leader had inspired in many of his followers, he never had any human reality for me. Had I been more informed, I probably would have been a bit horrified. The Hugh Hefner-type picture was one of few in which he didn't wear a bit of a scowl and often full-scale storm trooper regalia. I assume the scowl was an indication of his personality, but I don't know for sure. He was the occasion of what Bill Diehl called "a hell of a story," and that was that.

Even though details of Rockwell's beliefs weren't widely known, to say that people in Culpeper weren't pleased about the burial plans is an understatement. Robert Miller of Culpeper, a mild-mannered fellow who had fought in World War II and was chief of staff of the Veterans of Foreign Wars Department of Virginia, said his organization objected strongly that "a man living against the ideals we have fought for should be laid to rest by comrades who have given their lives for the country's freedom." D. French Slaughter, a Culpeper attorney who was in the Virginia House of Delegates and later served in the U.S. House of Representatives, contacted Sen. Harry Byrd Jr. to protest.

National news organizations were extremely interested in the controversy. The assassination had been on the front pages for a number of days before the burial was set. An AP story from Arlington detailed a reporter's visit to the Nazi Party headquarters. "The swaggering lad with the heavy pistol on his hip had a gleam in his eye as he announced 'Leaders of the Nazi world movement are coming here for this funeral, sir.'" The writer described a "ramshackle house that served as headquarters and barracks" for the party. Who knew? Apparently practically no one—it is a genuine tribute to American society's faith in freedom and self-expression that no one had bombed or shot at the place that soon after the war.

It quickly became apparent that the burial plans presented a real test of the system, and feelings ran high. Because the U.S. Defense Department was in charge of the cemetery, which lies on the east side of Culpeper, only blocks from Main Street, it was a Defense Department decision to allow the burial or not. Rockwell was a certifiable veteran, and they compromised.

Diehl wrote the lead story on Aug. 29, under the headline "Pentagon Bans Storm Troopers' Ceremonial Display." According to the story, "The Nazi flag was scheduled to wave today over Culpeper National Cemetery, where men who fought Nazi Germany in World War Two lie buried . . . but that won't happen now." The pentagon had ruled that no special ceremonies would take place, particularly involving the Nazi flag, but burial was duly set for 11 a.m.

I had been relegated to covering the planning commission on the day all this was developing, while the men, Bill and sports editor Don McCardle, concentrated on the Rockwell burial. I find it odd now to think back and realize I not only didn't protest the assertion of male prerogative, I didn't even think much about the unfairness—plus I would have been forced to admit in all fairness that McCardle had more experience than I did. But the planning commission meeting was later in the day, and on the morning of the event I was there, milling with everyone else, waiting for the funeral cortege. Even though I wasn't officially working, this was something not to be missed. Despite a request by the VFW for a boycott of the ceremony, there was a fair-sized crowd—for a town of 2,500, remember.

Actually, I guess there weren't a great many people there at first. The funeral party, coming from Arlington, arrived around 10:30 a.m. McCardle wrote that events "almost started off with a bang." The procession, including a large and doleful-looking hearse, came to the cemetery gates, where it was stopped by officials. "The hearse containing the dead Nazi leader's body then missed by seconds being mauled by a passing Southern Railway freight train," he wrote, since there were tracks to be crossed before entering the cemetery.

The driver managed to move, and then the standoff continued for the next five hours. To me, a person with a still-developing outlook on news events, it was by turns entertaining and tense, but, oddly, never frightening. The issue was that the burial permit had specified that the services be conducted with dignity and without demonstrations. But six uniformed "storm troopers" had accompanied the body, and they wore swastika armbands. No one really knew what they had planned, and whether there would be goose-stepping across a Virginia hillside that was in many ways sacred.

Cemetery superintendent Edward Maxwell barred the party from entering when they refused to remove the armbands. When he summoned help, army Maj. Gen. Carl C. Turner was flown in by helicopter. Everyone milled and waited.

The characters were both symbolic and interesting. General Turner, a smallish, extremely erect older man with a firmly set jaw and a uniform full of medals, had fought in World War II, and once on site he issued a written statement and made a matching declaration to the press. "I am here to protect Federal property. No one will be permitted inside this cemetery wearing either a Nazi Uniform or insignia. Otherwise, burial will not take place." He stationed one armed group of military police in front of the hearse, with the rest of the forty-one-member detachment who had been there all day blocking the road closer to the gates.

On the other side was Matt Koehl, who had inherited the position of commander of the American Nazis on Rockwell's death. He was then only thirty-two years old, and although he was to spend nearly fifty years in his unfortunate and hateful position, until his death in 2014, he came across during this crisis as a not unreasonable man. He seemed to be someone who wanted to do the right thing—and for him the right thing was burial with all the trimmings. His quote in the Associated Press story: "It is impossible to bury him without the proper insignia. The ceremonies call for six pallbearers in uniform. There is no reason or no why to these regulations, or to why he should not be buried here. He was a veteran of nineteen years of service to his country." There was an odd bewilderment, for a fanatic, as he confessed that he did not know what would be done with the body if the funeral were not permitted.

Five hours is a long time in August heat. A few small demonstrations arose, there were cries from the storm troopers of "We want in" and "Heil, Hitler," and four arrests were made. But the highlight, captured by an AP photographer, came when a young storm trooper spoke heatedly to the crowd while standing on top of the hearse. After declaring his loyalty to his country, but a surpassing loyalty to the party, he attempted to lead the way to the gates by leaping onto the hood of the hearse— and sort of bounced from there into the arms of waiting MPs. It was theater—slightly crazed youth versus the staunchness of a major general and his efficient and apparently unexcitable troops.

Of course the MPs were young men too, and were also probably worried about doing the right thing, but military training held and the crowd, which eventually grew to more than an estimated one thousand, never seemed fearful. Actually this wasn't very reasonable, given that the fray was a corollary to an assassination, that World War II was not that long ago, and that anyone on either side might have become trigger-happy.

At 3:30, General Turner spoke publicly to Koehl: "I give you fifteen minutes to comply with the instructions and regulations for burial. It is now 1530 hours. I told you what the regulations were, that you may bring the body in but no Nazi insignia, uniforms, or paraphernalia will be permitted. I have given you these instructions four times."

Koehl said simply "I cannot comply." Turner then declared that the burial would not take place, a local justice of the peace said the cemetery was closing for the day, and everyone dispersed. I went on to the planning commission as scheduled. The hearse was turned around and driven back to an Arlington funeral home, where reporters saw the "garage doors bang shut." Because, as Koehl said sadly, "We could not find a place to lay him to rest," Rockwell was later quietly cremated and his ashes scattered over the ocean.

So it wasn't a happy time for the young Nazis, with the American struggle to do right coming out ahead, the military handling everything safely and efficiently, and finally a flag-draped coffin headed back north with nowhere to go. But that wasn't my summation of the day, which came in a story that ran above the masthead in the morning paper. While McCardle had stayed close to the action, and even made it into an AP photo hurrying along only a few feet away from a stiffly walking Koehl, I had mingled all day with the crowd. The headline was "'I Truly Admire You,' Drunk Announces to Supporters of Slain Nazi." It was full of details from the ground, including that people were calm and tolerant, and nearly a half century later I think our small paper did a good job of portraying the entire weird yet well-handled happening.

In my little story, I noted that the audience was on the whole a good-tempered one, and that state troopers mingled here and there, no doubt adding to the impression of safety. I wrote that Koehl laid aside his worn copy of *Mein Kampf* to climb onto the roof of the hearse and urge his forces to push through. (This was before the leap of the young trooper into MP arms.) I recorded that CBS cameras pushed in front, trying to interview Koehl, who made no secret of not knowing how to proceed.

The man of doubtful sobriety, in spite of the volume of his expressions of admiration for the departed, was generally ignored. For lack of other action, some of the idle, waiting crowd turned to a boyish, very short Nazi trying to hold up a swastika flower arrangement. Far from wondering at such an item, apparently the work of what must have been a confused florist, the onlookers were somewhat sympathetic to his plight, and were obviously feeling secure enough to take as routine a symbolism that evoked war and horrors. "Poor little fella, I bet he's upset," was one remark. The rejoinder: "Yeah, I didn't know storm troopers came that small."

By then, the drunk who had drawn my attention was bothering the cameramen to interview him. He wanted his views heard, he wanted everyone to know that Rockwell was a great hero. Even TV people weren't that desperate, so I was apparently the only one who recorded him for posterity. One of the Nazis even took a moment to shush him, saying firmly "Okay, be quiet," while, as I wrote, "observing Koehl's performance critically."

Koehl was so not ready for prime time as a fanatic. It was a surprise to me when I looked him up on Yahoo half a century later and found that he was still head of what had become the New Order, with a web page that says "We are comprised of white men and women of all ages and social backgrounds who are committed to building a better world for future generations of their race." His rather sad, bewildered comment about finding a place for his leader to "rest" has stayed with me. The proverbial wrong side of history isn't comfortable.

Koehl has since died, in 2014 at the age of 79, still as head of the renamed organization. He was the longest serving leader of the group.

The press was later told by party members that Rockwell's ashes were being held "in sacred trust" until a planned court fight. Other details were quickly uncovered, including that a former party official who had been ousted for developing Marxist leanings, twenty-nine-year-old John Patler, was charged with the murder. He was eventually convicted and spent eight years in prison. On the website fifty years later, Rockwell continues to be revered in some circles as a martyr to the cause.

It was hard to let this story go, but it was over. Oh, Bill Diehl followed up somewhat later with a column on the legal battle over Rockwell. He wrote that the American Civil Liberties Union had backed the Nazi Party, saying that it was a legally established organization in the U.S. and that theoretically a swastika was no more objectionable than, say, a Lions Club pin. The opposing argument, ultimately successful, was that the U.S. Army had the authority to decide the rules in national cemeteries.

This amazing event followed closely on the heels of two other happenings that took over the front page mostly because of the size of the community. The first was in the July 11, 1967 paper, and had both a byline and a photo by Kathleen Crawford, mostly because of my proximity to what happened.

And proximity it was. Again, I was living in what had once been the carriage house at the North Main Street address that had been home to several generations of the Green newspaper family. In front of this tall, imposing brick edifice was a wrought-iron fence, and sadly, in front of that were some fairly unsightly big metal trash cans. Again unhappily for the old estate, the big cans were for the people who lived in the various apartments the house had been cheaply remodeled to provide.

Since my hours ran until midnight, I was peacefully sleeping in the very early morning when there was a resounding crash out in front of my little dwelling. A car stolen miles to the south had been driven into town, Main Street being then the only way north, since this was pre-bypass; a town police car driven by Officer Clyde Mays had been lying in wait for it because of a radio alert from Charlottesville.

The fugitive car had been stolen in Lynchburg, and the three men in it got through the larger city to our south, since Charlottesville had a few different routes that could be taken, but not, by gosh, through Culpeper. My long lead to the story, innocent of commas, summed up both what happened and my excitement: "The chase of three men in a stolen car who had fled from Lynchburg police several hours earlier at speeds up to 105 miles per hour ended in Culpeper early yesterday morning when their vehicle plunged into Mountain Run at the Rt. 29 North bridge."

The story added that the occurrence had cost the town a wrecked police car. The stolen vehicle had hit those big, solid trash cans, bounced back, and continued for two more blocks before skidding into a utility pole near Mountain Run, the fair-sized stream that snaked around the town. It then slid over the embankment. Mays had leaped out of the patrol car, which had been damaged by the careening runaway vehicle but not disabled, and run down the bank to extricate the three, meanwhile yelling at people to call the rescue squad. The stolen car was steaming and he thought it might catch fire.

The estimate was that it was going ninety miles per hour when it went out of control, sideswiping a building and leaving skid marks for a block on the wrong side of the street. The hill approaching the bridge had made the driver lose control.

Not only did I get a byline, but the story was in the featured position at the top right of the front page, with two photos across the top. (And this coveted position was mine despite coverage, in the same issue, of the county election to follow the next day, with candidates including the owner and publisher of the paper.) Better yet, since we had no news photographer, I was the one responsible for those on-the-spot pictures—humble Polaroids, but they told the story of the wreck pretty clearly.

Well, no one would have called me Flash in recognition of the way the pictures came about. The only Polaroid the office had went home most nights with Bill Diehl, who probably did think of himself as a potential Flash, and I knew that. Here I had carnage almost at my front door, including a mangled police car at a time when I was fascinated with the police, and no camera. I surveyed the scene with my reporter's eye, and then ran for my car and drove the half dozen blocks to Bill's house, rousing him from sleep.

The fact that my boss came to the door in boxer shorts didn't even make me draw breath in that moment (in spite of remembering that detail *forever*). I asked for the camera, he produced it—padding barefoot into another room to find it—and back I tore. The scene was undisturbed, and I got my pictures, counting carefully while the first developed until I could pull the protective cover away with shaking hands, and then taking more.

The next day was a letdown, in spite of another byline on a lead story. This one was about the county election, in which the publisher lost. It was of no benefit to him that his newspaper had done its job the day of the voting. There was an editorial, a gimme, saying that Clyde Mays, that brave young officer, had been a hero. The drop line said it was "his finest hour," and though he remained a good policeman for many, many more years, that chase probably was indeed the highlight of his career for pure adrenaline and excitement.

Then there was the second mostly-important-in-Culpeper event during that summer of '67, undeniably a good time to be a young fledgling reporter. Ten days after the fleeing car went into Mountain Run, I had a byline on a banner-head story, "Gayheart's Drug Store Held Up." You're thinking, okay, a drugstore was robbed, big deal, must have been a pretty small town for such a story to rate a banner head. But Gayheart's wasn't just a drugstore—it held an important position in the town in almost uncountable ways.

First, it was located dead center, occupying the southeast corner of Main and Davis, an intersection that was so central to Culpeper that Mary Stevens Jones used it as the title for her column. Main and Davis was where the police box stood—this was a phone-booth-shaped structure with big windows on all sides. Since Route 29, the north-south highway, came straight through town, and electronic controls to change stoplights depending on traffic seemingly hadn't yet been invented, a town police officer sat in the little booth at peak times and manually changed the traffic light. As Dave Barry would say, I am not making this up.

At any rate, Gayheart's was both in the middle of town and maybe thirty yards from the police box. It was operated by Marshall Gayheart Jr., son of founder "Doc" Gayheart. It included a little lunch counter, one of very few around at that point, and it stayed busy beginning with breakfast (with a menu that oddly didn't include doughnuts). That was where you heard what was going on in town. If the person next to you at the counter hadn't heard the latest, you and he or she might be clued in together by one of the waitresses. It may not have been a requirement that the women who worked the counter in Gayheart's be Culpeper natives, but if they weren't all born and bred there they certainly seemed to have been.

The July 21 story described how in broad daylight a lone gunman held up the drugstore and escaped on foot with an undisclosed amount of cash. "Police said it was perhaps the quietest armed robbery on record," the article noted. The man pointed a gun at the clerk, Mrs. Evie Myers, who was behind the counter at the front register. (I don't know now whether Mrs. Myers identified herself by first name, whether it was the proper thing in police reports, or whether I had finally had some faint glimmer of raised consciousness, but in my story she wasn't a husband-named woman.)

There was lots of good detail, presumably because it was such a huge story in the community and people talked about it. Plus, when I was walking home to supper that night just after 6 p.m. I went down West Street and caught up with a young woman who worked at the lunch counter at Gayheart's, headed the same way. She was understandably still in shock, and talked perhaps more than her employers would have liked. For many years I would see that woman around town and we would speak, but I don't think I ever knew her name. She was the robbery information source, and I protected her in the same way that Deep Throat would later be protected.

In getting information for the story, I learned that after the robber had taken the money from the cash register that Mrs. Myers had been routinely and peacefully operating, he walked her casually back to the rear cash register, without attracting the attention of the four customers sitting on the counter stools. At the back he had Mrs. Marshall Gayheart Jr. (who hadn't a prayer of escaping the husband-name custom in this story) and had her open up that register. Once he had added the new cash to his collection, he walked out the door and departed, looking back at the store as he hastened down the street—but not without pulling the phone out of the wall first. Ooh, a phone yanked out of the wall. Police, I was told, hoped for fingerprints, as well they might.

A couple of days later the paper printed a police artist's drawing of the gunman. He was youngish, described as five-foot-seven to five-foot-nine, with long black hair neatly combed back. He had a .22 revolver. While he was apparently a master of quiet stealth during the actual crime, he hadn't been very careful when it came to his preparations, and because of a pretty clear trail it didn't take long to track him down. In mid-August a headline said that a Walla Walla, Washington, man was charged in the Gayheart's Robbery (which by then rated capitalization of the second word, since it was always spoken of in that manner, in awestruck tones). A transfer to Culpeper was being sought for Theodore Jack Beltz of Walla Walla. The clue, it turned out, had been a maroon car with Pennsylvania plates. Beltz was stationed in Pennsylvania with the army, and had driven down to Culpeper to commit his by now almost mythical crime.

Disappointingly, I do not recall Beltz having his day in court, although I'm not sure why not. There were murmurs of a plea agreement, but after all by late summer we had become consumed by the Rockwell uproar and perhaps did not keep as close a watch as we should have. Certainly it was always taken for granted that he was guilty, what with fingerprints on the phone and all, but there was talk of family connections and buying his way out and the like. Or perhaps it had to do with his army status. At any rate, a month's time that featured the Gayheart's Robbery, the fleeing car crashing into trash cans in front of my house, and the Rockwell nonburial was really never equaled during the rest of my years on the job.

During that first summer of my newspaper career, I found it surprising that the paper had so many balls to keep in the air, of a variety of sizes. National politics shared space with photos of the freak vegetables that gardeners kept bringing proudly into the office. I had a byline on a story about another car crash, one in which four teenagers died, although none of them were local. That story ran on the front, sharing the page with a wire photo of a pretty girl sitting on a hippopotamus (kind of a Bill Diehl special), captioned "Happy Hippo." And speaking of Bill, he did a column on the phone calls received in the *Star-Exponent* office, from people claiming to have raised the biggest cucumber ever, or to have found a clover with the most leaves on record.

A story about the Culpeper-Madison-Rappahannock Farm Show, always worthy of much attention, included photos taken by young Alan Wohlleben, who would soon take over Goad Studio and operate it until his own retirement. Downtown got a new Leggett's store, and a new telephone-company center was planned, projected to cost $4.5 million.

I did a feature on Captain Felix Bradley of the Virginia State Police division office in Culpeper, and described him as a "big, blond, knowledgeable man." We had quickly become buddies, and he remained a friendly source until his untimely death—an altogether nice man who could run a police division. The principal of George Washington Carver High School, a facility that had been opened for black students years earlier, was found dead in the school hallway, but the death was from natural causes. Extension Agent Roy Heltzel, another very nice and very capable man, warned in his column, "Don't Chop Corn Too

Early." Those who ignored Roy and whipped out and chopped that corn would pay, everyone knew. People did know, because the community was a very agriculture-oriented one that knew the cycle of planting and harvest; the Baptist Home, one of the earliest retirement homes in the area for those who could afford it, attracted 1,500 people to its Harvest Days.

In national news that summer, LBJ was pushing for an income-tax increase. Detroit was rocked with race riots, and pundits blamed Stokely Carmichael and H. Rap Brown. George Wallace "almost" put his hat into the ring to run for president. Lynda Bird Johnson was to wed Marine Captain Charles Robb.

As fall neared, there was a new historical marker for Little Fork Church, Culpeper County's only Colonial church, completed in 1773 and well-worth a marker or two. It was declared that construction of Culpeper's new airport was coming along so well that "we'll be flying before the end of '68." A community park was urged by the Jaycees, to be developed at Mountain Run Lake. All of these got attention somewhere among the *Star-Exponent's* always-limited pages, sandwiched in with little worry about design, no fancy graphics Every night was a marathon of writing, calling people to check things, counting out headlines, watching and quibbling about the pasteup, and finally heading off home with the paper "put to bed," ready to go on the press. To me it was engaging, even exciting, day after day, and it was a bit hard to unwind and go to sleep. I was awake in my little former carriage house, but the town everywhere else was dark and quiet except for Main Street traffic. Briefly I took up smoking, but I found it seductively relaxing and realized that it wasn't something I could do and restrain myself to the rate of one each night, so I didn't do it anymore.

CHAPTER SEVEN

American History

B y anyone's definition, what was going on out beyond Culpeper during my first year as a reporter was real American history—events worth staying in the back shop until midnight to see that first rough draft being pasted up. We always acted on the premise that keeping a finger on the local pulse was what made the paper a community necessity. But the stories that filled in around this—and by filled in I actually mean got the big front-page heads most of the time by default and really occupied most of the space, even if everyone read about the in-town wrecks first—were a summary of what was going on in the state, the nation, and the world.

Readers learned in October of 1967 that Lee Harvey Oswald's brother Robert had been allowed a ten-minute meeting with the accused assassin not long after his arrest. Robert Oswald said his brother denied killing Kennedy, but told an interviewer that he personally thought he did it. Robert never saw his brother again, because Lee Oswald was gunned down the next day. The brother's opinion of the Warren commission: early on, he thought it failed to answer important questions, but eventually he said he was convinced that the commission's conclusions were correct.

Opposition to the Vietnam War was growing, with hundreds of students picketing the Pentagon. "Israeli and Arab Leaders Trade Hard Lines," declared a headline. There was a rare graphic, this one showing the planetary probe Mariner 5 orbiting Venus. Oh, and "Ode to Billy Joe" was at the top of the charts.

Still, while people could have learned about Mariner 5 or Bobbie Gentry in the *Washington Post*, the *Star-Exponent* was the only source of information about most local topics. One of these was the always-busy legal system, where news that mattered but appeared nowhere else could be gathered.

I have to say that court activities were a real revelation to me. They illuminated an underside of life that I had had no inkling about, a sort of parallel existence to the norm of people living in single-family houses, raising their children, having a mild interest in local politics, and maybe going to a church supper or a movie now and then. I was fascinated, and spent quite a few mornings when I wasn't officially on the clock sitting listening to testimony in either the general district court or the circuit court, trying to remain impassive and not show how flabbergasted I was.

My interest paid off. I had a byline on "Driver Fined After 100 mph Chase." A twenty-year-old was stopped by a state trooper, and tried to get up a gentlemen's agreement on the charge: he offered the trooper double or nothing in a drag race. Not surprisingly, Trooper L. N. Stevens declined.

Court activities often featured lengthy testimony about the events leading up to a crime of some type, events that generally included several people driving here and there in search of 7-Eleven wine. Often in the course of these late nights several groups who had been doing the same thing would wind up in the same parking lot, words would be exchanged, and there would be a fight—even, now and then, with firearms or knives produced.

There was no drug traffic to speak of in Culpeper in those days, although later on there would be tremendous amounts of buying and selling in pretty public spots. Crime consisted mostly of drinking, fights of varying degrees of seriousness, and then more drinking. Only occasionally were there women involved, and generally they stayed in the background and didn't get summonsed to court—but when they did, they came clad in ways that astounded me. "Let's see, I'm going before a judge, I want to look sober and credible, so I think I'll wear a tight T-shirt and these jeans that fit me twenty pounds ago." Embarrassingly, their testimony was pretty much disregarded since it invariably and sometimes confusingly favored a brother or boyfriend. It was all an in-depth and condensed education for me.

Sometimes testimony was rather frank, but people apparently read the articles avidly and no one complained about the occasional shocking disclosure. It was quite an exposure to the ways in which some citizens lived, but no one said "Hey, this stuff is too much." Nor did anyone with the paper ever think twice about sending me to gruesome happenings. A rare instance of Bill Diehl remembering that I was young and female occurred with an early summer plane crash near Etlan, in mountainous Rappahannock County. The pilot was killed, and Diehl sent both Don McCardle and me to ensure blanket coverage—but he called around to get someone else to give me a ride out to the area in the darkness. Don went up to the crash site, but I stayed at the Etlan store to talk to people. We had a joint byline the next day.

Happily, there was a lighter side to the local news that summer. Rehearsals were under way for the Culpeper Hospital Auxiliary's Pink Ladies Follies, a semiannual event for which a paid director was brought in to whip local talent into a fund-raising show at the downtown State Theater. In this case the director, Jud Davis, caught a virus on the way to town and was whisked by some of the auxiliary ladies to Culpeper Memorial, where he was given pills. He was "well pleased with the treatment he has found in Culpeper," according to an interview with Mary Stevens.

Mary Stevens also reported on the graduation at the Waite Kindergarten, a fine institution run by the librarian, Miss Crimora Waite, and her sister, Miss Kitty. It was operated in Miss Crimora's historic home on equally historic East Street, and was the alternative to the Baptist church kindergarten, considered a somewhat more businesslike institution in comparison. An alumnus of the Class of '60 spoke, according to the story, "waxing nostalgic" about finger painting and graham crackers. It was that kind of setup, with nap fairies and the like, and the account in the paper was readable and amusing, and no doubt ended up in scrapbooks all over town.

A nice diversion came when I, as the young female reporter, was chosen to accompany the Culpeper area's spelling champ to the National Spelling Bee in Washington. Dail Willis of Orange, a precocious thirteen-year-old, and I spent several days at the Mayflower Hotel. The winner was to get a three-day paid visit to Expo 67 in Montreal—and the escort would go too. I took my dog, John, down to stay with my parents for a few days, and we were off.

There was a Polaroid staff photo taken by Bill Diehl of Dail and me, getting ready to leave in my Volkswagen convertible. We were wearing dresses, and the adolescent Dail towered over me, as indeed most people did.

I wrote daily dispatches from our room at the Mayflower Hotel, and read them to someone at the office in the evenings to be typed out—no emailing. I included my own reminiscences of the trip our class made in seventh grade, which of course really hadn't been that long ago, of a trip a decade earlier, saying "I remember seeing Washington, D.C., with the eyes of a thirteen-year-old," and I described Dail as thrilled. The now worldly spellers visited the JFK grave site in Arlington and the FBI building. At the FBI there was a shooting demonstration with a tommy gun, something I wouldn't think they would do anymore. "I am," I quoted Dail as saying, "deafened but impressed." I also noted that we were "getting over our original awe at the rather resplendent surroundings . . . and ordering room service." Thirteen years old or not, our spelling champ was clever, and excellent company, and we had a splendid time.

Dail advanced triumphantly to the second round, which saw the group cut in half. But she missed "lapidary" in the eighth round, and there went the trip to Montreal. The stay in Washington did include a gathering with Vice President Hubert Humphrey on the Capitol steps. He seemed perfectly happy to be there, and very enthusiastic about the group of youngsters—I reported that he was "beaming with the true ardor of the politician."

CHAPTER EIGHT

Part of the Times

After the 1967 summer of excitement, things did quiet down, but the local subject matter continued, at least to my mind, to be interesting and readable—and in retrospect, reflective of its time. Mary Stevens wrote a feature that bore the head "Retarded Children's School Opens—at St. Stephen's." Not "special-needs," not even "handicapped" children, and they were pictured and identified. St. Stephen's was the Episcopal church, a bastion of Culpeper society, but nonetheless always in the lead on doing innovative good. There was a panel discussion by local police officials and Commonwealth's Attorney W. D. Reams Jr. on "How closely should the average citizen be 'involved' in law enforcement?" Culpeper itself was raising its consciousness in many ways.

A state story with a photo about newspaper boys visiting Virginia Gov. Mills Godwin ran in the paper, and Culpeper carriers were identified in the crowded photo. The paper's headlines went from up style to down style (that is, with only the first word capitalized, rather than every word), and back again. Occasionally in those early years the paper featured an exciting advance: a head was sometime printed in color. If the color was red, the story was shaded in a see-through red. This might be done because an advertiser had paid for color on a page that would go on the press as part of the Page 1 spread, so there was no extra cost. Extra costs were to be avoided; the paper wasn't broke, but the advertising base was small. Overall, changes in presentation of the news were few and far between.

Hard news kept adding up. Locally, I had a byline on a murder trial. Maurice Hundley was convicted by a jury of second-degree murder, for which no motive was ever established. The proceedings grimly outlined events that were like a black-and-white episode of *Gunsmoke*. Hundley, six-foot-three and downright scary looking (his appearance was the real genesis of the *Gunsmoke* comparison, I think), had been drinking when the death occurred, and said haltingly on the witness stand that he had forgotten exactly what had occurred when he shot his stepdaughter. The victim's half-sister testified, saying she went on her knees to beg when he threatened her as well. Interestingly, the dead woman had been acquitted some time before in Louisa County of murdering her husband; she had moved back to Culpeper and was living with her parents in their trailer home. As I explained earlier, court was a revelation.

When Hundley's case was sent to the grand jury, Goad Studio was lined up to get a photo of the accused when he was taken from the jail to the courthouse. In the photo, Hundley contrasts wildly with Sheriff Robert Peters, who was to be reelected until his own semi-old age, but at that time looked very young and innocent. The accused had actually been arrested by a state trooper, who testified that when he approached the trailer after the shooting, Hundley introduced himself and said "I just shot my daughter." In fact, Trooper Stevens said, he was "real cool." A cool customer himself, Stevens was the same officer who had turned down the offer of a double-or-nothing drag race.

Since it was a big election year, I became immersed in local politics, again a series of revelations. There was an election for board of supervisors in November, and I hastened to interview the two candidates for the Cedar Mountain District seat on the seven-man (literally men, of course) board. T. E. McMullan, a very quiet, shy man who operated a country store in tiny Mitchells, Virginia, practically tugged his nonexistent forelock at me in apology, but declined to express any viewpoints at all, really. He was the incumbent, having been appointed to replace his brother, who died in office. Mostly no one had a party affiliation—parties weren't necessary for the board.

On the side of progress, an electoral board vacancy was filled by an appointment made by Circuit Judge Harold H. Purcell. He named a woman, saying "The court has felt it advisable that a lady be appointed" because "they are as intelligent as or more so than the men." Purcell was a courtly man with great dignity, and he used Mrs. Russell Lane's first name in the proceedings—"Russell" was in fact the given name of this very bright businesswoman, but I don't think it was confusion on his part.

Politics on the state and national levels were more of the usual. There was a to-do made over the fact that Chuck Robb, the man notable for being engaged to Lynda Johnson and headed for a White House wedding, would not have to go to Vietnam as originally scheduled. *Richmond Times-Dispatch* columnist Charles McDowell came to the Culpeper Host Lions Club to talk about what he saw as the "greatest crisis since the Civil War" in American life, liberals versus conservations (can you imagine!). He also discussed the ability of the Republican Party to "make the worst of a good thing," losing elections "out of principle." Although I had been reading McDowell for years and was a fan, I didn't get to go see him because 1) it was the Lions, for goodness' sake, and 2) I was female, and 3) Bill wanted to go and someone had to work in the office. McDowell was on target; the Democrats swept the state elections. You have to wonder what the columnist would have made of the 2016 race.

Ronald Reagan, as governor of California, held a press conference to explain the sudden retirement of two staff members who had featured in a press account of a raucous homosexual party they had attended. The press conference didn't go as planned; it had been an effort to clarify that the men weren't fired for being gay, when in fact the public attention to their sexual orientation had led to their dismissal. When pressed, Reagan waffled, and then was allowed to say firmly "This subject as far as I'm concerned is closed," and it was in fact closed. A player from the past, Robert McNamara, went from being secretary of defense to president of the World Bank. The first human heart was transplanted in South Africa, only months after the U.S. prediction had been that such a success was perhaps five years off, and was given a lot of attention. Patient Louis Washkasky blazed a trail, and it was big news, although his death was recorded in a smaller bulletin just over two weeks later.

The mix of news on all levels was often striking, but as Christmas neared that year attention shifted more to the local. I had a byline on a story about a seventeen-year-old American Field Service student from Norway. I wrote that "Inge is, in summary, a large question mark. His ambition seems to be to gather up, in large pieces or small, all that is to be gained from the U.S."

I remember very little about him personally, except that he impressed me tremendously as a young man who was elated about his opportunities and enjoying them to the hilt. Something like this was news in the community, which was unabashedly interested in people from other countries, and very welcoming.

Community news continued as usual. Margaret Barron, who wrote the Jeffersonton News column about her northern Culpeper community for many years and was a stickler for accuracy as well as comprehensive coverage, made a vocation out of her efforts. She would hand-carry her reports to us, chat briefly, and then be on her way, a solid country-type woman who was obviously very intelligent and a generation later might have done much more with her writing. Anna Townsend Willis did a regular column, To Live in Virginia . . ., that tended to be about bird feeders and spring blooming, but occasionally tackled something beyond. She had begun her column asking for title suggestions, but the winner, she said, came from "the man"—her husband, sometime Culpeper Vice Mayor E. O. Willis. And maybe most down-home of all was Culpeper's Mixing Bowl, in which local women shared recipes. One reader was asked so often for her Jell-O "ribbon salad" recipe that she sent it in asking that it be printed to save her trouble.

A story I can't pass over, simply because it was so puzzling from so many angles, was written by Mary Stevens in her column, Culpeper's Main and Davis. It was titled "Dear Jess Bags Deer," and related how Jess Kennedy (Mrs. Garry G. Jr.) got a deer on a hunting trip for the second year in a row. Living up to the terms of her agreement with the men in the hunting party, she had to drag the deer out of the mountains to cleared ground. What exactly this said about the state of local society and its gender viewpoints I couldn't say then and can't now.

It's hard for me to understand now, but I used to go out and take Polaroids of hunters grinning over dead deer, rifles in hand. I did it any number of times, and mostly didn't think about the deer. Finally a hunter forced me to consider the realities of the thing by fetching in a couple of small, dead bears, one with its tongue lolling out. I took the photo, but that was it for me.

Anyway, Dear Jess notwithstanding, another accomplished woman was featured in a Bill Diehl story. "Being the mother for four children . . . and the grandmother of 10" hadn't meant the end of an athletic career for Mrs. W. R. (Lucy) Rose, he wrote. She was still bowling duckpins, and still scoring high; in 1943 she had been the nation's number-one-ranked duckpin bowler.

CHAPTER NINE
I'm a Newsperson

Culpeper people were undeniably interesting. 1968 began with a Diehl story, full of football references, about Deputy Robert W. Bobbitt, who ran down a prisoner after the miscreant escaped during a court transfer. The sprinting prisoner hit a slick spot and slipped, and according to the article—"touchdown . . . Deputy Bobbitt." Once again, there is some residual sadness in looking back; Bobbitt was a conscientious young man who took himself and his job seriously, but died early. The company of those who doubt that police officers lead difficult, complicated lives does not include me.

The Virginia Press Association held its annual banquet, with both Bill Diehl and Mary Stevens Jones coming home with awards. Mary Stevens won awards year after year for her column, and occasional ones for news or features, and I'm sure she surprised the press group at the banquets with her age and ladylike reserve. Newspeople were not noted for gentility, then or, I guess, now. We were at a VPA meeting some years later, spending the night in the hotel, and the newspaper people were so rowdy that someone came out in the hall and screamed at them. I of course was quietly in bed, but had been kind of enjoying the noise made by what had become my people. The yeller noted that they weren't as important as they thought and should shut up.

That first year, I didn't enter anything because it would have seemed pushy. Less than competitive in games (ask my brother about my approach to contract bridge) or possessions, I did know I wanted that recognition for what was important to me, and resolved as my second full year opened to produce something worthy of an award. It didn't happen with my first byline, which announced that J. B. Carpenter Jr.

had been elected mayor and E. O. Willis had replaced Giles Miller as vice mayor. Miller, a bank president who was to live to be 102 and was known in his later years as "Mr. Culpeper," had been named to the board of the Federal Reserve Bank of Richmond.

Some of the paper's filler coverage wasn't going to win anything either, particularly in the way of predictions. "Women No Threat to Men" said an AP story, and it elaborated: "If pants-wearing women are a threat to the masculinity of men . . . men can breathe easier. The threat appears to be over." This was because there were few pants in the spring fashion shows, which then—as, really, forever—had little to do with what Culpeper was wearing.

On Jan. 22 the paper carried a story with my byline that marked several firsts for me—I understood the pain that news coverage could mean for those involved, and the long-flickering background noise of the Vietnam War suddenly wasn't background anymore: Army Pfc. Edward Odell Spencer became another Culpeper casualty. He was a college student studying for the ministry, and could have claimed an exemption, but he went off to Asia as a matter of duty. "A Culpeper boy who didn't have to go to Vietnam but who went anyway, a soldier who meant not to kill people but to use his medical training to help those who might otherwise die; a boy who would not have been 20 until next month, has died in the war," I wrote, and I felt it, and hoped what I wrote did not add to the grief of his family. I later got to know his mother, Marge Prewoznik, somewhat, and she carried the grief with her always.

But life went on. Again illustrating the breadth of things a small-town newspaper reporter did, I went to my first steeplechase. I had been a horse person since I could remember, and when I learned about steeplechasing as a pursuit of the wealthy, landowning classes, I ignored the obvious elitism and spent quite a few late winter weekends watching and reporting on this ritual. An early 1968 account of a win by a horse named August Acorn—a pretty cool name—demonstrates some growing familiarity with the racing scene. Rereading the story many years later, I realized that at that point I knew which jumpers were supposed to duel for the win in the Ben Venue feature, and which hunts the horses were from. Ben Venue, incidentally, is a tiny community in

Rappahannock County, just below the Blue Ridge Mountains, and at least back then the race was normally the first meet in a busy circuit.

Horses were pretty much my limit when it came to sports. On rare occasions I got sent to a high school basketball game, and once I even asked my neighbor, my dog's friend Jack Hoffman, a major fan of all sports, to accompany me. It was sort of our first date, although neither of us would have described it that way. He later went to horse races with me, but his heart was never in it.

I continued my steeplechasing enthusiasm with a later story headlined "Walrus proves truly 'grand old man.'" The horse, owned by Mrs. T. A. Randolph, who must have had her own name although it was never mentioned, had used the phrase to describe the winner of the big, big area race, the Virginia Gold Cup. Walrus was in his fifteenth year of winning, I noted, and came in ahead by twenty-two lengths when much of the field didn't finish. The Gold Cup was held on the first Saturday in May, and still is, as is the Kentucky Derby. Walrus's glory didn't extend to the Derby winner that year, with Dancer's Image being disqualified after the win because of evidence of a painkilling drug.

Things moved along locally and nationally as winter went into spring. An $800,000 dam project got the go-ahead from town council, as the town looked forward to an adequate water supply. Don McCardle began writing a sports column called SpinOut—he was a car racing fan who trekked off regularly to Charles Town, West Virginia, where there was a busy track, and Diehl was a believer in letting people write about what they cared about. But I'll say this: after my coverage of the horse races, the local news mavens followed up with who had attended and who had had guests afterward. The opportunity to watch someone "spin out" in West Virginia wasn't as big a draw for society as Culpeper knew it.

Along with the accounts of local society and sports on all levels, the chronicling of history in the making continued. Richard Nixon declared he was a candidate for president, and said he had the answers. Virginia Del. D. French Slaughter and I got together to sum up the legislative session. An Associated Press story from Saigon was headed "American troops hand foe another decisive setback." A small Page 1 item noted that Lurleen Wallace's doctors were "concerned." And *Cool Hand Luke* was at the only theater in town.

Following an early presidential primary, Robert F. Kennedy said that "major obstacles" had been removed from his candidacy, but he then offered to stay out of presidential contention if LBJ would appoint a committee to change Vietnam War policy. LBJ, beset by the war but with one big success in hand after the passage of the largest Social Security expansion ever, refused.

About this time there appeared another front page recognizable as a Diehl special. It noted that Cuban president Fidel Castro was threatening to keep the U.S. planes that had been hijacked to Cuba, because the U.S. had not returned boats stolen on the island nation and used by refugees to head for Florida. As perhaps a counterbalance to threats and uncertainly, Diehl spiced up the page by turning to a standby, the wire-service photo of a pretty girl. This one was sitting "saucily" amidst car wheels at a Michigan plant. At least a hippopotamus was not required this time.

It was a big deal when construction of a shopping center on Business 29 South was proposed. The property in question was a pretty, green field at the south end of town, in front of Culpeper Memorial Hospital. The developer could do what he wanted by right, under the zoning, but almost 150 people came out to protest, a raucous crowd that surely had no inkling that the community would eventually have a half dozen shopping centers—including this one. Because the county was not far enough from Washington, it probably never had a chance to stay rural, but a highly verbal minority fought growth pretty hard. At that point, the developers said they weren't going ahead—but soon they did. That was the way with development.

A front-page item of the kind that was a hallmark of journalism as practiced by Bill Diehl (as much as pretty, saucy girls) can easily make me smile so many years later. A fisherman had seen a hairy object floating in a pond, looking for all the world like a poorly submerged drowning victim. He called the sheriff's office. W. D. Reams Jr., a lawyer who served as both commonwealth's attorney and judge during his career, was also an accomplished diver and was called upon to take action. He did, and found a dead muskrat. Pretty hard not to like that story, unless of course you were a muskrat.

What was really an upheaval in society was illustrated in the headlines soon afterward, one of the 1968 events that has made the year the subject of a number of books fifty years later. On April 5, the paper announced the assassination of Martin Luther King in Memphis. Street disturbances followed in Virginia cities. College students were in an uproar of protests against the Vietnam War and racial inequality, and the House of Representatives responded by refusing to permit any financial aid to go to any student who had participated in a demonstration. That war was a genuine crossroads in the ways people thought about a government's responsibilities to its citizens and to the world.

But in Culpeper, only a few people were very caught up in the turmoil of war resistance or protests against racism and the need for change on those fronts. A couple of weeks later a letter to the editor came from Mortimer Marshall, a black man who was a funeral director, deep thinker, and effective writer. "Negro blames isolation" was the gist of his communication. He made the case that other ethnic groups had been allowed to integrate into the community, but that his own race was held firmly apart.

No one wrote anything similar about women being held to their place, although they should have. In fact local writer Bernice Roer Neal said she considered herself honored by being slated to share the speaker's spot with Admiral Strauss at an author event. Of course, the event was sponsored by the local chapter of the American Association of University Women. This is by way of saying that the turbulent '60s did not necessarily filter down to small-town attitudes.

At about this juncture Lurleen Wallace died of her cancer, at forty-one years old, weighing sixty-five pounds. There had been no public mention that the cancer had returned after the February operation. She was credited with compassion toward the people of her state, particularly the mentally ill. Presumably after she died her husband was no longer the de facto governor. It was all a sad, sad story, and the news seemed generally pretty unhappy.

Dr. Spock was sentenced to two years for his anti-draft activities. In a news conference, he said there was "not a shred of legality" in the

Vietnam War. Still, the war went on. And in the more things change, the more they stay the same department, a May editorial cartoon pictured Congress as a silver-haired lawmaker wearing a string tie, having a shotgun held to his head by "The Gun Lobby." The shotgun wielder was explaining "It's only for a little sport, Sir."

Robert Kennedy "crushed" Eugene McCarthy in the Nebraska primary, the paper announced in May (note that the presidential campaign had not been annoying everyone for more than a year by then; unfortunately, there have been changes). McCarthy, who was viewed as the peace candidate, came to our office once or twice from his home in Rappahannock County, and somehow I was not a fan because of his aura of self-regard. I should have been a natural member of his constituency, since my college, Mary Washington, was close to the Marine Corps base at Quantico, and I had seen students weeping in class or heard whispers that someone was absent because a Marine boyfriend had shipped out or been wounded or killed. Peace had growing appeal locally as well as nationally, spurred on by things like a May 17 story that said the 562 American deaths that week in Vietnam had set a record.

The Poor People's March took place in Washington. That same day, Mary Stevens's Main and Davis column was about the association of bluebirds and happiness, with loads of details about bluebirds, including what I found to be a touching memory about her father lifting her up when she was a very small child so she could see inside a nest without in any way disturbing it. A jury was selected in the trial of Dr. Spock on charges of counseling American youths to avoid the draft. Bobby Unser won the Indianapolis 500, and a sports head proclaimed that as often happened "Mickey Mantle explodes at bat."

There was plenty of national life to keep up with, but it wasn't exactly the number one topic on Main Street. The paper not only mixed marches on Washington with bluebird thoughts, there was other important local news. A new animal hospital was approved for Route 522, and there was a feeder-pig sale. Moreover, "The sixth Nickel Crombie was at the corner of Main and Davis with a camera, looking for a 'crowded pavement' for a photograph," I wrote in a feature on another visitor from another land, this one a Scotsman improbably named Nickel, whose father and grandfather and so on had shared the name. Culpeper was pretty proud of its own history, but this was a man whose family name began in 1743, when the first Nickel Crombie was born. Turned out a "crowded pavement" was a gathering of people on a sidewalk, and that was a hard thing to find in Culpeper then.

Local and national ran together in early June, when the publisher interrupted a personal trip to cover a McCarthy speech in California. He wrote his contribution to run with an editorial-page byline, and therefore was permitted to express his strong opinion, and he did: "One must hope that people will truly listen to what he says rather than be mesmerized by his voice." Colonel Potter was a military man, and he didn't share the McCarthy "peace at any price" stance.

Robert Kennedy did of course win the California primary, and seemed to be on his way; then suddenly, direly, the June 6, 1968, banner head read "Sen. Kennedy clings to life." An editorial reflecting those troubled times noted that the shooting of Kennedy might have been expected. Illustrating the thought was a picture of RFK in a beam of light after his primary win. My neighbor Jack and I, by then on the way to being a local item, watched the coverage on his (better) TV, and were shocked beyond words by the images on the screen. This was way different from the assassination of a weird Nazi type I had barely heard of.

On the day the Kennedy jet returned the body to New York, there was a jarring story-picture combo. A Humphrey–Ted Kennedy ticket was being urged, and the story ran just below a photo of Robert Kennedy lying mortally wounded. Inside the paper, Kilpatrick wrote warmly of RFK: "He had a revivalist's sure sense of timing in his badinage with the crowds . . . a brave and brilliant man who died too soon, too soon." Kilpo was capable of both rhetoric and poetry when necessary, and did not fail to make use of them in a deserved tribute simply because he had staked out the "conservative view" side of the divide between himself and the liberal Democrats who backed the Kennedys. The divide stayed mostly unspoken in those troubled and frightening times, because it was so clear that the country could not afford to lose Kennedys and their kind in this way.

Troubled times indeed. The U.S. was trying to extradite Martin Luther King's accused slayer, James Earl Ray, from London. Ray had disappeared for two months after the shooting, and was found in London trying to board a plane. He had a pistol in his pocket. An editorial cartoon showed a little boy happily unwrapping a gift of a toy pistol, as his parents beamed. "As the twig is bent . . ." read the caption, expressing the national worry about guns. LBJ reluctantly signed a crime control bill that was short of what he had sought, and there was still disappointment among many lawmakers because Congress failed to enact full control of mail-order gun sales.

The political situation was much as usual in town, regardless of the national picture. A black man, lunchroom and poolroom proprietor Gerard Jennings, was given a strong chance of actually getting on the town council. The turnout was so heavy, with people lined up to mark their paper ballots and insert them into the slots in wooden boxes, that the vote count was delayed. But once everything was tabulated Jennings had fallen far short, and four of five incumbents were reelected. Apparently the "new town" created by annexation was satisfied with the old town. There had been few specific issues, and as the paper summed up, "The challengers promised to do a better job with less money if elected, with the incumbents standing for continued progress and economy." Local politics didn't touch on gun control or assassination.

CHAPTER TEN
Part One Ends

As the presidential race really geared up, local partisanship got into full swing. "Humphrey and Nixon edge nearer to party nominations," a July head said. Culpeper party leaders became embroiled, trying to get the community to pay close attention to their own versions of the campaigns while evading the most sensitive areas.

Leaving a certain amount of confusion in their wake, the assassinations had ripple effects on local and national campaigning. Resurrection City, the encampment conceived by King, melted away in a leadership void. Night riders arose in Meridian, Mississippi. It was on record that "Mac could support Rocky," meaning Eugene McCarthy was willing to back Nelson Rockefeller. An editorial cartoon had McCarthy holding a rabbit labeled "Vietnam policy" and saying "Now if I can just find a hat to pull this out of." It's a bit hard now to imagine, but there was a recall petition in California to oust then-governor Ronald Reagan.

Close attention to it all was paid by quite a few activists in Culpeper. John Moffett Brown, an elderly and outspoken local and chairman of the Culpeper committee of the American Independent Party, made a speech hailing George Wallace as David battling a "federal Goliath." I went to interview the rather dapper Brown, reminding myself that I was an unbiased reporter even though Brown's positions reminded me of my own fanatical father and anyway Wallace was pretty loathsome—and wound up entirely charmed by the AIP spokesman, who was bright, funny, and sincerely convinced, and besides that could turn a phrase.

Looking away from the national scene, as the paper did every day and generally on every page, one could read that the town was acting to save historic East Street through zoning (there was also a West Street; both ran parallel to Main and were pretty much it for north-south travel). It was an early move to use zoning laws to do something rather than prevent something. Part of the street was designated commercial, but there were wonderful old houses there that deserved protection. One of them, the Burgandine House, was being restored; the house was reputed to be the oldest in Culpeper, and Mrs. Elizabeth Burgandine Coons had deeded it to the town for use by the adjoining library. It now houses the Culpeper museum.

Politics and zoning aside, there was a photo of a *Star-Exponent* pressman, Jack Griffin, recognizing the "young fire eater" after he and others had put out a blaze on a passing train engine. Griffin, fifty years later, having spent all that time as both an employee of the paper and a top fire department volunteer and later officer, was pretty much in charge at the printing plant, although the paper had someone called a "general manager." People like Jack are really, truly the heart of a community, those who quietly keep it going by doing their jobs and considering the welfare of others.

Interestingly, Diehl used the term "massive resistance" in a headline about a huge poplar tree at a South East Street home (the enormous tree had taken days to cut down). This was only a decade after the Virginia policy of massive resistance to integration, but the state had moved along with surprising speed.

It was about that time that we got a new reporter, young Sean Kilpatrick, son of the columnist and therefore with newspapering in his blood. He was assigned to cover the first presidential campaign speech by Wallace advocate and my newfound friend John Moffett Brown, but we tended to share the political stuff as time went on.

There was another huge event in the life of the *Star-Exponent*: a six-thousand-pound Goss press was installed, an enormous investment for a small-town paper. When I was back in the offices doing research in 2013, a young pressman, Billy Roper, told me in response to an inquiry about the press "That's the Goss printing the *Belvoir Eagle*," although it may not have been the same Goss.

In spite of some excitement over a new press, it never seemed to us that we were in any kind of a backwater; things happened every day that needed coverage, and evenings putting the paper together included a constant and eager reading of the wire-service machine that rattled steadily in the cramped and paper-strewn newsroom. Some things were more exciting than others, but looking back I can see change after change in development. An item from Philadelphia merited a Page 1 box: "Boys with hair like girls have to wear caps" in pools in that city's recreation centers, it had been decided.

Big headline news illuminated various questions that were perhaps more important than swimming caps. Because of the shooting death of presumed presidential assassin Jack Ruby, security was very heavy for Sirhan Sirhan, who had shot Robert Kennedy. James Earl Ray gave up his fight against extradition and was about to return to the U.S. In Cleveland, snipers killed four and wounded ten, using automatic weapons, in a black district of that city. Whites were banned from the area until things could calm down. Pope Paul VI rejected the birth control pill and all contraceptive devices. Campus unrest continued. The old cartoon *Tizzy* had its high-school-girl heroine saying to her father "I don't think I'll really want to go to college. I can't stand bloodshed."

There was no actual bloodshed in the run-up to the Republican nomination, but a story described the machinations of rivals struggling to stop the front-running Nixon. Ronald Reagan tossed his hat into the ring, and then Maryland favorite son (sorry, Maryland, but he was in fact just that) Spiro Agnew joined forces with Tricky Dickie.

In Miami Beach, the wire stories reported, Nixon was nominated in a first-ballot blitz. He was, as the paper noted, "master of the political comeback." Agnew offered Nixon's name in nomination. A liberal move (yep, at the *Republican* convention) failed to put George Romney on the ticket, and Agnew was nominated for vice president.

Life went on outside our shuttered and invariably dusty doors, as a column by the librarian, Crimora Waite, attested: the library had a new copy of the *Encyclopaedia Britannica*. There was a short piece on a note left in the poor box at the Catholic church. Father Maurice duCastillion, a kindly, gentle man with a heavy accent, I think Belgian, had left a note at the box, "If you need help, come to me." A written reply had been left, saying "I'm pregnant and have to get out of town" and then asking for $200. No $200 was left for the alleged pregnant person, and the next note left at the box said "You're a liar," presumably objecting to the non-appearance of the $200. Boys were suspected.

Construction was continuing on Culpeper's future airport. The sale of beer on Sunday was okayed, and a sow earned deserved recognition with a nineteen-piglet litter. Just consider for a moment how firmly the newspaper had to be connected to the community for someone to bring it to the attention of the news desk—and consider the responsiveness of the editor who never doubted for a moment that the prolific porcine mother belonged in the paper as much as the new encyclopedia did.

Back to politics, Kilpatrick wrote that McCarthy was down the drain; his reasoning was that the Soviet Union had invaded Czechoslovakia, and the chances of a peace candidate were nil. There was a plan under way at the Democratic convention to draft Ted Kennedy, but it was soon down the drain as well. Virginia, we dutifully reported, was sticking by its favorite son, Governor Godwin, although Godwin had had to rush home when his fourteen-year-old adopted daughter Becky was hit by lightning. A running spot on the left bottom of page 1 tracked Becky's progress for days, until very sadly she died.

Democrat Hubert Humphrey was nominated on the first ballot, with Edmund Muskie as his running mate. There was bitter street violence in Chicago, where the convention was held. The paper began its separate but demonstrably equal coverage of the election campaigns in earnest on Sept. 4 of that year, with Nixon stories running on one side of the front page and HHH stories on the other. No one got extra space simply for being outrageous.

Harbingers of things to come appeared that fall. On Sept. 5 there was a story describing a bus-terminal bombing in Tel Aviv that killed one person and injured forty-nine others. Mayor Richard J. Daley continued to defend his Chicago police against the "new media scolds." And speaking of scolds, Agnew pronounced that Humphrey was "squishy soft" on Vietnam.

A charming harbinger was a Kilpo column on Lee Smith, who worked at the *Richmond News Leader* for a while and who was to become a really great Southern novelist. The conservative columnist wrote "I have fallen in love with a lady novelist." Her first book, *The Last Day the Dogbushes Bloomed,* had just been published, and Kilpatrick found it "so good I could cry," and predicted, correctly, "At 23, she is headed for the bright circle of shining stars." At the Richmond newspaper, while Kilpo still worked there, their girl Friday job had fallen open. Lee was recommended and showed up, having been suspended from Hollins College for staying out all night during a group student foray in Paris. She had spent ten days in her new job teaching herself to type, the columnist wrote, and worked very hard until she went back to Hollins. As an intern, among the things she did were kind of the lower echelon of my duties—writing heads, laying out pages, no doubt typing up obituaries. When she returned to college, the columnist wrote, she was "taking 52 hearts with her," obviously including his.

Harbingers often got space when there was a drought of local hard news. The Rental Uniform Service annual football contest was announced (a fine thing for the paper, since the sports page got enthusiastic attention from its readers with all sorts of local predictions and then proper heralding of the winners, and thus drew lots of ads), and there were photos of Mrs. Michael March and Mrs. Phil Irwin, slender in stylish clothes at a Sperryville tennis tournament. Mary Stevens produced her column on a tour of the Pacific Northwest including Canada and Lake Louise, but there wasn't much else for a while.

Because there wasn't a lot happening in the local political or crime arena, I got a byline on a small boxed item. "Pausing at the intersection of Main and Davis to look in a store window was the escapee's undoing," I wrote. Officer R. H. Ford had spotted a Holstein cow, ambling south down Main, at the moment she was peering into J. J. Newberry & Co. He herded her into the fenced courthouse yard, from whence she was claimed.

Cow attendant Roscoe Ford was a story himself. He was the town's first black policeman, so far as I know, a cheerful, committed man who seemed pretty comfortable walking what in the '60s and '70s must have been a difficult line. When he was stationed at the traffic control box at Main and Davis, I would often stop on my rounds to chat with him. This was not only because he was bright and interesting, but also because very occasionally he would kindly let drop a hint that was useful to a news reporter. Ford apparently possessed the agility needed to sidestep the questions that arose because of his race and position of authority, although an elderly white lady once gave indications of hitting me with her umbrella because of the obvious camaraderie I felt with this very black man.

In his personal life, Ford was evidently a wonderful father and a reliable caretaker of infirm animals of all kinds. He was also best buds with a white officer, R. R. Campbell, and he eventually was promoted to sergeant. After he died many years later, the new town police station was named for him; Chris Jenkins, chief at the time, wrote proudly that the name honored a "35-year veteran of the department, Sgt. Roscoe H. Ford."

The big-events drought of '68 ended, and local news returned with a vengeance in the form of a story that I remember with excitement, even while asking myself in retrospect what was wrong with me at the time. Some Angus cattle had breached a tumbled-down fence at the north end of town and managed to make their way onto the railroad trestle, when naturally a train came along. Four of the cows were killed and tumbled into Mountain Run, which flowed beneath the trestle. I was there, in the dark down the banks, rather thrilled while watching the town police and others poling a boat directed by a single flashlight, trying to determine which animals were alive and which were dead. As I say, a questionable reaction on my part to a grisly scene.

Turning from dead cows to live politicians, the paper printed a presidential poll on the front page to fill out and mail in. The list included George Wallace, who to the credit of John Moffett Brown was the local winner, with 180 votes to 91 for Nixon and 30 for Humphrey. Wallace backers were evidently very willing to go to that kind of trouble—that was a lot of mailed-in ballots for a community of that size (county voters were included too, of course, but the county wasn't exactly overrun with people either).

A six-column head on a Sean Kilpatrick story described the vandalism of Fairview Cemetery, with sixty-five monuments overturned. Fairview, now on the National Register of Historic Places, is owned by the town, and includes a large mass burial site of unknown Civil War casualties and a memorial monument added in 1881. Readers were pretty horrified. Happily, justice was swift. Three weeks later several high school students, one from Madison, were sentenced in district court to work at the cemetery as punishment for the vandalism. The Madison lad, whom I described as a "big boy who nevertheless looks younger than 18," brought his mother and stepfather to testify. He said he leaned on a tombstone and it fell over, and one of the other boys toppled one and "it just happened." Judge Reams, of muskrat-diving fame, was not impressed, noting that the lad had "64 chances to change his mind."

Politics in one form or another gained volume. I had a byline on the three-way presidential debate among Democrat Wayne Duncan, Republican Claude Smith, and Brown of the American Independent Party. The story was long and wordy, but I was pleased with it then and, I admit, now. The rambling lead didn't begin with any of the campaign points made. It said that the audience for the debate included "a man who had a son killed in Vietnam, a woman whose child recently brought home a slip of paper requesting signed parental permission for her to participate in prayer in school, a retired man who is watching inflation eat away at his investment income . . ." These were the local issues, encapsulated.

Other news was ongoing. There was an auto show on Davis Street, with a Goad Studio photo of Mrs. Ellen Gimble and her very nice legs getting out of a car. It was announced that Jackie Kennedy would wed Aristotle Onassis, and several days later, to the quiet disappointment of all, she did. Apollo 7 came back after a perfect eleven-day mission, and Admiral Strauss's Brandy Rock Farm held another sale, at which Sen. Albert Gore bought a heifer for $2,900.

A longtime *SE* character whom I haven't mentioned made a number of contributions to local lore, and helped make the paper pretty consistently down-home. I first met Donnie Johnston, then an eighteen- or nineteen-year-old lad, in my early weeks at work. He was in the office to have a photo taken to illustrate a story about a project he and a brother had undertaken, a long walk to publicize something or other. He had his feet propped up toward the camera and wanted the photo to hone in on them to emphasize how tired and sore they were.

He eventually became probably our most popular sports editor ever, and did a closely-followed column on other topics. One of his most memorable was about elderly relatives who wanted to expose the walk on the moon for what it was, a sham, and the moon rocks brought back as fakes. Donnie had one foot in the semi-mythical Eggbornsville that his country relatives called home and one in a world where he was adventuresome enough to go take a picture of Hank Aaron hitting his record-setting home run—a photo that was displayed at Cooperstown. Over the years he was also a disk jockey, photographer, and novelist at various times.

Anyway, back to the big election as a Culpeper happening—who remembers that the 1968 presidential race was undecided for a time? The local news was that "Nixon wins Culpeper," and my lead was that "Culpeper County surprised itself yesterday by giving" the GOP "a sweeping victory with an almost 2–1 margin over" Humphrey, who barely beat out Wallace and his surprisingly viable third party for second place. The national story was that Humphrey had edged ahead in the popular vote but there was a seesaw with Nixon for the electoral win. Not until the next day did our stories describe Nixon as "back from oblivion" and pledging to unify the nation, while locally there was a "surprising lack of rancor on all sides and even a genuine atmosphere of good will" toward the new president-elect. There was a wholesome family picture, and the day after, a rarity: a full-color photo of the Nixons, poor quality but in print.

Sometime during the election cycle there had come a letter to the editor from a writer with a Richmond address, advocating "Negro freedom." It had been duly printed, because letters always were, but drew no comments. Just after Election Day, Bill did an article on Ruby Beck, a black woman who owned the now long-gone Boxwood Restaurant and its little adjoining motel. The head, "I'm just me—that's all," set the tone, that this fifty-nine-year-old former domestic saw no racial problem in Culpeper whatever: "At the restaurant you just serve people, not races." It was a bit of a summary of the prevailing attitude, that there was no problem as long as one wasn't stirred up. Ruby Beck and Roscoe Ford, not stirring things up, got along fine, thinking what thoughts no one knew.

On Nov. 13 there was a dual byline on a snowstorm story, "By Kathleen Hoffman and Sean Kilpatrick." Also appearing in that issue was an announcement of my wedding, explaining the name change.

The young man who was nice to my dog and I had taken a brief trip on our wedding day to Skyline Drive, and that was the day the snow season started.

It was a major storm and should have been a bad omen for a marriage, but forty-nine years later I guess maybe not. We set up housekeeping in my former carriage house with the snow coming down, and were fine with power supplied by the town, which uniquely had its own power plant. Elsewhere, power lines were down all over, and people struggled with the cold and dark. The paper happily covered it when an irate man delivered a wreath to Northern Piedmont Electric, the local co-op. He hung it on the door of their Madison Road offices. "Everybody there," he explained sadly, "must be dead." We also covered the round-the-clock efforts to restore power, with men out in the snow doing their best.

It is a measure of the role the *Star-Exponent* played in the community that we not only wrote about the hardworking linemen, but then gave equal time to the co-op manager, Edwin Kann. He described in detail the measures that had been taken, the difficult struggles in the snow and cold, and the man-hours spent, and expressed great unhappiness because the wreath story had hit the AP wire. He knew instantly that we were the source; there wasn't any mysterious "going viral" with no traceable starting point. "Sorry, but you shall never bury us because we refuse to lie down and die," was his somewhat stuffy rejoinder to the memorial gift. Power people hit by early winter storms have no sense of humor.

Wreathgate over with, the paper continued to be filled with unrelated happenings that were important to someone. The moon flight was slated at last, and less than a year later Neil Armstrong would take his "small step." O. J. Simpson, with a gimpy leg, was playing excellent football; "Partial O.J. is enough," a headline quoted the coach as saying. Another plane was hijacked to Cuba, with the claim that there was a bomb on board. Perhaps most culturally telling was the declaration that "Next time Heidi has to wait," announcing the TV networks' decision that Joe Namath and an exciting gridiron clash would never again give way to a movie at a decisive moment. John Lennon was convicted, surprise, of a drug charge. There was a photo in the paper of H. R. Haldeman, then an unfamiliar name who was to be the presidential assistant. The

Germanna Foundation, a group with ties to the German settlers who had been the forefathers of many local families, donated a hundred acres to be used for the area community college.

The third barn in a short while was destroyed in a suspicious fire, and Rev. R. C. Davis of the black Antioch Baptist Church was to preach the community Thanksgiving sermon at Culpeper United Methodist Church (fairly groundbreaking). A fierce wind blew down the less-than-sound ceiling in the sanctuary of Culpeper Presbyterian Church on Main Street. It was a rather strange thing to look into that church and see the ceiling settled over the pews amidst some pretty old dust, and that was one of the times I felt keenly the lack of the "photo" part of the photojournalist I later considered myself. The Presbyterians moved their services to the basement, and Goad Studio took the needed photo.

There was another color picture on Page 1 in December. The Apollo 8 astronauts who would orbit the moon, William A. Anders, James Lovell Jr., and Frank Borman, posed in their space suits. Borman would later come down with the flu during the flight; another frustration for the astronauts was their attempt to broadcast a view of Earth from halfway to the moon. It didn't work properly, although something did come through just before Christmas.

And in yet another of those haunting recurrences, indicating that sadly not much changes, a five-year-old boy was playing with his father's shotgun in a house near the village of Winston when it went off. The child's twenty-three-year-old mother died. And tempting as it is to think the dangers of terrorist attacks are new, the start of the 1969 Superbowl was delayed by a bomb threat that turned out to be false. The New York Jets won over the Baltimore Colts and Johnny Unitas.

Early that year there was ample proof that women really hadn't gotten far in the national perception. A cartoon showed a woman talking on the phone with considerable irritation: "Look, Charles, I don't call you during board meetings, you don't call me during 'Peyton Place.'" This was interesting to me, since I had never watched *Peyton Place* in my life, but my new husband was startlingly conversant with it.

I wrote a story on two high-achieving and very pretty high school seniors, Alison Graves and Pattie Ankers. I can't swear I didn't write the head, but I hope not. It said "So beauty and brains don't mix?"

Sean Kilpatrick demonstrated that despite his youth he was a member of the male old guard that included his father by doing a sports story on a female jockey who was then riding at Charles Town (home of both auto and horse racing). He described her as a "striking girl" and then compounded this by calling the nineteen-year-old a "delightfully feminine gal." I'm not sure when the word "gal" began to whomp me over the head like a large mackerel, but I doubt that it did then. I liked Sean and we got along well—he was rather charming, articulate, easy to talk to, and fond of dogs, all good things.

The mix of news in the usually eight-page paper continued to be diverse. A jump-page head, heralding what the story that didn't all fit on Page 1 was about, said "Nixon expected to remain man of caution throughout administration." And so he did, sort of. The tearful skipper of the USS Pueblo described his torture during his interrogation by North Korean captors. North Carolina state police battled black students who had seized an administration building at Duke University, while the National Guard stood by. Students, mostly white, shouted "Pig" at the police. It was revealed that Sirhan Sirhan had practiced at a shooting range the day before he assassinated Robert Kennedy. Plane number nine was hijacked to Cuba.

Locally, there was "an intensive, three-day manhunt in the Richardsville area" when two cornered fugitives used weapons to hold off police. They turned out to be a fifteen-year-old with a .22 rifle and an eleven-year-old with a bayonet. They had come to Culpeper from Maryland, and had broken into a house. A big funeral was held for Miss Mary Gertrude Durant, 101, the subject earlier of a Mary Stevens Jones feature, who was then the oldest county resident.

Mary Stevens did a feature on Peter Leach-Lewis, an Englishman who was charged with reckless driving while passing through Culpeper. He liked Culpeper and his courteous treatment so much that he stayed— and starred in a production of "The Man Who Came to Dinner." Interviews with citizens in the recently annexed part of the town indicated that they liked the setup fine, particularly trash collection and new streetlights. The town office was "swamped," with "only four girls" to handle the doubled volume of phone calls.

Page 3 had a series on historic homes. Anna Townsend Willis wrote in To Live in Virginia . . . that a visiting lady oriole (a bird, not a ballplayer) liked lemon meringue pie. And in a relatively unusual move, Bill Diehl's column, Dealing It Out, was about ten children, several under the age of five, who had been left at home alone when their mother was hospitalized. The father was said to be "just not around." Local women took them in—Culpeper was a close and involved community, for sure—and Dealing It Out gently pushed for the welfare folks to do more, with carefully chosen quotes from the women who were looking after the kids.

At almost the same time, Anna Willis' column turned from birds to the genesis of a new county animal shelter, as Culpeper's awareness of its community responsibilities grew. She called it "a living memorial to good dogs," and recommended commemoration of a beloved canine with a gift of cash for the shelter. For her part, she had a good dog to remember: "For more than a year now, there has been something missing from our house . . . since the snowy day the little black cocker trotted down the path to go on her last ride." Who doesn't remember the sorrow of such a day? What better way to collect funds? Of raising the money for such a cause, she declared "We can do it; of course we can," speaking directly to the community as one could do in a local newspaper column then. And we could and did, and the shelter was established.

In March of 1969 the assassinations (horribly, plural) were back in the news. In New Orleans, Clay Shaw, who had the dubious distinction of being the only person ever prosecuted in the death of JFK, had been cleared of the conspiracy charges brought by New Orleans prosecutor Jim Garrison. But then he was charged anew, this time with perjury. Sirhan quietly confessed to the murder of the younger Kennedy. Asked if he was sorry his victim was dead, he was quoted as saying "No, I'm not sorry, but I'm not proud of it, because I have no exact knowledge of having killed him." He said he was drunk, and was willing to die for the Arab cause. He never indicated much clarity on the topic—he was Palestinian with Jordanian citizenship, and his court appearances were memorable particularly for a diatribe about Israel. As Robert Kennedy Jr. expressed doubts about Sirhan's sole guilt in 2018, the man's story about having no memory of shooting the presidential candidate remained unchanged.

There came at this point another crossroads in my career, such as it was. I was pregnant, constantly throwing up and suffering from various respiratory ailments. My husband and I felt pretty firmly that a mother should stay home with her children until they went to school, so again acting in ways that I would not have admired thirty or even twenty years later, I decided the time had come to give up my seat at the battered partners desk and turn to the more domestic role that seemed proper. Now anytime I see a young woman work up until the week before her due date I want to applaud, and I feel more than a bit mortified by my own wimpiness, but then it seemed like the reasonable thing.

In truth, I felt inclined to shirk not only because working until the last minute wasn't done, but also because I was so bad at being pregnant. Throwing up had become a way of life, whether it was in the bathroom at work, the one at home, or a paper bag inside a drugstore. I wasn't getting much warning and was taking it badly. I believed in being healthy and taking these things in stride, but it wasn't happening.

My last memorable story in 1969 was about a tour of the Mount Pony Federal Reserve facility, memorable partly because this unlikely structure became a major part of Culpeper's identity and partly because the climate of secrecy surrounding it made me want to know stuff. "The world of the future has come in the form of a hugely expensive communications center," I wrote, making Culpeper "one up on most of the world" in terms of computer capability. Built into the side of a steep hill on farmland that wasn't much good for farming, the thing was supposed to house the big computers that the Fed required to transact its business. The first thing anyone involved said, over and over, was that there would be no money kept there.

I could understand the reservations that the banking system had about every Tom, Dick, and *Star-Exponent* reporter who wanted to know about the place, but they were so paranoid and rigid that it was irritating. Sean and I went, and met with the vice president in charge, Gordon Dickerson, a man who later retired to Culpeper and started a bookstore and who was in fact a fine person. But he was a bit jumpy, and defensive to the point that I felt physically protective of the Polaroid

I was carrying but was forbidden to use. He told us little except that the facility was wired to the economic workings of the nation, and we went nowhere beyond his office.

I knew more than perhaps the average person about the structure, because it was the last job that my father, a union pipe fitter, worked on before his retirement. He told of carefully separated work groups, each confined to an area, and of the inclusion of lots of showers and other amenities. And no, I didn't mention this to Gordon Dickerson.

The perversity that all the secrecy aroused in me (plus a dearth of information) led to this, in the story: "It is easy to imagine a handful of computer experts, the only men left in the world after a nuclear attack who can hope to communicate with the complex machine, fearfully entering the heavily shaded glass front doors and walking with palpitating hearts down empty corridors to the waiting brain. There they would hope to wring from its memory centers enough knowledge to start the world in motion again."

When we left, with Sean driving, I sneaked a photo of surveillance equipment at the entrance, taken at the odd angle I needed to conceal the camera from the man in the guardhouse, and the paper used it, a small triumph. Years later it came to light that I hadn't been far off, because the structure was the intended refuge for the federal government's financial titans in the event of nuclear war, complete with radiation-proof window linings and desks with names of various Federal Reserve bigwigs who would work at them, in between using the showers and living quarters. Still later it apparently housed a mountain of out-of-circulation pennies, despite the "no money, ever, absolutely no money" mantra. Sometime in the '90s it even took over as the switching station for the whole Fed system when the Chicago Federal Reserve Bank was flooded. Finally, with the realization that computers didn't need much space and that their physical locations were the least of their vulnerabilities, the expansive building ended up as part of the Smithsonian Institution, housing a wonderful film preservation facility.

At any rate, a few weeks later Sean was writing about the new redistricting plan and I was home making preparations to move and to have a baby.

CHAPTER ELEVEN
I Return; the News
Is Still There

During the two years I spent as a homebody I certainly did the best I could, baking bread from scratch, carefully monitoring my child, keeping things cleaner than I would ever do again. Yes, I felt a loss— we were way, way out in the country, had only one car, and couldn't see another house from our rented porch.

Obviously I was isolated; certainly I missed my job, and I knew progress was going on without me. It left a huge hole in my heart when John, by then three years old, was shot to death in the driveway of our house, presumably by a wandering hunter, presumably in hell now. All this led to a major depression, a loathing of our rented house, and then a move to a house that we bought in a Culpeper subdivision. Then I was back.

In addition to the Mount Pony story, my first calendar year as a reporter had wound up with a byline about the town's annexation and its plans for expanded services. The drop head said "Local Population Will Climb to Nearly 6,000." That was amazing, and it meant there would be no going back. When I moved to town, people knew one another—when I first went to pay my natural-gas bill at the Main Street office, the clerk looked at me closely and remarked firmly and in surprise "I don't know you." I had to explain that I was an Ann Graves tenant, or I don't think I would have been accepted as a paying customer.

But growth came, and I was back to write about it. Fast-forward about two years after my departure from the scene, and I was again at work, again on the night shift, an arrangement that allowed us to leave our toddler daughter in day care only two hours a day. I went to work at three, and Jack got off at five. He went by the sitter's to pick Jennifer up; I'd come home and cook a quick dinner, and then go back to the office while Jack attended to bath and bedtime. The anxious mother (and I certainly was that) was still around, but I managed to pick up my reporter persona where I had abandoned it. Again I was pulled firmly into the day-to-day routine and occasional drama of doing what needed to be done to put the paper to bed by midnight—hopefully much later than my child's bedtime.

A lot of changes in society had been vaguely developing during those first two years of my introduction to news and newsgathering. But between the time I returned in 1971 and the time I left the *Star-Exponent* for good in 1984, there were some major shifts in the mood of America, as well as in the business of newspapers. Really, that dozen years wasn't much time to adjust. I can see it incrementally now, but of course while it was happening I was too enmeshed to step back and say to myself, Oh, this is different, and yay for it. Well, yay for some of it; not for what happened with community newspapering, which was extreme and kind of a tragedy.

Certainly I understand at this point that I might have foreseen that my daughter would grow up in a fundamentally altered society. She wasn't going to have as her only acceptable career choices teacher, nurse, secretary, or homemaker—not that I had been limited to those choices, as it happened, but I had done a little thinking about it. Not deep thinking, admittedly, because for most of us not a lot of that goes on in our early twenties, but there was something I was not quite willing to fall in line with, even if my different path wasn't really radically different.

And let's face it, I had been giving very little consideration to whether I could make a long-term, permanent living. There is no denying that my lack of thought about paying my bills, buying a house, having a car that started consistently, and that kind of thing was partly because hovering on the periphery of my choices was the thought that yes, I'd probably get married, and yes, my husband would make more money than I did.

So my daughter was to have the more challenging situation of unlimited options for a career, but she would enter the world of work thinking she would have to make a living. I could never forget, though, that all those choices were made easier because of "those who had gone before," role models who wouldn't have thought of themselves that way but were so firmly themselves that there was no other way to see them. I don't count myself among them, because my steps were small and intermediate. Mary Stevens Jones was certainly a role model, as were longtime newspaper veteran Lucy Catherine Bowie and, less immediately, Ann Green Graves, my landlady, who was retired but had worked on the Green publishing empire's various papers in the early days.

I have a suspicion none of them thought much about what they were doing: becoming women who held responsible jobs out in the thick of things when women mostly didn't. Regrettably, it never occurred to me to talk to them about it, but I wonder now whether they found themselves noticing that the unexpectedness of their roles was fading as more women took less traditional roles.

My role models were far outnumbered by the husband-named women whose public lives were bound up with having presentable children and nice homes for them, helping out at school as room mothers, and making those holiday decorations. Still, also working in journalism in Culpeper were Martha Ross, a long-married teacher who had turned to newspapering with the *SE* as a retirement job, several women who were stringers for bigger papers, women who sold advertising, and of course the indispensable typesetters. Following in their wake in the coming years would be a growing number of young reporters for the paper, then a first female editor and then another. There were also dozens of women I wrote about, people doing unusual things like running for town council, or even simply living a long time on their own, unmarried or widowed, and when I interviewed them I took in the lives they had lived. There was depth to those people, depth of a kind that had difficulty expressing itself while they were being expected to live up to, and through, a secondary identity taken from a husband.

Mary Stevens wrote about anything and everything for many years, first on a weekly paper and then on the daily. Her final Christmas opus was published on Dec. 24, 1975, and included this couplet:

"To all officials reelected

"A fine performance is expected."

She did expect fine performances, from those in government, those teaching children, and those working for newspapers. The questionable morals and ethics of the twenty-first century would have given her heart palpitations, but she would have expressed her displeasure with no more than a well-bred sniff and then a brief dismissal. For her, there were no two paths—people should behave themselves and do absolutely the right thing.

Her personal soapbox, the Culpeper's Main and Davis column, was recognized as a winner in many state and national newspaper competitions. Its content ranged from appreciations of beauty and the occasional wry comment about local politics to reminiscences of an earlier time. One such was about opening gates of the past, as she remembered the trips from her home east of Culpeper to the tiny community of Lignum to go to school. She and her sister Mildred drove a horse, and someone had to get down from the buggy to open the gates as they passed through pastures and woodland. That by-definition "backwoods" education was an obvious success in opening a fine mind.

After she retired, though, there was a January 1976 story in the paper about a party that other staff attended to honor her at the Holiday Inn. She had begun work with the *Culpeper Exponent* in the '40s. Still, the story about this tower of strength, accuracy, and reliability was relegated to Page 3, sharing space with Public Pulpit. Had she been a longtime male employee it would have been on the front, and I did grouse some over that at the time.

To compensate, I wrote a feature story on Mary Stevens that spring, although it also was relegated to Page 3. It began with the fact that she had returned from a trip to Jamaica, and that *Star-Exponent* readers hadn't gotten the usual account of her trip because the traveler had retired, and some were disappointed. According to my story, her writing career began when the owner of the old weekly *Exponent* died somewhat unexpectedly. As befits a small-town lady, Mary Stevens went to offer her sympathy and to ask if there was anything she could do to help. She was told with some directness "You could help get the paper out this week." She and Lucy Catherine produced the paper for two weeks, and then Lucy Catherine went to take another job as previously scheduled. Mary Stevens pitched in and proceeded to produce most of the paper by herself for a time; unlike Lucy Catherine, she never learned to operate a Linotype.

Over the years she won more than thirty-five state and national writing awards, and was in *Who's Who Among American Women,* not bad for a child of rural Virginia. I wrote my heartfelt opinion: "People will tell you right off that MSJ is a lady, but being a lady can be done with an active mind, quick judgment and some acerbic views."

The only real disagreement we ever had was during the few years when she and I shared the women's page and daytime news, both part-time, she in semi-retirement and I as the mother of a preschooler. She had much stricter rules about wedding coverage (often long, detailed articles and of course photos of the bride, all published without charge then) than I was willing to enforce. Our only noticeable contretemps came about because she opposed publishing pictures of bride and groom posing together, and I really couldn't bring myself to care or to take the fierce stand needed to resist a bride who wanted a couple picture or else.

If Mary Stevens's retirement wasn't given the space I felt it deserved, a bigger splash was made when the admirable Lucy Catherine resigned as editor of the *Madison Eagle* in 1976. She said publicly that she had been ordered by the ownership not to print any more "controversial articles" about the Madison school board. Lucy Catherine admitted that legal action had been threatened against the paper, but declared that the articles were factual and no lawsuit was going anywhere—and of course it didn't.

She explained that the school board had been disguising illegal closed sessions by declaring the closures to be for personnel reasons (an exception permitted by the Freedom of Information Act), with the explanation that they were in the process of hiring substitute teachers. But, Miss Bowie remarked tartly, they could have "hired 1,000 substitute teachers by now." In reply, the owners said they had only ordered the withholding of unsigned letters to the editor. Lucy Catherine admitted that one unsigned letter had indeed been used, on a different topic; that one was about pornography, and the writer, while feeling strongly about the subject, was embarrassed to have her name associated with it.

After thirty-three years in the news business, Lucy Catherine said firmly "I can't live with the policy that I must print only what someone wants to see." Still, upholding the committed journalist's belief that the paper-and-ink show must go on, she worked without pay to train her successor.

The year before, I had done a feature article on her, with the headline "Miss Lucy Catherine Bowie—no one ever called the lady dull." It began with the quote that inspired the head: "'I'm dull and I'm ordinary,' mourns Lucy Catherine Bowie, skilled Linotype operator, editor of the Madison County newspaper, quilting expert and Culpeper historian." It went on with my happy conclusion from my association with her: "Hand her a topic and you get back a neatly packaged spoken essay, including a ream of quotable quotes." One such: "A Linotype is a beautiful piece of machinery. It has 40,000 moving parts and takes 18 months to learn how to operate. After you do learn, you have a renewed respect for your fellow man's mind." Another: "I always go to work neither male nor female."

On one of her favorite subjects, Culpeper, she said that it was "adolescent. It has all the ills of the big city, like overcrowding, but none of the benefits, like museums." She was then about sixty years old. She and her brother Bruce, who had died a short while earlier, had started the tiny weekly *Rappahannock News* in nearby Sperryville and run it for years.

Looking back, it seems I sought out older women who had made their own way, some married at least briefly, some never, to interview. Or it may be that readers brought these people to my attention once I had written up a few of them. I talked to Nora Kendall, who was ninety-three and lived in Little Washington, as the town in Rappahannock County with the founding father's name is known locally. Her husband had been a chauffeur for the Tiffany family of jewelry fame. Nora had been friends with the daughter of the house, but as things worked out she couldn't be merely a wife and a friend. Her husband had returned safely from World War I, only to die in a plane crash soon afterward. Nora had been an army nurse in the war, so she had traditional skills to keep herself going, and that's what she did.

Another woman, also an army wife, who referred to herself no matter what as Mrs. Alfred J. Booth, merited a story on reaching one hundred years old. In spite of the "Mrs. Alfred," her husband had died when she was in her forties, leaving her with a daughter to raise, and she too had done it, alone.

And there was Nan Frazier, also possessed of nearly a century of memories. Her parents met at a dance in a house on Culpeper's Main Street during the Civil War. At ninety-two she still managed to live by herself in a home on Asher Street. A member of the United Daughters of the Confederacy, she was possessed of a prodigious memory and enough friends to keep her "aging in place," to use a relatively new term that she would not have known but would have favored.

One of my favorites, ever, was Eckis Simms. I talked with her for print when she was eighty, but I had known her to say hello to for a while. She lived in a Main Street house close to the first Culpeper Library building, and she kept chickens there, streetwise chickens with which she had a fine relationship—some would sit on her lap, and cooperatively did so for a photo. Parts of her story were pretty unique. She never learned to drive, and walked everywhere. Fairly late in life she was hit by a car while crossing Main Street. She survived, and did not give up her constant walking; the strange thing was that many years before, her nine-year-old only daughter had been hit by a car and killed in almost the same location. As a child, she said, she had been a champion speller, inheriting an interest in words from her mother, who said she had taken the name Eckis from a novel. Unique women, apparently, both of them.

And I wrote about women who were beginning to step up, groping toward a form of equality or at least the coveted seat at the table. In 1971 I wrote about Gladys Bowie, who was married to Lucy Catherine's brother Bruce and was the first of her gender to hold a seat on the city council. "As a freshman councilwoman in 1966 and 1967, [she] lost no time making it clear that she was on the formerly all-male town governing group for other than decorative purposes," I wrote. "She has considered herself a person working with people, rather than a woman competing against men." She was reliably outspoken, innovative, and conscientious, and was a champion of such causes as recreational facilities.

Gladys was quite a bit younger than her husband, and he had become ill. The needs of a business—the Bowies had a print shop on East Street—and an ailing husband had left her worried that "personal affairs" might interfere with doing a first-rate job for the town, so she was leaving the council. She certainly had always expected herself to give one of Mary Stevens's "fine performances" for those who had elected her.

Another unorthodox subject was Mary Ann McCarthy, who at fifty-eight was teaching self-defense for women, sponsored by the Culpeper chapter of the National Organization for Women in 1974. "She looks something like a Sears Gramma Doll," I noted (the Gramma rag doll was a bespectacled, gray-bun-coiffed creation that was popular at the time), "but would have you know she possesses the reputation of being 'the dirtiest fighter east of the Mississippi,' and besides she curses a lot." Not surprisingly, I found her "gleeful over the disparity between her appearance and her avocation."

A young woman who had been swept up by the changes in attitudes was Margaret Phillips, the curate at St. Stephen's Episcopal Church. She told me about taking an unusual route to where she was. Her seminary life had been undertaken without heartfelt commitment, but had turned out to be a slow building toward the ministry. Her faith had left her for a while during her college years, and right at the time she felt it returning, the church stepped up the stakes by approving the ordination of women. "Suddenly," she said, "it was not a question of whether we [women] could be ordained, but *when* I should." Impressively, considering the small, traditional community, she felt welcomed by the local congregation.

I wrote about Billie Lee Dunford-Jackson, thirty-three, who was the still-rare female attorney with a local firm, and who even had the temerity to hyphenate her last name after marrying her husband, Stan; about Lois Harden, who was breeding Morgan horses at Lignum; about Ann Browning, who had worked for her father's lumber company and was elected to the county board of supervisors and served on the welfare board.

Toward the end of my daily-paper servitude, there were three stories within a few months that demonstrated the complications of lives traditionally entwined (or not) with men. Miss Crimora Waite, the longtime librarian, retired. The library had begun with donations of books and of space on Davis Street. Miss Crimora became the official librarian in 1933, five years after the book-lending service had moved to the town municipal building. She was the daughter of Charles Waite, a prominent attorney, and everyone in town knew her, but her age was something never to be revealed. When she stepped aside for a new librarian, there was an editorial in the paper: "Thanks, Miss Crimora."

Miss Crimora's other means of support was the Waite Kindergarten, which she operated with her sister, Miss Kitty, who had married but was there to help run an educational effort that included elaborate art creations and, as I mentioned before, because it stuck firmly in my mind, a "nap fairy." Our daughter spent her five-year-old year there, and enjoyed the nap fairy, the art shows, and the spirited dancing at graduation. Miss Crimora was an unapologetic gossip who was devoted to all things Culpeper and was tuned in to all sorts of details about the town. She once told me that she had been worried that my predecessor, Gary Ebbels, was "going to write a book and 'spose us all."

Another revolutionary woman, on her own terms, was Anna Ruth Inskeep, the first female member of Culpeper's board of supervisors. Pleasant and smiling and apparently at ease with herself and her life, she had a bedrock realism that came from living into the beginnings of her golden years a few miles from where she grew up. She was the hardworking wife of a dairy farmer, a man who did not limit his and his family's efforts to humbly tilling the soil but who joined various relatives in diverse investments including the local Holiday Inn. She insisted she was not political, and described the agricultural youth organization 4-H as a big force in her life. Still, she easily grasped the issues of a growing community and voted her opinions firmly.

An accidental revolutionary, but the real thing nevertheless, was the charming Sally Lea, one of my subjects for Women on the Go, a tabloid special section invented not really to honor women but to sell ads. She had made herself a successful real estate agent, although somewhat to her own surprise. She explained to me, who was close to her contemporary, that she grew up a sheltered only child, and went to college mostly for fun and to position herself for marriage, rather than with a career in mind. Her marriage ended, and she had to earn a living for herself and her children. She had dabbled in real estate, but was so uncertain of herself that she went back to school and finished her degree in case she had to teach.

Sally, who did remarry, but a ways down the road, indicated in her low, measured, rather sweet tones, with a note almost of surprise, that as a real estate agent she was not a sales superstar, but "I can do for myself." Actually, she was very good at her job, and continued to do well for many years until she retired. "I can do for myself"—a succinct statement of what was changing for women.

There were gender-related breakthroughs reported in the local, national, and international news, as well as some backlash evident here and there, and a sampling of all this was of course crammed into the local newspaper. Mary Stevens wrote in early 1971 about Betty Webb, the bookkeeper and secretary at Culpeper Building and Supply, who came down with mumps and had to miss work—for the first time in twenty-two years. A woman faithfully hanging in on the job was a good thing, and the job she had was perhaps not recognized but was important.

Retired teacher turned reporter Martha Ross was then covering the supervisors in her part-time job, indicating that Mary Stevens's elevation to hard-news reporter status wasn't a fluke. Ross, a woman considered part of local society but possessed of an unrestrained and even rowdy sense of humor, was sent out to write about the area bull-testing station. Happily her thoughts about what kind of testing she had thought went on there didn't make it into print. (For those who also thought the potency of the bulls might have been the subject, or maybe the strength of their reaction to a comely heifer, no, it had to do with weight gain on a particular diet, as I recall, since fattening up rapidly was a good trait for cattle to pass on.)

Pioneer attorney Carroll Kem Shackelford became the first woman substitute judge in Culpeper, although she had already acted in a similar capacity elsewhere in the state. Women did begin to get their own names in photo captions—Gladys Bowie on her own as councilwoman, and Mrs. "Kit" Robinson, wife of congressman J. Kenneth Robinson. Still, women pictured in group photos along with these privileged few were often still identified by a husband name. Kay Potter, wife of the publisher, had begun covering a few things here and there, and eventually stopped being Mrs. Walter Potter. To all appearances she enjoyed the work, and certainly the paper had use for the womanpower. She related quickly to people, and was a more natural newspaper person than her publisher husband.

The women's and Focus pages held out on the first-name issue for as long as Mary Stevens stayed. So Councilwoman Bowie was "Mrs. Bruce" when she lauded Southern women at a United Daughters of the Confederacy meeting that got a few inches in the paper. She was quoted as telling her audience that a few women even participated in the fighting during the Civil War, although they would have preferred settling things at the conference table. Certainly in the 1860s "a seat at the table" before the killing began would have been a good use of a sensible woman or two.

The Roman Catholic Church and its stance on reproduction and women came in for local coverage. Bishop Walter Sullivan visited Culpeper and spoke about birth control. Although Pope Paul VI was still strongly opposed to it, Sullivan noted interestingly that there were "occasions that mitigate the norm." There was also something of a war between the Catholic Church and the miniskirt, with photo proof of young women being stopped for wearing short skirts as they were about to enter the Vatican.

Still, in the first half of the '70s a woman named Alene Bertha Duerk became the U.S. Navy's first female admiral, but shortly afterward the newspaper did a dispiriting about-face. There was a front-page picture of the first female to deploy aboard a U.S. Navy warship, but she posed in boots and a miniskirt. "Join the Navy and see the pilots" was the headline, with the recommendation that that should be the Navy's new recruiting slogan because, well, because there was a pretty girl.

A quick cyber check years later revealed that the attractive young servicewoman, one of eight to be naval pilots by that point, was promoted to commander and then captain. Joellen Drag, who had worn the miniskirt while waving from a plane wing, was well aware of the big picture, it seemed, and a later photo showed her in the cockpit wearing a helmet with a large flower. Interestingly, she used her married name in her career, and as Captain Joellen Oslund became a plaintiff in Owens v. Brown, a lawsuit that challenged the combat and shipboard assignment restrictions on women in the navy.

A twentysomething named Pekay Pettus (she never said whether this was a nickname, and I never knew) began writing for the paper, indicating that female reporters were there to stay—of course they were, because they worked for less. A recent graduate of Mary Baldwin College, an all-women school, she had really wanted to write, so she did. In 1973 I managed to be something of an illustration of where things were on the timeline of steady progress by female journalists by winning a National Association of Press Women award for a story about a big trial—moving on from a win in the state—while working part-time so I could stay home more with my child. In the photo with the Page 1 announcement I wore a paisley dress, which I remember fondly, and black cat's-eye glasses. The story noted that I was sharing editorial duties on the Focus page with Mary Stevens.

Most tellingly, the award came because I hadn't totally surrendered to the Focus page and its activities, which I could have done and still kept my part-time job. Trials in the two courts, of course, were a daytime happening, as were meetings of town committees, so I set out to build myself a news beat to keep from being held to wedding rewrites and editing of who-visited-whom news. I was pretty proud of that award, because I knew when I wrote about the murder trial of Clarence Linwood Bowen that it was a good story and that I had gotten to the heart of it. (More about it later.)

A trial worthy of a big front-page head was a rarity, though. I guess the restrictions that I felt were dishearteningly in tune with the times, since a 1974 national poll found that only fourteen percent of women said they preferred "Ms." as a form of address over "Miss" or "Mrs.," and that more than half wanted to combine marriage, a family, and a career.

On the other hand, I had begun a column, Wandering Mind, which ran on the Focus page and was often about children and the war between the sexes, treated with humor. "Any man who watches six consecutive halves of football can be declared legally dead," I asserted, and I still believe that. But while I long ago surrendered to the reality of interminable TV sports, there is no doubt that somewhere along the decades I ceased to find it funny.

Things cried out to be included in the column. The "Total Woman" phenomenon began, stemming from the book written by Marabel Morgan of Miami. It was a marriage enrichment course, dedicated to the proposition that whatever makes the husband happy will make the wife happy, so she should concentrate on doing things his way. The most famous recommendation was to greet the home-coming husband clad in Saran wrap; satisfying his libido was the key to obtaining the material things that would make the little woman happy.

In the best-selling nonfiction book of 1974, Morgan wrote "It's only when a woman surrenders her life to her husband, reveres and worships him and is willing to serve him, that she becomes really beautiful to him." Honest, she wrote that, and there were women then who fully embraced it. The splendid movie *Fried Green Tomatoes* took note of this awful antifeminist phenomenon by having actress Kathy Bates as a housewife go to such a seminar and become inspired to greet her husband in plastic wrap. His quick response: "Have you gone insane? Someone might see you. What if I'd been a paper boy or something, honey?" A Total Woman program was taught in my own neighborhood, West Lakes, although I declined to attend.

Possibly as an offshoot, a neighbor came up with a beauty gathering for women. I did go to that, and wrote about it. There was instruction and hands-on practice in applying slathered-on green mudpacks, pale masks that made someone observe that everyone's noses stuck out. I frolicked heedlessly among the quotable remarks while compiling my next column, and as a result lost the esteem of and interaction with the woman who was the hostess.

Again as a daytime endeavor, I began a series under the general heading Woman Working, writing about women I knew who were involved in government or business in some way. Mary Lou Mullins, manager of the planning and zoning office, was an early choice. Juvenile probation officer Bev Robson was an interesting one; her job was something that hadn't actually ever been closed to women, so far as I could learn, and was one that women instinctively handled well—it just wasn't a choice the average young girl graduating from Mary Baldwin might readily consider. Another area of female strength was demonstrated in a story about Frances Goddard of the department of social services, who confirmed the existence of irregular adoption services not overseen by her agency. She was to figure in my future twenty years later, when the time came to transfer to employment that paid better than the community newspaper pittance.

To show the other side of non-gender-based employment, I did a story about Ronald Ceremele, who at twenty-five became the first male telephone operator in Culpeper. That was a giant step for mankind, indeed, since the female, whiny-voiced phone operator had been a joke long before Lily Tomlin created Ernestine.

Even the ongoing Watergate drama was not without its female players, who were duly given their own time in the news. In June of 1973 a story noted that "Martha Mitchell, once the darling of the Nixon administration, now travels a lonely, bitter road." She was mad, and said her husband, Nixon Attorney General John Mitchell, was guilty and that the president should resign. Rosemary Woods, the president's secretary, came in for her share of attention with the "Rosemary stretch," in which she reenacted her version of how that incriminating tape got erased. A traditional, loyal woman with a male boss, she became a footnote in history and a staple of late-night television comedy. It seemed women couldn't win in the national news. There was an onslaught of media attention when Symbionese Liberation Army captive and then apparent cult participant Patty Hearst recorded a message to her parents saying the FBI was trying to murder her.

In Culpeper, though, things were going a bit better from year to year. Anna Marie Stringfellow served a term on the town council, but declined to run again. In the next election, Kay Potter came in second in a seven-person field, and began her own term. A young Culpeper woman was organizing a Montessori school, one that didn't succeed but was a brave attempt. Some young mothers also established a babysitting co-op.

I was to run across one of those co-op members forty years later in a Culpeper shop, and she recognized my name on a credit card and recalled that article fondly. We were both absurdly pleased by the incident.

An ongoing Homemakers' Column from Virginia Cooperative Extension was written by my friend Brenda Olafsen, the only female agent in that agriculturally essential office, which traditionally dealt with when to plow one's winter crops under and how to make use of the new concept of rotational grazing. While Brenda wrote mostly about decorating and baking, she was willing to touch on education and that sort of thing.

Cooking and similar activities were all pretty women-centered. There was the *Star-Exponent's* Adventures in Cooking local recipe contest, held each year for a while, attracting quite a bit of interest while generating lots of advertising for the special section in which the recipes were printed. The community was still small enough that people knew many of the entrants and even in many cases had tasted the dishes at church potlucks. I don't remember any men entering; it would probably have been an admission of something dread if they had. Eventually the recipe section began to shrink, as ads became fewer. Newspapers of, by, and for communities had to live by the rule of advertising inches, because they were businesses—local, homegrown businesses, but businesses.

By the mid-'70s I had happily been added to the lists of Virginia Press Association and Virginia Press Women winners in most years. In 1976 I won first place for news coverage in our circulation category in the VPW contest. I got front-page coverage all by myself, with a nice photo of me with long, biggish hair. When we went to the conventions to receive the awards, I saw lots of women doing very well in my profession, and I tried not to feel too smug about being among those who were quietly part of evolution.

Women began to crop up in somewhat new ways in my stories and those written by others. Sharon Stone Kilpatrick, sometime reporter who had married editor Sean, was named as a state running mate for Sen. Eugene McCarthy in his doomed race to be the Democratic nominee for president. "I can't foresee any trouble presiding over the Senate," opined Kilpatrick. "I used to teach junior high school."

A former narcotics agent, Donna Rice Boone, still in law enforcement of some kind, came to her nephew's schoolroom in Culpeper to talk about her work. She was known as the "freaky chick" and wore a holstered six-gun. An undercover agent, she dressed and talked the drug culture, and I found her a bit scary. Two young women from New York stopped in town on their way to Mardi Gras in New Orleans; they were traveling by horseback, riding mostly on the Appalachian Trail.

Another subject was a "lady vet," and the story ran with a picture taken by me of Dr. Fayette Witherell with a Great Dane pup. Her practice was a one-woman operation, she said; she mopped floors and answered the phone. She also worked with large animals, and gender wasn't a big deal, she said, because sometimes horses in particular found a woman soothing, and anyway if a horse was going to be difficult one person couldn't handle it without help.

In that same vein was a feature about a young woman horseshoer. The woman, girl, really, said she had been discouraged in her first forays into the business by the men she was trying to learn from while watching them labor over hooves. But by the time of our meeting she was doing it herself, despite a size and fragility that reminded one of Mary Martin playing Peter Pan. I even interviewed, with considerable interest, a woman worm rancher. It turned out she had discovered a major problem with that as a business venture—since the ranch was established in open ground, the worms ignored her offerings of coffee grounds and manure and decamped en masse from time to time and she was left without foundation stock.

But an accurate look into the future, in retrospect, was offered in a short item that was submitted by the family of the subject, Josie Ballato. The head was "Culpeper girl will be AF academy cadet." (This was in 1977, and no one thought twice about calling her a girl; she was fortunate not to be a "gal.") A web search for Josie Ballato many years later revealed that she had not only been a success at the Air Force Academy, but had gone on to the University of Maryland for a law degree and become an attorney with the Patent and Trademark Office.

Not that the paper, and its female reporter, had resolved to write only about women who were being untraditional. There was a story on Lady Bird Johnson and her daughter Lynda, in Culpeper at the train station to campaign for Lynda's husband, Chuck Robb, for Virginia lieutenant governor. They were re-creating the whistle-stop trip Lady Bird and husband Lyndon made in 1960, when he was seeking the presidency. Molly and Robin Fray, daughters of Mr. and Mrs. Jack Fray, presented flowers as they had seventeen years before.

The larger context of change was illustrated in 1978, with the silly but not unreasonable accession to the demand that hurricanes should also have male names. Women's groups had actually exerted some pressure, and the headline noted that while there had been only "herricanes," now there would also be "himmicanes." Well, yay again, I guess. In my column I noted that men were in fact now changing their tactics to a more devious approach, with the bellwether of change being the advertising industry. My proof was the ad in which a man praises his wife for all that she does. "My wife—I think I'll keep her," he says proudly. Women, I noted, were actually falling for this stuff.

One early year's Women on the Go section had as its cover art an athletic woman out running, with her hair tossing. More prosaically, I wrote about Virginia Clybern, who as office manager of the *Star-Exponent* was then the woman highest in the pecking order there.

Another noticeable step, in 1981: an editorial appeared, done in-house for the *SE* although I don't recall who produced it, highlighting a remark by the new Miss America, Elizabeth Ward of Arkansas. Ward said that unlike some recent title-holders, she didn't expect to be "controversial." And whoa, the editorial pointed out that Supreme Court nominee Sandra Day O'Connor was fielding question after question about her thoughts on abortion. Women are different from men, the editorial acknowledged, and there was perhaps a need for their viewpoint on the Supreme Court: "A woman may bring talents and ideas representing the hitherto unrepresented half of the population to that important body."

And if such a jurist wants to be a bit controversial and different, it's okay, because, after all, "She's not trying to be Miss America" (take that, Elizabeth Ward). I am mortified to say that I noticed that only while doing research, and don't remember it being published, or the major thrill I should have gotten from it. But in 1981 that was great, revolutionary thought.

A recent college graduate named Sue Freakley had somehow become the sports editor, I think the first female in that role, and that December another young woman, Bev Winston, was made the *SE* editor. She was not the first, but the first had been years before and hadn't worked out. Bev was then twenty-five years old, and one had to wonder where the Lou Grant authority figure was headed in the age of conglomerate news media. Young, single people were willing to work the night shift, and combined with the low salaries, the scheduling tended to discourage older, more experienced journalists. So possibly being a newspaper editor wasn't really a particularly noteworthy milestone anymore.

The difficulty of hitting the right note and actually recognizing progress that women were experiencing as the tide moved slowly toward their recognition as people can be illustrated with a long-forgotten but then-major to-do in 1983 involving a civil servant named Barbara Honegger. Honegger, an employee of the U.S. Department of Justice, had denounced the Reagan administration's approach to women's rights. She even called Reagan the Wizard of Oz, for not making good on promises to speed up review on the issue.

In the ensuing flurry of sound-bite Wizard of Oz references, a Justice Department spokesman made the mistake of referring to Honegger, who was not a very tall woman, as a "low-level munchkin," and I expect he was sorry. Honegger got her fifteen minutes of fame. At some point she refused to climb onto a box to be more visible at a press conference, crying "It's the wrong symbol," which it probably was, but it seemed to me that she enjoyed her temporary celebrity a bit too much. At that point the *Star-Exponent* was publishing an occasional reporter's column on the editorial page when appropriate, and I had one on the topic of the reluctant munchkin. It's the American way, I admitted, squeaky-wheel syndrome in service to a good cause, but you kind of wished it didn't have to work that way.

Another column on the topic was written by a local woman who was Western District vice chair for the Virginia Republican Party. "Who does speak for women?" she wondered, concluding that she herself wasn't being spoken for by Honegger, who was touring the country with a little road show centered on herself. The writer remarked that she was interested in many issues, not only women's issues, so there. Women's reasonable contributions to the dialog tended to get a little indignant and high-handed, but allowances could be made under the circumstances.

Neither of us quite hit what was wrong there, but I still think I may have been closer. It was embarrassing that those tactics were needed—but they were. Honegger later wrote a conspiracy-theory book about the Iranian hostage rescue attempt, and then went whole-hog into conspiracy promotion (while keeping a federal job), but she never regained her previous celebrity status.

Looking back, it seems incredible to me that one of the last stories I did at the paper was a feature on "Mail Woman Samantha Shifflette." The twenty-four-year-old was the first female mail carrier in Culpeper. Those were good jobs, and that was 1984.

So women were making some progress then, when I was about forty years old, but racial equality still had a ways to go. That was twenty years after school integration became widespread in Virginia, and back-of-the-bus confrontations were over. Race relations were peaceful, the black and white parts of the community seemed tolerant of each other, but mostly they were as separate as ever. Black teachers now and then drew attention for achievements, as did black students, but we had to look to find many stories about interesting African-Americans because they were mostly under the radar.

One of the most memorable contacts I made was with Mortimer Marshall, the town's truly remarkable black mortician. Although local, he firmly believed in a D.C. connection—his young mother was enslaved before the Civil War on the Fauquier estate owned by a family named Marshall, and Mortimer had always been told that Chief Justice John Marshall was his ancestor. I interviewed him when he was ninety years old, and he truly was something.

My lead was easy: "A mortician, he does not believe in death. The grandson of an eleven-year-old black slave and an unknown white man, he does not believe in the past." He had room for plenty of other contradictions in a busy mind, still lucid at ninety. I wrote that he was a "constant berater and doom-crier over government and its doings," as well as a frequent author of outraged letters to the editor on those subjects. But he was also convinced that the United States was not only the finest country ever to exist, but was "only at the beginning of its evolvement into something far finer." Pretty good stuff, then and much later.

Marshall had had an interesting life. He had a wartime appointment in World War I with the Department of Justice as an investigator, and he had been interviewed by Alex Haley in the course of background work on *Roots*. Of course my interview was partly because of his age, and he did die in the next year. But he was an inspiration—one who rattled on with great fire and truly was sure he was right about most things, but nonetheless an inspiration.

CHAPTER TWELVE
Location, Location,
Location

O ne of the elements that made
newspaper work in Culpeper
particularly interesting was the town's
location, only about sixty miles from Washington,
D.C. This meant that some fairly strange people passed
through on their way to the capital city seeking attention
for various causes. A more lasting impact was made by
those who wanted to be near the city but looked outside it
for cheaper places to establish homes or businesses. When they
looked south, where things were traditionally less expensive, they
found Culpeper.

Sometimes those bearing well-known names sought country living
in the area; there were weekend homes, or hideaways. People from the
national political scene also looked not far away for retirement locations,
thinking they could keep in touch or get back to the city in just over
an hour. This of course was before traffic built up and made the hour
estimate a dim memory. These people would look at a map, draw a circle
of the acceptable radius, and there was Culpeper, part of the metro orbit.

The nonburial of George Lincoln Rockwell described earlier was
a D.C.-orbit story, since the American Nazi Party had its headquarters
close to the capital and Culpeper National Cemetery was the closest
federal burial place after Arlington ran out of space. The cemetery was
frequently newsworthy. In 1972 I wrote a story about what then was
expected to be the last funeral in the Culpeper cemetery. Staff Sgt.
Henry S. Trumbar, who died in a West Virginia veterans hospital without
a next of kin, was assigned the one remaining burial site available until
there was an expansion.

The federal burial place, on hilly land running along the eastern edge of the old town, had been available for veterans since the dead from the Civil War fighting at nearby Cedar Run were moved to the newly purchased spot more than a century before, in 1867. But the room had been rapidly used up after the Rockwell fracas, because the location came to the attention of those up north looking for a resting place for their service members that was not too far away. An option had been taken out by the local VFW on sixty acres adjoining the old cemetery, but the option hadn't been picked up by the parsimonious federal government. Nothing personal toward the local VFW; it had been the policy of Congress for the past twenty years not to expand cemeteries.

This rather depressing story did have a good ending. The VFW continued for years trying to get the cemetery enlarged, without making any progress, but a man named Joe Gardner, president of the long-established local gas and oil fitments manufacturer Bingham and Taylor, donated ten and a half acres to the local Burton-Hammond VFW Post 2524 in 1975. The portion of the cemetery that had been declared closed in 1972 was filled with 3,796 graves, including Sgt. Trumbar's. Once space was added, the occasional high-profile burial continued to receive coverage for the rest of my time with the paper.

In fact, the national cemetery again brought attention to Culpeper in September of 1981. Lt. Col. David L. Smith, commander of the U.S. Air Force stunt flyers the Thunderbirds, had been killed when his jet crashed shortly after takeoff in Cleveland. Television was represented by Harry Reasoner, who probably hadn't been in Culpeper before. The dignity and restrained pageantry are still powerfully alive in my memory. I wrote about the sad, quiet family, but the real catch in the throat came as the Thunderbirds flew overhead in the missing-man formation: one plane peeled off from the group and didn't return. "The depiction of loss and end was almost stunning," I wrote.

Just as stunning was the fact that a second such ceremony was held at the snow-covered cemetery in January 1982. A second Thunderbird pilot was buried there, near Colonel Smith's grave, and again the missing-man formation was flown. This time the sorrow was for Capt. Joseph

N. Peterson III, who had attended the funeral for the commander who died before him. Captain Peterson died on a training mission in Nevada.

My story again tried to convey the solemnity surrounding a death that had occurred too soon. "The whiteness of the cemetery, paler than the line of headstones, added a starkness to the military movements, as when a small detachment of blue-clad men marched across the hillside to take their position for the firing of the salute. Crusted snow cracked with each step, and bits of ice slid rustling through the rows of markers to the bottom of the slope." There was an unforgettable illustration— an *SE* photo by Ray Saunders of the marchers in the snow, etched in a darkness that belied the humanity of the figures, even while their struggle for dignity in the deep snow said clearly that they were feeling, reacting beings.

One of the Washington-related local news staples in my early years, as mentioned before, was Adm. Lewis L. Strauss, the man standing with the prize bull on the front page as I began work on the *SE*. Strauss had been the chair of the Atomic Energy Commission, and was deeply involved in the development of nuclear weapons and then in the use of nuclear power in peacetime. Perhaps as an antidote, he retired to Brandy Station to raise prize Angus cattle on his Brandy Rock Farm. He made news with his cattle auctions, which drew state politicians as well as former president and fellow Angus aficionado Dwight Eisenhower. In retirement he merited an Associated Press story by George Wilbur in 1971. Strauss was described by Wilbur as seeing the end of wars. "I suspect that the great wars are over," he told the AP writer. He was hoping that the Nixon visit to China would open up the path to disarmament.

Oh, well.

I did a story on the 1978 day when the Brandy Rock herd was sold at auction. It had been operating for forty-five years, and at one point was the largest Angus operation in the state. Mamie Eisenhower attended, as did Senator and Mrs. Gore. Local cattleman Bill Eggborn, one in a long line of farmers of that name who ran the Eggborn homeplace on Route 729, was saddened, saying he had always bought his bulls from Brandy Rock. The sale realized almost $250,000.

I never got to meet Strauss, who died in January of 1974. But a couple of years later I did talk to another political player from the past, Welly Hopkins, a Justice Department attorney and later counsel to labor leader John L. Lewis. He was then seventy-eight, and lived at his farm Rest Harrow, to the west of town. He considered Lewis a very great man, of "impeccable character," he told me. Lewis of course led the Congress of Industrial Organizations and the United Mine Workers, and was perhaps a bit too ruthless to be exactly of impeccable character.

Another nationally known name drawn to the area by the proximity of the seat of power was John Fisher. He was in *Who's Who in the World*, and was fifty-seven when I first met him in 1979. The Freedom Studies Center near Boston, Virginia, on the way to Sperryville, was a big Cold War player. Fisher was president of the American Security Council and the American Security Council Education Foundation, both located on the estate originally called Longlea, the home of Alice Glass, mistress of Lyndon Johnson—speaking of convenient yet out-of-the-way locations with access to the powerful.

It was Robert Caro's mention of Longlea, in the 1982 first volume of his planned five-volume series on LBJ, that set up an occurrence which clarified for me that newspapers belonged in the hands of newspeople, not ad people who had gotten a promotion from a corporate owner for, presumably, selling a bunch of ads. I read the book, having quite an interest in the shortcomings of the thirty-sixth president, and was pretty excited by the discovery of his visits to our environs while still in the Senate. I went out and busily interviewed people—Welly Hopkins again, and a Durant, a member of an aristocratic family that owned land just east of Longlea. They all remembered Alice Glass as beautiful and high-spirited and pretty much wonderful.

According to Caro, Johnson met Miss Glass in 1937 at the Longlea estate when he was a newly elected congressman. She lived there as a companion to wealthy Texas newspaper and oil man Charles E. Marsh. Caro described an unsavory triangle in his book, *The Years of Lyndon Johnson*. LBJ got both financial and political help from Marsh, while conducting a secret affair with the woman the man loved and wanted to marry, I wrote.

When I went to talk with Alice Hopkins, Welly's wife, then living at Rest Harrow, she recalled Alice as "very close, like a sister," and in fact there was a distant and tangled family connection. She said Caro had stayed at the old Lord Culpeper Hotel, and spent quite a bit of time talking with them: "He was a brain-picker." Caro surmised that Alice fell in love with Johnson because she was moved by his stories of working to get federal programs such as dams for the very poor people of the Texas Hill Country. She thought he was a different kind of politician.

I worked diligently on the story and wrote up my findings with considerable pleasure, and waited for the article to appear. But the then-publisher reviewed it and declined to allow it into print. It might upset some people, he said. Needless to say I was furious, partly because of the publisher's lack of the perspective that would have told him very few people would be bothered, and that most of them were old and had lost any protectiveness of Lyndon Johnson many years before.

Anyway, that was the background of the estate where John Fisher ran his interconnected enterprises. He was from Ohio, and had gotten involved with the idea of national security when he was Sears Roebuck's representative to the Institute for American Strategy in Chicago in 1955. He was then loaned by Sears to the organization, and "never got untangled." The thrust of his message was "peace through strength" via a strong military, and he put the Freedom Studies Center on the national map in many ways. There was a Graduate Center for International Security Studies offering a master's degree in cooperation with Georgetown University, and many seminars and classes were held at the Boston campus. He was consulted by various national leaders, and was recognized for his efforts by President Ronald Reagan.

So much printed information was generated at the center that there was an entire printing and mailing operation. It all went great guns for a long time, and Fisher was its heart and soul. He was a mild man, not an intrusive personality, sure-footed in his arguments and ideas, and good at relating one-on-one because he tried hard, even with reporters from local papers. It could be argued that his success was partly his undoing, as national security issues got attention from Reagan and others and the Soviet threat went away—for a while.

The tide of name visitors and even part-time residents wasn't a recent phenomenon in the '70s and '80s. Quite a few years before, a president had had a retreat in Madison County; Herbert Hoover built Camp Rapidan on the edge of what became Shenandoah National Park, and in a wonderful chapter of the county's history his wife, Lou, had a school built for the children growing up in the far-flung mountain hollows without an education. She even recruited a teacher. In May of 1979, President Jimmy Carter spent a bit of time at Camp Rapidan, arriving forty-seven years after Hoover had last slept over. Since then the camp has been renovated and is the destination of a regular visitor bus trip from Big Meadows on Skyline Drive.

I, and Culpeper, had a bit of a narrative of brushes with other presidents—two of them Theodore Roosevelt and Woodrow Wilson. My indirect contact with both was admittedly many years after their time, when I visited Salubria down on Route 3, the family home of Dr. Cary T. Grayson. Grayson was a navy surgeon and rear admiral who was the physician to presidents Theodore Roosevelt, William Howard Taft, and Woodrow Wilson. He became Wilson's personal aide, and was an influential man. Actually, I did my story mostly on P. T. Fitzhugh, who managed the place then. The house was built during the 1740s, and Fitzhugh said he looked on it as a "venerable old ancestor." He spent time shooing people away but occasionally conducted tours just because he thought the structure was so special. Eventually the Grayson family donated the estate to the Germanna Foundation because of the German connections.

As I mentioned earlier, Eugene McCarthy had lived for a while just to the west in Rappahannock County, not far from longtime newspaperman and syndicated columnist James J. Kilpatrick. Kilpo used the dateline "Scrabble" for his column, although he actually lived closer to a tiny community with the less distinctive name of Woodville.

A story done by a relatively new reporter with an interest in the elder Kilpatrick appeared in the regular section Northern Piedmont Personalities, finally explaining what the TV commentator was doing in Rappahannock. He had seen an ad for a house on thirty-six acres, called White Walnut Hill, in a newspaper while living in Washington, gone out and looked at it, and bought it. For a while he lived in Alexandria, with weekends on the farm, before making it his permanent home for a long while.

At perhaps the other end of some spectrum from those prominent, erudite men was one I wrote about the same year the Kilpo feature was done. Dale Crowley was D.C.'s "radio minister," and apparently felt the need to head to more peaceful climes in Culpeper. I had my reservations about radio ministers, particularly those who, like Crowley, opposed the teaching of evolution, but I found him an oddly interesting, amusing, and downright nice man. Born in Indian territory, he was the son of an alcoholic father. A Fundamentalist with a capital F, he was always quitting jobs and organizations rather than be muzzled. He eventually wrote a book, *On the Wrong Side of Just About Everything but Right About It All.* And isn't that how most of us feel? I don't think Jerry Falwell could have written that book, or at least not with that title.

Crowley was then, I think, not quite fifty, on the way to making it to eighty-seven. I included his great story about two men who forced their way into his house in Washington, beating him violently. "I kicked the stuffing out of them," remarked the man of God. One of them pulled a knife; recognizing a change in circumstances, the minister said he then prayed for them with equal vigor. He didn't pray for himself, apparently having faith in his own well-being.

Another excellent Crowley story involved his courtship of his second wife, Ruth, who moved to Culpeper with him. A widow, Ruth had said she would remarry "only if God put the man on her doorstep," and Dale was aware of this as well as of the mysterious workings of God. He went to her house, rang the doorbell, and then hastily sat down on her front steps. Ruth was, of course, a goner.

The story of businesses, operations vaguely related to the government, and just plain entrepreneurs who used the Washington-radius approach to finding a place to establish themselves is more or less endless. From the computer brain center of an international banking network to a large-scale nursery, the spot just seemed like a reasonable choice.

SWIFT, the Society for Worldwide Interbank Financial Telecommunication, came because of Virginia's fiscal policies, said Gov. John Dalton when he attended the grand opening. The organization observed secrecy akin to that of the Federal Reserve a mile or so away, and while the community was welcomed for the opening, that was pretty much it for access. The paper did a big spread on the grand opening, with a page of photos of the interior, but after that it was off limits, with a guardhouse for enforcement. Hmm, two guardhouses for Culpeper.

The nursery was Van Wingerden's, owned by a family described as a "plant dynasty." The founder was one of those who looked at the map, drove down, made an offer for a property, and began construction. In less than two years the operation had grown to nearly two hundred thousand square feet of greenhouses, and that was just the beginning.

Various sorts of land booms occurred here and there, possibly because people thought the urban neighborhoods were on their way south. A German citizen, Carl F. Tenge-Rietburg, had brought his area holdings to 3,700 acres by summer of 1981. He owned Spring Hill Farm, Chateau-Briand, and Horseshoe Farm near Rapidan. And speaking of national connections, Horseshoe Farm had been the early retirement home of Edward Stettinius Jr., U.S. secretary of state under presidents Franklin D. Roosevelt and Harry S. Truman from 1944 to 1945, and U.S. ambassador to the United Nations from 1945 to 1946.

CHAPTER THIRTEEN
People Are the News

Well after Admiral Strauss's time, the *Star-Exponent* pages were still often spiced up with accounts of people like him, local retirees with government pasts. One of my favorites was John Dailey of Kelly's Ford. Dailey was on the LBJ presidential advisory committee in 1966. He and Johnson went to the same school, which became Southwest Texas State University, in San Marcos. Dailey, a man ahead of his time, was considered the father of the magnetometer approach to screening for hijackers. He retired from the Federal Aviation Administration as chief of Biomedical and Behavioral Science Division.

He and his wife, Helen, following the pattern of Kilpatrick and many others, bought an area estate, this one called Beaufort, first as an escape from Washington and then as a permanent home. I interviewed him as the author of the book *The Pioneer Heritage*, which was self-published. Although Dailey held a doctorate, he had retained the traces of his Texas background, and the book was anecdotal and almost folksy. He wrote about coon dogs, twenty-five-pound catfish, eccentric uncles, and black cowboys. But he made clear that while the lore about such subjects was interesting, "It is the life force of these things that really counts."

Another interesting character was Donn Grand Pre, a military man whose ongoing personal connections to the U.S. government were described in his book, *Confessions of an Arms Peddler.* I mentioned in print that Grand Pre would have made a great Marlboro man. Originally from somewhere in the Dakotas, he was a horseman with a bit of an eye for image, and he established a school in Madison County for children with severe disabilities. Looking around at his beautiful farm, he then became a land developer. Madison County as well as Culpeper drew people like that.

Grand Pre had a stroke in 2001, at the time of the 9/11 terrorist attacks. Several years later he resurfaced to promote the belief that there was a government conspiracy involving the attacks, and that a coup was coming. He had a long radio interview with conspiracy promoter Alex Jones, who didn't have the excuse of a recent stroke. It was disappointing to see a man with such varied interests and abilities go down the rabbit hole like that, and I don't mean Alex Jones, who continues to make a living off this sort of thing.

There were other odd connections, not only with the government but with the capital city. An example was seen in coverage of a local woman who testified in the lawsuit brought by comedienne Carol Burnett against the *National Enquirer*. Mary Jo Dorman, wife of Town Manager Jack Dorman, was flown to Los Angeles to testify about her talk with the *Enquirer* reporter. She was director of public relations for the restaurant Rive Gauche in Washington, and testified that she had insisted to the reporter that Carol Burnett was not boisterous in her behavior at the restaurant. The magazine had nevertheless published an account of the star being drunk and rowdy, leading to an altercation with Henry Kissinger, oddly enough.

Burnett won a $1.6 million libel judgment, and was quoted in a wire story as remarking "If they had given me a dollar plus carfare, I would have been happy." It was the principle. Something like the Carol Burnett story, told from a local angle, was always well received by our readers. I mean, who didn't want to know about Carol Burnett?

Painter Adolf Sehring didn't start out in Washington, but the location of Culpeper not far from urban life, arts, and transportation no doubt played a part in his choice of the area. He said, according to my feature article, that he lived there for the "paintability." Way back in the early '80s his paintings were selling for $50,000 or more, many to international buyers. He and his wife, Renate, had a small farm near town, and he used local children and his son Marc as models. He gained a burst of national fame with a portrait of Pope John Paul, which he presented personally at the Vatican.

Born in Russia to a Russian mother and a German father who was an art director in the German movie industry, Adolf won prizes for drawing from earliest childhood. Throughout his boyhood and during World War II, he studied art in Berlin and assisted his father with his theatrical designs.

By the time he was working in Culpeper, his paintings were in the Victoria and Albert Museum, the Grand Palais in Paris, the Chrysler Museum, the Mellon Galleries at the Virginia Museum of Fine Arts, and many other public and private collections. But the portrait of John Paul was very special to him—he had spent enough time with the pontiff to be sure that the holy father was destined for a major place in church history. Not a man given to smiling, Sehring grew especially solemn as he spoke about John Paul. The impression had gone deep.

A cultural distance away from the pope-related interview was a visit by television's Eddie Albert, again presumably because of the county's proximity to D.C. central. The Future Farmers of America was filming a series of TV spots in the county, at the Baptist Home, Ebenezer Heights Greenhouse, and Battle Creek Farm near the Midway Store. My story about Albert noted that the message on behalf of the FFA came from Albert's own convictions, as perhaps did his signature character on his very popular rural-life-based show *Green Acres*.

I was more than charmed by the man when I went out to see him in a crop field. He stood for a while looking serious and noble while surveying waist-high barley. When the filming was done for the moment, he came back to the roadside happy to talk with me a bit. Asked to pose for a photo or two, he paused for a moment, then said "I can give you several things. Serious"—and he looked instantly and incredibly grave—"or"—grimacing into the lens—"stark terror." Yep, he was an actor all right, with a wider range than his TV series indicated. He remarked solemnly that Arnold, the *Green Acres* pig, was in a retirement home in Santa Barbara, and that Eva Gabor was as incredibly lovely as she looked on the small screen.

Aware that he was a man delivering a message, he said that government policies in regard to the American farmer for the past thirty years had been "brutal and counterproductive," and he also had a second message: that modern TV was without creativity or thought. And this was before the age of reboots.

If being close to the center of many things could bring a reporter the fun of a television star, it could also bring reminders of more solemn elements of national life. In November of 1983, the twentieth anniversary of the assassination of JFK, I interviewed a local man who said he owned the plank that the thirty-fifth president had stood on to watch his inaugural parade. He had bought the board from the demolition company, after figuring out which one it presumably was by the markings left over from the big day. This local resident had been an administrative assistant for members of Congress, and then an insurance lobbyist. Eventually he had moved out to the country, no doubt after consulting a map of places within a certain radius of the capital.

While well-known and unusual people often came from the outside, occasionally one was born in the community. Such a person was Adam Hill Gilbert. Born William Dudley Gilbert in 1935, he left Duke University at the end of his sophomore year to enroll with the Pasadena Playhouse and study playwriting and theater. He died at eighty years old in 2016, but in 1980 he returned to Culpeper to visit his parents, and the *SE* (but not me) scored an interview. It appeared with a photo of Gilbert with Brooke Shields and Rock Hudson.

At Duke he had originated a radio show, *Campusology*. He worked on it with his friend and college big brother, David Hartman, who went on to host *Good Morning, America*. He did some acting, on *NBC Matinee Theatre, The Lawrence Welk Show,* and *The Virginian*, before beginning his writing career on the adventure series *Ripcord*. Later he was a production supervisor, and then associate producer for *Circus of the Stars*. He was a busy man with a long and successful career, and he was from Culpeper. Everyone was rather proud.

Again because of convenience, Culpeper was surveyed in 1981 for use as a relocation shelter area for people from urban places to the north in case of nuclear catastrophe—with no mention of the relocation arrangements already in place on a hillside right outside of town. That place, built in the '60s for the Federal Reserve, was always mysterious, and I described it earlier as the subject of the last major story I did for the paper before I went off to motherhood. When I did a much later story, after the facility's cover had been blown, the piece appeared in the Piedmont Living section and the head was "That Place Under the Mountain." It noted that Barbie dolls and computers were once ready for the nuclear holocaust.

Al Tinkelenburg, the Federal Reserve senior vice president who then headed the center, said that the auditors had questioned the purchase of the dolls. It was a bit funny, bean-counters saying to themselves "Dolls?" On the other hand, it wasn't very funny at all—people had envisioned children waiting out a nuclear disaster at the center with their parents.

The matter-of-fact explanation was that while Mount Pony had served openly as a center of nationwide financial communications since about 1970, it also was the planned hideout and emergency operations center for the Fed's board of governors. There were 135,000 square feet built into the side of a very small mountain, and incidentally there were ways to close off the outside with radiation-proof barriers. *Esquire* magazine had mentioned the facility as the main relocation center, and the horse was out of the several levels of living space in the place under the mountain, cavernous enough to be barn-like.

CHAPTER FOURTEEN
About that Iranian Hostage Crisis

There was another federal connection, a big and generally kind of undercover thing. A known location for the gathering of "intel" was the Warrenton Training Center, something I first became aware of when we lived in the West Lakes subdivision. Quite a few of the residents worked at the training center, and other people spoke of them a bit covertly as "the code-crackers." They did some kind of computer searching or analyzing or something, and never talked about it. It all loomed as a question mark.

It wasn't until 1980 that there came some revelations about the mysterious government connections of people in our area, mostly recent arrivals. Culpeper got attention with the Iranian hostage crisis, and became a center of attention like it had never been before.

When the American hostages were seized in Iran in late 1979, it all began relatively quietly. There was indignation, but as time went on and there were few developments there was no rising tide of demand that something be done. Months after the imprisonment of the Americans, there was a story in the *Star-Exponent* that noted that the Red Cross, during a seven-hour visit, had found the hostages in good condition. There was an aborted rescue attempt in which eight American servicemen were killed because of the freakish malfunction of three of eight helicopters. And then Ayatollah Khomeini threatened to kill the hostages if there was another try.

By then, Worrell Newspapers had taken over the *SE* in the ever-morphing merging of media, and had begun a practice aimed at wooing the locals that I found particularly irritating: featuring "man-on-the-street" comments about various issues. There were not a lot of illuminating comments even about local issues, and when people were asked "What do you think of the unsuccessful attempt to free the hostages?" guess what, not much illumination. But they were local names, and that was the goal.

As the hellish hostage situation continued, it was hard to imagine what people were experiencing. The paper was running a graphic at the bottom of the front page, a slightly impressionistic stone prison with the tagline "U.S. hostages, day ____." But after Election Day 1980, the Iranian militants relinquished "responsibility" for their captives, turning them over to the Iranian government. Ronald Reagan had been elected to replace Carter, and the thought was that he would by gosh do something. After all, look how well he did in all those war movies.

And then on December 27, the paper was able to declare that a Culpeper man had been identified as one of the fifty-two hostages who had been held the entire time. There was no byline on the story, and I don't remember whether I wrote it. But much earlier than that, the staff had known the identity of the prisoner, and in order to protect the man and his family, had actually forgone the tremendous temptation to publish something that no one else had.

Phillip Ward was identified just before the new year. The story included a picture from TV monitors of a dark-haired, mustached man with dark-ringed eyes. He joined the other hostages in sending Christmas greetings to his family during a TV broadcast: "Hi, Connie and Scott. As you can see, I'm healthy and well, so don't worry about me . . . and Scott, I expect you to continue the good work at school and help mom around the house and don't forget to feed the birds this winter."

Phil Ward became The Story, and I became the reporter on The Story. I'm not sure any credit was due, though—then-reporter Carolyn Banks had called Phil's wife, Connie, and had a conversation at some point early in the crisis. I had spoken with Connie myself even earlier, at the first inkling of her husband's being among the hostages, but had received such a frightened response that I had backed off instantly with an apology for bothering her.

But Carolyn, a refugee novelist and magazine writer who lived in Rappahannock and took the Culpeper job to make the ends that often escape a struggling writer meet, was a master talker and begged Connie to let her do an interview, staying on the phone long enough to perhaps form a connection. But then she too had recognized the woman's fear, had to respect it, and went no further. At least that's what I think happened; Connie Ward apparently didn't get her name, or mine stayed with her longer, and when it came time for a contact on the paper Carolyn was gone and I was the female in residence. So when the Wards became the story, it was mine.

I saw Phil a number of times during the homecoming hurrah, met him briefly, but didn't exchange more than a few desultory words with him until a later interview, after he had been back for a while. And I felt sorrow and sympathy for him the way I have for few of my fellow men and women, ever. It was the kind of looming, helpless grief that I get from a photo of a desperate dog pressing against an animal-shelter fence—his eyes were that haunting. He had in fact given all he could to his country, and it really was all.

Just as the movie *Argo*, about a part of the hostage crisis, came out in 2012, attorney Tom Lankford, who was representing the hostages in seeking reparations from Iran, minced no words about what the men had gone through. "They were beaten; they played Russian roulette with them, they stood them up against walls as if they were killing them in mock firing squads," he said. "They destroyed in many cases not only their bodies, but their souls."

But I'm ahead of myself. On January 2, 1981, less than a week after the hostages were identified, the paper reported that Iran had threatened spy trials if its demands were not met by the U.S. Then Carter gave Iran a deadline of Jan. 16—a week before Reagan took office—for the release. The hostage graphic the day before the deadline said it was the 439th day of their captivity. Although Jan. 16 came and went without resolution, a story on Jan. 17 said the hostages' return seemed certain. A final agreement from the U.S. had been sent. The Associated Press furnished a list of "Who we're waiting for," and Phil Ward appeared, alphabetically, at the end. There were several residents listed from Falls Church, and others came from Quantico, Maryland, and D.C. itself.

Inauguration '81 was shadowed by what a headline called an "inherited crisis." Jody Powell, White House press secretary, noted that the incoming president had "no obligation" to honor the agreement that was under negotiation. The return still was expected, though, and a Brownie troop put up doorway decorations in town, featuring little American flags in a frame and declaring "Welcome home Phillip Ward and hostages."

And finally, on Jan. 21, a banner over the *Star-Exponent* masthead read "Free at Last." Yellow ribbons (there were hundreds up in town) and tears of joy featured in the coverage, as the hostages were reported to have reached Algiers. Ward was identified but not pictured in the vast coverage. Culpeper began its homecoming celebration plans, and Connie Ward released a statement: "First, I would like to say a very special thanks to the Culpeper Star-Exponent, who respected my desire for privacy throughout this trying ordeal. Also to others in the community for support. Scott and I were able to maintain somewhat of a normal lifestyle for the past 14 months." She said she had talked to her husband the night before, and felt "emotionally drained."

I was invited to the Ward home the evening of Friday, Jan. 23, and my story, "Ward's home an elated place," was carefully copyrighted by *Culpeper Star-Exponent*/Worrell Newspapers. It described a festive house with a Christmas tree decorated with fifty-two yellow ribbons, and an overwhelmed woman in the midst of friends.

Not often in the world of sewage-plant discussions, land transfers, and district court actions does a small-town reporter get much of this sort of thing, but I recall a nagging discomfort with being there. The stakes had been so high, the possibilities so dire, the cost to the little family so heavy that an undercurrent of unease jangled the nerves a bit.

When my story appeared the next day, it said that Phillip Ward "left his wife and young son, a family dog and cat, and a garden spot famed for prolific eggplant, and went off to serve as communications specialist for the U.S. embassy in Iran, just ten days before militant students stormed the embassy and began the long siege of holding the Americans hostage."

Scott Ward was just nine years old. Early in the crisis, his mother had called Pearl Sample Elementary School, where he was a student. She had explained the situation and forewarned the principal and teachers about possible difficulties with her son. Everything was kept low-key, and copies of school materials and a school picture had made their way to the captive. In fact, Connie Ward said that during those emotional fourteen months Scott's apparent optimism had been very sustaining to her when "more times than I like to think about" she wasn't sure she could get through another day.

The Wards had traveled a great deal for his job, mainly in the Far East. They had moved to Culpeper in March 1978. Connie explained that they had still been getting settled when Phil had to leave, and hadn't even finished the interior painting in their house. All of them had enjoyed the community, and an enthusiastic Phil had put into practice the saying that in planting a garden you plant "a seed for the birds, one for the worms, and one to grow." He really was interested in feeding wild birds, as he said in the brief Christmas message he was allowed.

Attention had come to the family from all over the world in the days before the actual release, and Connie had even gotten a call to be on a talk show in Australia. She didn't want to. She only wanted the Wards to be together again.

We talked about her reactions when at 2:30 a.m., just a few days earlier, Connie was "spending one of a series of almost sleepless nights" flicking through television stations seeking a glimpse of her husband in the constantly repeated film of the just-released hostages. The phone rang and Phil said simply "Hello." And now Connie was sitting with friends, in a house that fit that description of "elated." Everyone laughed as stories were recounted about ardent gardener Phil, now forty years old, trying to give away baskets of his homegrown eggplant.

Many of them had been there on Inauguration Day, trying to pay attention to television coverage of the new president taking the oath of office, waiting mostly for the hostage updates, trying not to consider what might go wrong. Connie said they had all clapped spontaneously as each new, encouraging event was highlighted, watched eagerly as the news cameras turned to the group of former captives, and then groaned inwardly when the lens turned away without showing their friend and neighbor.

Connie said there had been few letters during the long captivity. The Wards had been married nineteen years, after meeting in high school in Proctorsville, Ohio. In the calls they had been able to have since that first one at 2:30 a.m., "I've just let him talk," she said. She had not asked whether he was badly treated, or whether he spent time in solitary confinement. She was aware that he had lost sixty or seventy pounds, and of the hard-to-process detail that his shoes had worn out and not been replaced.

I did a second piece that appeared the same day. "Inauguration Day 'emotional high'" quoted sometime *SE* editorial-page writer Emily Steger and her husband, Garland, as local GOP officials who had been on the National Mall for the event. They described the dramatic intensity of the day, and the sense of history mixed with joy and relief over the hostages. When the national anthem was sung, the Stegers said, people wept in united joy. They saw Robert Goulet, Charlton Heston, Frank Sinatra, and best of all, the Reagans themselves at a ball.

The Jan. 27 paper ran a wire story, "Returnees seek time to adjust." But the artwork was very local, a photo of a huge banner saying "Welcome Home Phil – Culpeper Jayceettes." And yes, the paper took the admittedly self-serving opportunity to talk about the harassment by reporters of many of the hostages' families. In discussing "What's News," the editorial upheld the First Amendment rights and obligations of news media, but declared that "reporters, editors and news executives need to develop their own realistic guidelines as to where news ceases to be news."

Two thoughts about this, many years later: First, it was prescient to include "news executives" among those who need to develop good guidelines before the days of obvious content control for political bias. The need for profit, won by wooing specific audiences, now wins out over any thought of restraint.

But the more important point would have been the opportunity to open a discussion about cogent, rational, and even measurable limits to where a newshound should go, how much the identity of someone who might be endangered should be protected, or where the lines of legitimate family privacy might be drawn. How ruthless should reporting be? Somehow, there would have to be agreement on these questions, like the general avoidance of printing the names of rape victims. The fact is that news remains news, but the devil is in the details.

By the time of this proud editorial the paper kind of felt it had a major claim on Phil Ward and the story, and it went all out on the day before the former hostage was to arrive. There was a top box proclaiming "Welcome Home Phil!" with of course a big yellow ribbon. The yellow ribbon symbol was repeated all over town, a really nice little image that far outlived the trio Tony Orlando and Dawn, whose song originated it. The Holiday Inn had a sign out, and there were flags all over. The front page that day featured a photo of the freed hostages listening to Reagan. Phil was in front, second from right, in a suit and tie.

Somewhat piling it on, the editorial was titled "Welcome Home, Phil," and noted that "The *Star-Exponent* has long championed your family's need for privacy," adding that it hoped that privacy would continue to be granted. The writer (not me) then once again welcomed all the hostages back to the U.S., and particularly Phil to Culpeper. It concluded by showing off Phil Ward familiarity by promising that after the welcome, it would be time to go "back to the eggplant." Or not, since it was January.

I wasn't allowed to write editorials, but I did the story on the actual homecoming. Ray Saunders again demonstrated his considerable ability with nice photos of the day, particularly one of the Wards together looking on edge but also thrilled. Ward had slipped quietly into town for a brief but very warm reception from local officials, and had "received with hesitant appreciation the idea of a Phil Ward Day on Saturday." I remember being in sensory overload from the strength of the feelings being projected. "Almost shaky with fatigue and the strain of the last 14 months and now rapid adjustment," I wrote, he told the small group he was not used to public attention and was nervous about speaking to people.

"But no scriptwriter could have come up with more appropriate and direct words," I noted. What he said was quietly dignified, and grateful. "I'm overwhelmed by your welcome," he said, having just ridden down Main Street with its banner, yellow ribbons, and signs. "*You* gave us support," he added. "You're the real heroes." And I was deeply touched by one response from the local officials. Council member John T. S. Kearns was a retired Navy captain, and despite a genuine dedication to public service in his retirement he was known for being outspoken and at times even a tad rude. "We know who the real heroes are," he told Phil gently, and he was a man in a position to know something about heroes.

So Phil Ward Day did happen on Saturday, and it was a banner day in every sense. The photo of the courthouse being draped with an outsized American flag was mine, and it seemed to sum up a lot—rarely in the American experience is there that kind of unity. The paper raked in the profits from a slew of "Welcome home, Phil" ads, but that was okay. David Autry of the *SE* staff wrote about the ceremony, noting that the Wards received a fruit basket and a Sons of the American Revolution good-citizen award (Captain Kearns was big in the SAR). I wrote about the reception afterward—"Returnee greets 100 at Reception"—and described Ward as rested by a few days at home, and visibly more relaxed.

The former hostage shook hands, cut the celebratory cake, and talked sports. Both Phil and Connie "admitted their day in the public eye wasn't as frightening as they had expected," the story reported. Everyone was absolutely aglow. State Sen. Nathan Miller spoke briefly, saying he had been amazed by the turnout for the event, and that "people are high on America again."

Like most highs, though, this one didn't last. Coverage in magazines and newspapers tended to be upbeat on what was then called the "final reunion" of the hostages (it came one hundred days after their return to the U.S.) at the posh Greenbrier resort in West Virginia, and then one 30 years later that indicated the first one wasn't all that final. Stories generally included an admission that people don't get through these things unscathed. Phil Ward was quoted as saying that his son Scott clung to his belt loop and wouldn't let him get any distance away for quite some time.

Since, what was happening to many of these people has been codified as post-traumatic stress disorder, and the stress of torture, constant loss of any feeling of security and deep worry and depression along with the thought that at any moment their captors might kill them was a guaranteed recipe. Psychiatrists interviewed by the media had predicted a bad time for the returning hostages. Any portion of what they had gone through could have been expected to produce many kinds of emotional turmoil, but this had gone on for well over a year.

The hostages did seem to enjoy the Greenbrier event, but perhaps the reunion at West Point, the site of their original homecoming, was both blessed and cursed by the passage of time. While the gathering at the resort resounded with jokes about food and actual bedsheets, the West Point event was more somber. Aging came up, and there were regrets that the shadow of Iran was so long.

Phil was quoted in a few of the earlier stories, admitting that he had had problems with readjustment. His return to private life included hospitalization and his new work assignments were kept light.

I wrote a story on him early the next year, on the anniversary of his release. He said he had spent the day before splitting wood with Scott. Looking back, he said the all-out greeting in Culpeper had been great—"I can't explain how really good it made me feel"—and he wanted to retire in Culpeper. Starvation was pretty close in Iran, he said, and he still had dreams about things that happened there. He said it took months for his body to "remember what to do with food." He also confirmed news reports that loud noises tended to make him jump.

The former hostage was quiet and reticent, willing to talk with a local reporter because of gratitude to the community, but not really forthcoming about his problems.

Later news items quoted him as saying he had received lots and lots of help, and was fine. But news stories after his death in 2012 at age seventy-two said he had committed suicide. He had been beaten in his cell and subjected to mock executions during captivity, said hostage attorney Lankford, and as time went on, he became more and more a recluse and an alcoholic. "In reality, his life was taken from him thirty-three years ago," the lawyer wrote in a tribute in *Roll Call*. He had become an alcoholic and was unable to hold a regular job.

Phil Ward died at his home in Culpeper, and as an Air Force veteran was buried, of course, in Culpeper National Cemetery.

My lasting picture of him is not of the man standing firm and saying thank-yous at a reception, or of the father who had been cutting wood to share the outdoors with his son, but of the almost spectral being with dark, apprehensive eyes hovering around guests in his own living room as though he didn't belong.

In fact, his death occurred in the same month as the release of the film *Argo,* which was about the crisis. The movie went into theaters just a few weeks after the attack by militants on the U.S. mission in Benghazi, Libya. The dangers to diplomatic security were strongly in the air and the news about then.

A final note on all this: A month later we received a letter to the editor from a woman in Alexandria. "Congratulations," she wrote. "You kept secret the news that Mr. Phil Ward was one of the Iranian hostages because Mrs. Ward requested privacy. Your act helps to rebuild our confidence in the news media. Thanks." Well. I always had reservations—I was taught that information is not for newspapers to withhold, but to put out there, regardless. But when was the last time those words—"confidence in the news media"—were strung together without a "no" in front of them?

CHAPTER FIFTEEN
The Court System Works

A more theoretically routine aspect of newspapering that never failed to interest me was the courts. I have explained the no doubt inappropriate glee that I felt on my earliest introduction to the reality of the various courtrooms, since it was a view of parts of society that I had had no inkling of. Admittedly it was at bottom serious stuff, and often veered into the painfully tragic, as in a malpractice case when a woman described the death of her child because of poor medical care.

Generally, though, I always managed to maintain a certain amount of distance from what was happening, the inevitable result of being a designated observer. It was not unlike the ability to look through a camera lens at a fairly gruesome scene and see only a photo that I was expected to take—or maybe it was at first that I was young and had little empathy, but then it continued as a protective layer.

At any rate, the legal system was a close-up look at life as it is often (unfortunately) lived. And it rarely disappointed. In my years of sitting in the tiny district court space on the south side of Davis Street, or across the street in the dignity of the circuit courtroom with its ancient portraits and air of dedication to justice, I saw things that were funny, things that were tragic, things that were frightening, and things that were thought-provoking.

Court activity in a small community is presumably not very different from legal matters in larger places, and Culpeper cases sometimes moved on to the state court level, and even very occasionally received national attention in the development of law. During my years of covering the courts, a man who could pass the admittedly not very stringent mental health standards only under drug treatment was tried there, and another defendant was sentenced for a murder he did not commit. Inadequate court-appointed counsel was sometimes an issue, and sometimes was not recognized when it should have been a clear basis for appeal. There was obvious lying, and there was the convoluted atmosphere of a truth that was true only in the eyes of the accused or of witnesses for or against the defendant.

There were gory cases and tragic cases, but I'll start with one of my favorites that was neither, and was an excellent illustration of the difficulty of applying law to people with little sense of it. It happened in 1971, soon after my return to work, and was in district court. The headline was about "how to drive a judge bananas," and it was a judicial nightmare, a struggle by a then very rare female judge to make sense of various accounts of a semi-riot on a Saturday night.

Judge Carroll Kem Shackelford found about a dozen people before her in the little informal courtroom, some of whom were to be tried on various charges of disorderly conduct filed after a disruption developed on East Davis Street, a block or so from the town's center, and continued at the local hospital. Judge Shackelford, a member of a family of attorneys, was a woman of considerable genuine dignity and self-control, well aware of her position as a pioneer female.

On the fall day when efforts were made to drive her bananas, she worked very hard to figure out the causes of this particular melee. "An attempt to sort out the accused through the testimony of a single witness . . . failed hopelessly," I wrote. A woman had sworn out a warrant against her husband on the morning of the day in question, and unfortunately said husband caught up with her at the end of Davis Street that evening. He began hitting her, and two other women, one named Margo, intervened. Knives were produced, and in the confusion Margo "got cut." Someone drove Margo to Culpeper Memorial Hospital, and two carloads of people from the original fight followed them.

As all swarmed out of various vehicles, the star witness explained, a woman named Barbara Ann—family connection somewhat confused— "started hitting" anyone who was handy. The scene of this turbulence was outside the hospital, with Margo being treated inside, and a would-be peacemaker aimed a shotgun at everyone to protect Barbara Ann—or something.

At this point, according to my story, "Mrs. Shackelford inquired desperately 'Who hit Margo? Exactly who assaulted whom?'" And then came the oddly tangled answer: "Barbara Ann either hit me with a shoe or bit me, I'm not sure." The judge tried to regroup by addressing the Davis Street incident first. She had everyone who was involved only in the hospital battle sit down, then read through the warrants to find out who among those still standing was actually charged.

The charge of assaulting Margo turned out to have been brought against a seventeen-year-old, who of course as a juvenile was in the wrong court. The husband, not surprisingly, was also accused of assault against his wife. One man with a heavily bandaged arm and a look of bewilderment turned out to be an excess defendant. He was standing, so Judge Shackelford asked what he was charged with. "I don't know myself," he said in an injured tone. The rest of the defendants stood together during this exchange, giggling among themselves as they exchanged what apparently were pretty good witticisms. By very late afternoon the judge had been reduced to asking hopefully "Are you Big Frank or Little Frank?" Once Big Frank had admitted that yes, that was how he was known, the next step was sorting out Big and Little Barbaras.

And yes, it was funny, but it also spoke well of the legal system, because wrong had been done and guilt had to be determined, and eventually it was. A judge was willing to take the time and endure the frustration of delving into a world different from the one she had learned about both from personal experience and no doubt from her law school classes. There was no fight on Davis the next week, and presumably Margo was properly healed and there was at least a temporary end to public biting or hitting with shoes.

In fact, in 1975 I wrote a column titled "Our system, it's working." I noted that a court reporter has to be all too objective, and that it can play with a person's head. "In seeking everyone's best points," as the reporter does in order to quote them, he or she can pretty much ignore the weak ones. I admitted that partly because of my nature, partly as learned behavior (I had been covering the courts for a while by then), "For my own part, I invariably think everyone is telling the truth . . . if someone says he blacked out and can't remember committing an axe murder, I think, the poor guy, with a problem like that."

Our area certainly had its share of serious cases, many of them distressingly awful. Again in my earlier years, I watched as a jury found Robert Stanton of Culpeper guilty of the murder of Zula May Long, the mother of five small children. This was in the solemnity of the circuit courtroom, where Judge Harold H. Purcell presided over the dreadful case. He had little difficulty, since the jury (all male, it was 1971) heard eyewitness testimony from two young neighbors, and Stanton had confessed on-scene at the Spencer Street apartment. He was given life in prison.

Murders, I learned, were almost all unbelievably tragic, and often involved unhappy families. They also illuminated the pressures and stresses that all humans and all human relationships endure. That same year, Mr. and Mrs. Clarence Randolph Bowen were shot to death in bed in their home near Mitchells, and their son, twenty-six-year-old Clarence Linwood Bowen, was charged with the shotgun killings. Their daughter, Mrs. Frances Spradlin, found the bodies. The trial was one that vibrated with off-kilter family connections and opened a door on the "quiet desperation" that characterizes many lives. I was caught up in the two-day proceedings with a fervor that probably wasn't really a good thing, was threatened with jail by a judge who wanted a news blackout rather than a sequestered jury, and ultimately won both state and national press awards for the story. Frankly, it would have been hard not to produce a good account out of the proceedings.

The immediate news story that appeared after the shooting, on July 19, 1971, was pretty bare-bones. It said that the two had been shot, that the son was charged, and that Frances Spradlin had found the bodies. It added that the young woman and her small child had been sleeping upstairs in the small green frame house where they all lived, with the parents sleeping on the first floor, and Mrs. Spradlin had not been disturbed by the shots. The son who was charged had a "history of mental disturbances," and deputies found him asleep in a barn.

A pretty dire happening, but family murders were not rare and no one grew excited or fearful as they would have with a random killing. The trial, though, could have been a movie of the week, and even included that judicial threat to freedom of the press when Judge Purcell demanded in open court that there be no coverage of the first day's proceedings. I went ahead and wrote the story, and was told by Bill Diehl to be prepared to go to jail for said freedom. I guess I was, although I was in a panic—I had seen the cells in the jail. Bill, on the other hand, was envisioning the coverage: "Mother of two-year-old held for publishing the truth" or something similar, illustrated with a touching photo of my baby girl, alone.

It all began quietly enough, with court called to order on Monday, March 20, 1972. Clarence Linwood "Linnie" Bowen never took the stand, and sat quietly throughout, but his sister provided the prosecution's main evidence.

From the time she reportedly asked "Why, Linnie, why?" while he was being questioned in the sheriff's office on that July day, she never expressed any doubt that her brother had blasted their parents into eternity. Nor, according to her testimony, had she had any doubts when she found the bodies in the morning.

Questioned by Culpeper Commonwealth's Attorney John L. Jeffries III, with help from Orange County Commonwealth's Attorney A. Plunket Beirne, she explained that she had gone into town that night with her father, and they had brought home beer for Linnie. But as the evening progressed, the father became agitated and said there would be no more alcohol for his son, because he was drinking too much and "had to straighten up." Linnie, in response, had thrown some beer on the floor, but that was as far as the disagreement went. Frances Spradlin testified that later in the evening the two had companionably watched television, laughing and talking as usual. The family had gone to bed at about 10 p.m., with Frances's young son sleeping on a couch in the room with his grandparents while her tiny daughter shared Frances's bedroom.

Sometime during the night, Frances said, she had awakened without knowing the cause, and had sat up in bed. Her brother came upstairs and into her room; he had to go through her bedroom to get to his own. The two-year-old daughter woke up and wanted her bottle. The young woman went downstairs to get it, with Linnie accompanying her. When she had gotten the bottle, she saw him come out of the parents' room, and then he went back upstairs with her.

He then asked to sit on her bed and talk, which she said was not unusual when he was experiencing a case of "nerves." He told her he felt like something was crawling on him. And then, she said impassively, "My brother tried to rape me." She threw him out, and was going to leave the house, but he insisted she stay and promised he wouldn't bother her anymore.

It was morning when she awoke again, and she went to see why her parents weren't up. She said that when she found the unimaginable scene she checked for a pulse, without expecting to find one in either body. She then covered them with a sheet so her six-year-old son would not see them. The child had still not awakened, although he was sleeping within six feet of his grandparents' bed.

Then this girl, only in her mid-twenties, locked her children in the house and looked quickly around for her brother. She got the children up and drove them into town in her father's pickup, and went to the sheriff's office. Deputy R. W. Bobbitt testified that when he and another deputy came out and woke Linnie in the barn he was impassive, and denied only the attempted rape.

So that was the scenario. The thing that made the trial so riveting was the two principals, the young man and the sister who said he was a murderer. The two were strikingly similar in appearance and demeanor, neither ever showing any anxiety, reluctance, or emotion. A young woman in such a shattering position might have been expected to weep; her brother might have been expected to shake his head in denial, or leap up in objection, particularly since he was reported to have been excitable enough to have also felt things "crawling on him" in a past incident.

They sat only about six feet apart during her testimony. Cross-examination by defense attorney Gordon B. Gay of Fredericksburg, himself not much older than the two siblings, was tough; he probed around the possibility that Frances herself expected to gain financially from her father's death. The witness was noticeably pregnant, and had been separated from her husband for two years, as Gay brought out in questioning. He also brought out that she was on bad terms with the elder Clarence Bowen, who did not approve of her current boyfriend and was very displeased about the pregnancy.

But the movie-of-the-week quality came from the brother and sister. Both were very attractive people, and very much alike. In the story, I described them as "almost mirroring" each other. Both had deep-set blue eyes, short, straight brows, and "especially a firm, steady chin-up tilt of the head." That and their impassive demeanor during the proceedings were spellbinding.

The chin-up tilt remained in place as Frances gave her testimony. She did twist her rings, but never dropped her gaze. Even when she slid her blue eyes toward the similar eyes of the defendant, fixed on her, seeking silent corroboration for remarks like "Sure, we played in the barn when we were kids" or "Yes, he used to hunt," no emotions sparked from either.

Frances was on the stand for more than an hour. Gay brought forth her admission that she also owned a shotgun, and could shoot it, having at least once in the past killed a deer. Linnie had quit hunting, his sister said, because he no longer wanted to kill animals. The jury also heard testimony that Frances had come to an aunt's home the night before and made several phone calls. Hugh Beaver, owner of the E-Z Ranch, the farm where the elder Bowen had worked, testified that Frances had told him on the day of the murder that she was sure of getting her father's Social Security for the children "because he was raising them."

If Linnie had anything to say about his sister's testimony, or her motives, he never took the stand to do it. Gay, who fought hard against the two older prosecutors, could have been expected to have the attractive young man speak up for himself, had the defendant been willing.

The drama of the Monday proceedings didn't stop when Judge Purcell called a halt for the day. He announced in open court that news reports were forbidden until the conclusion of the trial, because he felt such reports might improperly influence the jury. It was a bombshell, the only time I had witnessed such a thing or ever would.

I went back to the office and announced this to my boss. He immediately leaped onto his high horse, and told me to go ahead and write the story. He then put in a call to Purcell, who wasn't home yet. It never occurred to me not to do as he said. Not only was he my boss and in effect my mentor, we both believed strongly that the press was not under the control of officialdom, and that included judges.

Later than evening I went home to my husband and not-yet-three-year-old, leaving the typewritten story behind on the usual pages of cut-up newsprint paper. It was close to bedtime when there was a phone call. "This is the sheriff," said the voice. "We have orders to bring you to the jail." It took me a breath-catching minute to recognize the gruffly disguised voice of Ed Seneff, the other reporter, but even then I thought it was kind of funny. Judge Purcell had called, described himself as between a rock and a hard place because of threats from the defense if there were premature publicity, almost apologized, and persuaded Bill that holding the story was the thing to do. And I was relieved, although I hadn't ever really thought Sheriff Peters would let me have an unpleasant time in jail. Not only was he a nice guy, he understood fully the power of the local press.

Anyway, the next day Linnie Bowen was found guilty and sentenced to twenty years for each murder, and Judge Purcell, at the insistence of the jury, ordered the sentences to run concurrently. Whether the jury was not quite convinced, or figured he wasn't going to kill anyone else, I never learned.

My story said that the defendant stood quietly as always while he heard the verdict of guilty of both first-degree murders. Asked if he had anything to say, he did speak briefly, saying "Only that I want to appeal." He then shook hands with a friend over the court railing, and for the first time, I wrote, he "appeared shaken."

Years later, a man named Clarence Linwood Bowen figured in a landmark Virginia case in which some details of what constituted stalking were determined. The man had been hanging around the home of an ex-girlfriend, and I think it had to have been him; it was more than twenty years after his sentencing, so he would have had time to get out of prison. At younger than fifty, he probably still had his good looks and would have had no trouble finding girlfriends, but he had assaulted this one (although his claim was that he hadn't done it, and was only near her house because he had to walk by it on the way to work).

Another criminal case that was horrible beyond belief occurred in 1978. Three young men, including one juvenile, were charged with the murder of seventeen-year-old Roxanne Pullen in a rock quarry near the Culpeper community of Raccoon Ford. Robert Lee "Bucky" Jenkins and Donald Wayne Hoffman, both of Madison, were arrested after the girl's body was found in the quarry, run over by a car. The rural life was no protection against ghastly crime.

It got worse. An unnamed juvenile who had been with the two adult men testified at the district court hearing that resulted in certification of the case to circuit court. According to his testimony, the three had picked up Roxanne and her brother at the Main Street corner by the Culpeper Post Office. The brother had flagged them down, saying he and Roxanne were looking for pot. All drove to the quarry. The witness said the other two were going to rape the girl and he was to kill the brother. But once Hoffman and Jenkins were out of sight, the witness said, he told the brother to leave.

Needless to say, he did, and hastened to call the police. After the rapes, all three—Hoffman, Jenkins, and the juvenile—got back into the car, with Hoffman driving, and he ran the vehicle over the victim. Exhibiting the same mentality that had allowed the brother to escape, the group then got their car stuck and had to flee on foot. During the trial the car was in the town police garage, with further tests to be done on it.

At the hearing, defense attorney John J. "Butch" Davies, who always took his duties very seriously, said he had "severe reservations" about Jenkins's mental capacity. No one ever indicated that Hoffman was anything but mean.

Legal maneuvering was duly carried out, with both defendants found sane after examination, and a venue change duly ordered as asked. Commonwealth's Attorney John Bennett and Robert Horan, a big-city prosecutor from Fairfax, were to pursue the case together. The move was made to Fluvanna County, where the *Star-Exponent* did not send anyone since the jury trial for Hoffman, scheduled to come first, was cancelled. He pleaded guilty to first-degree murder under a plea agreement. The eventual sentence was life, but he was eligible for parole. Somewhat later, Jenkins pleaded guilty to rape. He had only one misdemeanor on his record, and Hoffman was considered the "murder agent." Jenkins's sentence was forty-five years, but he would have been eligible for parole in a little over eleven years. An Internet search years later revealed that Jenkins had died in 2008 and was buried in a Madison cemetery. Hoffman was listed as living in Richmond, but at least he was a registered sex offender.

While these two cases were moving through the courts, though, there was another unthinkable murder in Culpeper. T. E. McMullan, former chair of the Culpeper Board of Supervisors, a quiet, responsible, gentle man who had politely declined to answer questions during my attempt at a political interview, was shot in the head in his store at Mitchells. The original story, which was bylined by *SE* reporter Gary Rhoades, said that two black men had entered the small country establishment and shot not only "Mr. Mac" but also a customer, Russell Shaw. An unnervingly similar report had come in from Orange County, where two storekeepers at another small country store near True Blue had been shot.

There were so many angles to the shooting spree that reporter Becky Clayton and I were both listed as contributors to the story. Because of the prominence of Mr. Mac, also known as Buck, the article ran under a two-deck banner head. Only one of the four victims, Mrs. E. E. Chambers from the Orange store, died immediately, with McMullan following a few days later. These were crimes of the sort associated with television violence come to life, with the vulnerable crossroads stores targeted by reckless and unfeeling men. A week later the newspaper ran a story headlined "Shootings frighten neighbors." People in both areas were indeed afraid, since no one knew where the robbers had gone, and it had been discovered that they had roots in the local community. What had happened to Russell Shaw was terrifying—an elderly man goes to a store several houses away from his own home, around lunchtime, to pass the time of day with a contemporary, and finds himself and his old friend in a surreal nightmare.

The crimes occurred on April 20. It wasn't until mid-May that a suspect, James Simpson, was apprehended late on a Friday night a short distance from town on the road to Sperryville. The next day it was announced that a second suspect, David Payton Thompson, was in custody in Chicago, where he had been arrested for kidnapping a taxi driver. It wasn't until months later that legal maneuvering ended, with Thompson being brought back to appear at the Simpson trial in Culpeper.

I didn't see much of the trial, but the testimony as reported was grim, not surprisingly. Shaw described being escorted with McMullan to a room in back of the store. Thompson stayed out front, rifling the cash register before heading for the back. His ill-gotten gains, according to the court records, came to $70 and six cans of beer. Possibly not happy with his haul, Thompson remarked "I hate to do this but I have to." He then shot both victims. Shaw later testified that Buck McMullan was shot in the forehead from directly in front, and that he turned his own head away just enough to keep the next bullet from being fatal.

Both defendants received life sentences—Thompson in a plea agreement, since all testimony was that he was the shooter. When Judge Vance Fry spoke to Simpson, he spoke quietly at first of the "callous taking of life." Then, raising his voice, he declared "You did not need to do it." There were appeals to the Virginia Supreme Court, but the sentences stood.

Defense attorney Robert Niles did his best, but there was testimony not only from Shaw but from Thompson's father, who lived locally. The appeals in particular were contained in a fairly brief written record, laying out drily what the men were charged with doing.

News does indeed occur in cycles, and in early fall of the year of the Simpson and Thompson trials, a case that was to hang around forever had begun, with a man accused of beating his father and sister to death. There was never much doubt of what had occurred, or why—Joseph Earl Nibblins was a young black man with an apparently caring family but a very limited grip on sanity. Because it was a potentially important case, it brought out thought, effort, and perseverance in court-appointed attorney Davies, and the paper—mostly me—followed it closely. The question involved was one of both human and legal complexity, and turned on the still fairly recent development of psychotropic drugs—and the definition of sanity.

The deaths occurred in the fall of 1979, at a home off Route 229 north of Culpeper. Nibblins was sent fairly promptly to Central State Hospital in Petersburg, a mental treatment facility, and it wasn't until the next summer that he was returned for trial. The staff at the hospital had decided he was legally competent, although his mother said he had been to all three state mental hospitals and was on a lot of medication. The medication was critical—on it, he apparently knew right from wrong and could assist in his defense, thus meeting the legal definition of sanity. Without it, he couldn't be said to clear that admittedly low bar.

Deliberation of his fate went back and forth, in what certainly seemed to be dogged and good-faith struggles involving Davies and the court, with no thought of a good outcome for anyone. It was the whole human tragedy bound up in one gangly young man who at some point turned an unself-conscious smile on a news photographer.

Davies was appointed when Nibblins first appeared in court in October of 1979. It was the beginning of a lot of time that the popular attorney put in. The defendant was sent off for testing and treatment, and was returned in the summer of 1980 after staff at Central State at last decided he was competent to stand trial—despite behavior that plainly indicated otherwise. That August, Davies asked that his client be reexamined locally, citing his actions in the local jail, where he had quit taking his meds. It was said off the record that the young man had stood up on a toilet seat and walked endlessly around it. No one at the jail had any idea what he would do next.

It wasn't until that October that the questions began to jell. The headline on my story said "Court ponders Nibblins," and indeed it was pondering away. This case was a big reason for my faith in American institutions because of the time, thought, and probing that went into it. Davies, who was later elected to the state legislature to represent the area, explained the case carefully in an interview with me, and the courts struggled to make a decision on this new question.

The problem really wasn't one of guilt or innocence, all sides agreed, and even in the early days of psychotropic medications everyone knew it was an important question to figure out. Nibblins might not continue to meet the mental standards to stand trial long enough to get through the proceedings, but he did not seem to be provably incompetent enough to be committed to a state mental institution—which in any case had limited space that perhaps should be reserved for someone with a better prognosis. Still, it was doubtful that Nibblins could fend for himself if he was found guilty and sent into the prison system.

He had been involved with the mental health clinic in Culpeper since 1971, and his "adaptation to the world has been marginal," local officials said. The planning district doctor who worked with him said there was "essentially no change" in him as a result of his stay in the hospital, and that without the "security of the mental hospital there is a strong possibility of violence." On the strength of such testimony, the defendant was sent back yet again to Central State.

It wasn't until the next April that Nibblins surfaced in the news again. He was being charged with the slaying of another patient at Central State; apparently the assessment of a propensity to violence was right on. He was described as being of subnormal intelligence, autistic, and limited by rigid ideas. Doctors now agreed that he had a preoccupation with violence and retribution. Any other details stayed under wraps at the hospital, but that fall he was to go to trial. Dr. William H. Young, the local psychiatrist who had seen him before, said that he was competent by definition, but only with large doses of antipsychotic medication. By that time the issue was a matter of public debate nationally, but no conclusions had been drawn.

With medication and treatment at Central State Nibblins was once more able to convince a special justice at a hearing that he could stand trial, and in early September he had his day in court. He received two life terms after a jury took only twenty minutes at the end of a two-day trial to convict him. Davies had immediate plans for an appeal, but Nibblins, by then twenty-six, wanted no part of it. He thought the decision was all right, and he was looking forward to playing basketball in the penitentiary.

Reservations about his survival in the corrections system seemed to have disappeared with the killing at Central State. Commonwealth's Attorney John Bennett argued that Nibblins's out-of-control behavior was often directed at getting what he wanted, which was residence at the mental hospital, with its pool and gym, rather than in the very limiting cell at the Culpeper jail. Once he understood that there was basketball in the penitentiary, he was willing to go there.

It seems unlikely that Nibblins was sane by any reasonable definition. Dr. Young said he had seen Nibblins off and on since adolescence, because his family did their best for him, and that he was never in anything but a psychotic state. He added that as a youth the defendant had killed dogs and cats, telltale behavior. The Central State doctor said interviews had convinced him that Nibblins had made a conscious decision to get rid of his father and sister.

Eventually there was an appeal, the joy of basketball notwithstanding. It went to the Virginia Supreme Court, but was turned down there for further hearing. Nibblins was given the two life sentences for the family murders, and also pleaded guilty in the death of his fellow patient at Central State. In 2018 he was still there, and parole cases listed as considered by the Greensville Correctional Center some years before included that of Joseph Earl Nibblins; it was concluded that he had "no interest in parole."

One of the strangest cases ever, another one with enough twists to qualify as a movie of the week, was that of Jack O. Lam. Lam was a Madison County man, and the murder for which he was eventually tried took place in the small town of Madison, at a Main Street apartment. The first mention in the *Star-Exponent* seems to have been on July 8, 1980, several months after William Darnell Barbour was shot to death on the back porch of the apartment. Kurt Bacci wrote the story, and I have no memory of how it came to the paper's attention, since Madison coverage was sporadic at that point. According to the article, a well-known Madison businessman was initially indicted for the murder. But somewhat later Jack Lam and another witness were indicted for committing perjury in the first grand jury hearing, and the case against the businessman was dropped. The next year, the perjurer, Lam, appeared in court to plead guilty to the voluntary manslaughter of Barbour.

I never covered any of Lam's court appearances, but since I lived in Madison I was aware of gossipy stories regarding the mysteries of the case. Lam was taking a fall for someone else, was one version; another was that everyone was so drunk on the night in question that no one really knew what happened and any one of a number of people could have been the shooter. At any rate, when Lam was sentenced a while later, he received a much-reduced sentence of ten years, with seven suspended.

He actually served less than a year before being paroled, but freedom didn't work out for the forty-two-year-old; in January of 1983 Lam was found dead of a gunshot wound to the head, sitting in his old car in the parking lot of the store at Wolftown, a tiny Madison County community. He was believed to have been waiting for the man he usually rode with to their jobs at Virginia Metal Products in Orange. It looked like a hit, and speculation began in earnest. The place where he waited for his ride was exposed to the road on all sides, providing a location where a drive-by shooting would have worked splendidly. There was $500 in cash found on the body, so robbery was not the motive. A murder investigation was under way, and began with an early morning traffic stop at Wolftown, where police questioned passers-by about what they had seen.

As the story developed, it came to light that vandalism of his car had recently made Lam move to the Wolftown site as a place to leave it parked. He had recently been dismissed from a civil suit brought by Barbour's mother, and had been expected to be subpoenaed to testify against someone else in the suit.

Castings of tracks found near the parked car matched the tires on a yellow pickup belonging to a man from Stanardsville in Greene County, but several witnesses agreed that the suspect hadn't bought those particular tires until months after the shooting. That sent the sheriff's department looking elsewhere, but then an eyewitness came forward. This new character knew both the suspect and Lam, and he finally told someone from the sheriff's office that he was there next to Lam's car when the accused shot and killed him.

Reporter Bethann Griffin was dispatched to attend the preliminary hearing, since interest in the strange tale had grown exponentially. She wrote that according to testimony, there had been yet another group drinking spree the night before the death occurred, since no one seemed to have learned much from the fallout caused by the original drunkfest that had resulted in Barbour's shooting death. In the early morning by the very rural road, the purported eyewitness said, Lam was sitting in his car and the accused man was talking with him from where he was sitting in his own truck. The witness testified that he was standing between the two vehicles when a bullet went past his ear and hit Lam.

When the trial was held in late September, I finally was there. My first-day story noted that early testimony might turn suspicion toward the alleged eyewitness. According to testimony, the man on trial had been home in bed with his wife at 6 a.m.; someone had talked with him on the phone there. He had an understandable reason for sleeping in a bit—he said he had been coon hunting the night before and was out late. There were thirty witnesses, I wrote, many of them contradicting each other. The defense said that without the theoretical eyewitness there was no case, and some of the others who testified corroborated the defense description of the witness—that he was a "harsh, hard, wily man." The jury found that the defendant did not kill Lam, and to my knowledge, no one was ever convicted.

Possibly the Culpeper murder with the most widespread effects was the death in the early summer of 1982 of a young mother of three, nineteen-year-old Rebecca Lynn Williams. Neighbors found her in a pool of blood outside her Village Apartments home on the south side of town. She had been stabbed repeatedly and viciously, and there was a reported sighting of a bearded black man in the area.

When an arrest was finally made, nearly a year later, the man charged was twenty-two-year-old Earl Washington Jr. of Bealeton. He had been arrested by sheriff's department officers in Fauquier for breaking into the home of a seventy-three-year-old woman, stealing a gun and money from her, beating her with a chair, and then shooting his brother with the stolen gun, and was identified in a photo lineup by the elderly victim. It was while he was being interrogated by officers in Fauquier that he was said to have confessed to the Culpeper murder. When Culpeper officials first went to interview the suspect, they were told he had been drinking very heavily (and yes, there is a theme here) for at least a day before the crimes, and that he had been questioned at length and had gotten little sleep. The Culpeper officers waited until the next day to talk with him.

Washington was transferred to Culpeper as the location of the more serious case. Bond was, not surprisingly, denied, after Washington had done the "perp walk" and been photographed being escorted from jail to court by Sheriff Peters. It was July of 1983 when he was indicted for the Williams murder. While reporter (and later commonwealth's attorney) Gary Close did the early stories, by the time court activities were in full swing the case had been passed to me for coverage. The story explaining that Earl Washington had been ruled competent was mine, and it included the argument by defense attorney John W. Scott Jr. of Fredericksburg that statements from his client after he was arrested were taken over a long period without proper food or sleep and without proper Miranda warnings.

Not surprisingly, memories of the threat of jailing reporters in the earlier two-day trial returned as I listened to an argument for a change of venue for Washington. The defense asserted that press coverage was inflammatory, but Judge David Berry relieved my misgivings when he said that he had read the printed coverage and it was "factual." Factual was a good thing, especially in a case as extreme as this one.

When the trial started in Culpeper, Washington had apparently had many second thoughts, and denied everything when he took the stand for only a half hour on the first day of the proceedings, in January 1984. By then twenty-three years old, he was shepherded by Scott through testimony that he had stayed home that day and cleaned up the yard. He added that he did not know state police investigator C. J. Wilmore, who had testified in detail about his confession.

Wilmore said that Washington had told him about coming to town with a friend, going to the apartment, and seeing Rebecca Williams with her two small children (the third was safely in school.) Other details were apparently confused, but according to Wilmore, Washington told of kicking in the door, and then said he "stuck her" one time and assaulted her. Scott argued that Washington's low IQ had confused him into making the confession, while Bennett, the prosecutor, countered that if the jury was willing to accept that, it would have to believe that "police in two different counties had some sort of massive conspiracy" to convict the defendant. The circuit judge in Culpeper, F. Ward Harkrader, ruled that there was no indication of such behavior by officials. But these details were to hover around the case when it was reopened in 2000.

In the newspaper of Jan. 21, 1984, I wrote that the first death sentence returned in Culpeper in thirty years had come back with the Washington jury. There was a new photo of Washington walking surrounded by deputies, tall and thin, with bushy, tall hair, his dark eyes shifting nervously above a beard.

For that paper, I also produced a sidebar on the last execution in a county case. But when I wrote those two stories, I was already wondering about the fairness of the trial. I'll swear that was my impression, and it didn't take the freeing of Washington all those years later to give me that idea. I knew I was a gullible audience for even a mediocre lawyer, and while the prosecution was winding up what was unquestionably a pretty good case I wondered whom the defense would call. Who might have seen Washington during the day, who might have talked to him by phone, who might have seen him later on the date in question without bloodstains on his clothing? And what of friends and relatives, who might testify to the nonviolence of his nature? Where was the discussion of how drunk he was when he committed the offense for which he was originally arrested? Remember, no testimony about his other charges was allowed, since that could unfairly influence the jury.

It seemed to me the defense rested almost before it started, although I think there was a great deal of dependence on the argument of Washington's diminished capacity and his confusion when he was arrested. I had been expecting the seesawing back and forth of my own opinion, something I was accustomed to experiencing in court as a parade of witnesses, or at least behavioral experts such as Davies had presented for Nibblins, came forth. It always amazes me what a defense can gather, if only as a smokescreen. But in this case, there didn't seem to be much.

This does raise questions about possible racial considerations in court proceedings. Certainly Scott, then in his early 30s, would have been court-appointed; he was black, and presumably the effort to find someone to represent a black defendant considered to be probably guilty of an outrageous crime had resulted in recruiting from a distance. Scott went on to become the area's first black judge, sitting in the General District Court in Stafford and then in 1996, being appointed as a circuit court judge.

A civil rights pioneer who was one of several students who won a federal civil rights lawsuit for the right to attend then all-white James

Monroe High School, he suffered from severe eye problems and died in April 2008 at 59 years old, following eye surgery. When Fredericksburg built a new courthouse, it honored Scott by including a bust of the black jurist, and following his death he was praised as a judge by other attorneys citing his knowledge of law.

But he was young when he represented Washington, and the resources provided to him may have been inadequate when compared to those of the state and the number of officers and detectives involved. Moreover, the quality of the trial itself was not cited by the Innocence Project in reopening the case so many years later. Questions were raised about procedures by police and the accuracy of testimony about the defendant's questioning. Washington was found to have an IQ of 69, and police reported that he had confessed to a total of five crimes. The Innocence Project attorneys described him as eager to please authorities and therefore willing to agree with whatever was presented to him.

He came within nine days of being executed in 1985, although the defense used all opportunities within the system to have his convictions thrown out or reduced. His sentence was confirmed after a hearing in which he was described by former employers and a probation officer as a "pleasant young man," although the probation officer said he was "slow in responses." Appeals and hearings notwithstanding, he stayed in prison for more than 17 years.

But in 2000, with the involvement of the Innocence Project, then only eight years old and with a record of exonerating prisoners with DNA testing, such testing implicated another man. Gov. Douglas Wilder had already commuted the death sentence, and a later governor, James Gilmore, pardoned Washington in 2002. A lawsuit was then filed to clear his name, and some years later Virginia struck a deal to pay $1.9 million to him, not a lot less than the $2.25 million figure a federal jury had come up with.

Then in 2007 the man implicated by the DNA, Kenneth Maurice Tinsley, pleaded guilty to the rape and murder of Rebecca Williams. He was already serving two life terms for a rape in Albemarle County, three counties south, and from his wheelchair he told the court "I'm sorry for everything I did." It was determined by a jury in Charlottesville that during the interrogation police had perhaps inadvertently given

Washington details of the crime, details that only the killer could have known. Because of his mental makeup, Washington had become confused during the very difficult and long interrogation over the attack on the elderly woman, and had confessed just because it seemed easier than continuing the questioning. He did recant later, but it took the reopened investigation to produce the pardon.

CHAPTER SIXTEEN

More About the Courts

And there were more murder cases. *Star-Exponent* readers in that span of a couple of years might have been forgiven for deciding that their world was not a safe place, that it was full of truly unbalanced killers. In early September of 1983, eighteen-year-old Joseph Maybury of Falls Church died from a shotgun blast at a Reva area pond. The young man was there with other teenagers and twentysomethings for a party before most of the kids went off to college.

Accused was Eugene Wells, forty-two, who owned property almost adjoining the pond. He had had a 1969 Renault parked there, overgrown with weeds and obviously the worse for wear. The partiers, off on a hike, had smashed in the back window, evidently just because the old car was there.

I picked up the story when Wells was brought to court for a bond hearing. He said he had heard glass breaking and gone down to see what had happened. Oddly, he also told the court he had "considered his options," listing them as calling the sheriff, contacting the boys' parents, beating them up to the extent they would have to go to the hospital, or "something worse." Four hours later, he said, after drinking four beers and a couple of glasses of wine, he fired warning shots at the group by the pond. Maybury approached him, perhaps to knock the gun out of his hands, and it discharged, according to Wells. The judge's decision was to reduce bond.

But Wells was quickly indicted, and the trial began in early December. *SE* photographer Steve Mawyer took a good shot of the bearded Wells, looking like a minister who had perhaps made up his own religion, walking toward the courthouse flanked as always by self-conscious-looking deputies.

The focus of much of the argument was on the weapon. Defense attorney Richard Dulaney noted that two of the partiers had knives, and said Wells had brought the gun because he felt outnumbered. He had approached the group of young people, at that point mostly swimming in the pond, to ask for restitution for the car. Commonwealth's Attorney John Bennett declared that Maybury had come to the fore, saying "I'll pay for it," only to be pushed back by the gun. There was discussion of the unreliability of the weapon; experts had examined it, but the testimony was not admitted because it was inconclusive and there was no finding that the gun could have gone off if dropped or handled roughly.

The most memorable testimony, certainly, came from Wells, who talked for an hour, doing himself no good in spite of demonstrating that he was articulate and wasn't a *Deliverance*-style country backwoodsman. Gesturing and dramatizing, he said he had come upon the boys "trashing" the car, and had expected an apology or an offer to pay for the damage. He said in didactic tones that his convictions required that he provide time and opportunity for "reconciliation" before he involved the police or the young people's parents.

His reason for taking the gun along? Well, so he wouldn't be "reviled or rebuked," and could keep them at bay. The scenario he foresaw involved sitting down with a couple of beers to talk the matter over (no word of what he'd do with the gun during the negotiations, or indeed why he needed more beer), and would have accepted $25 and an apology. "Hey, I'm easy," he added, pausing for effect—or maybe applause.

Throughout his time on the stand, Wells altered his voice to reflect who was speaking, and described a struggle which obviously had come to be played out in his mind almost as if choreographed. The gun, he said, was "old and dangerous." At one point he referred to the people he had gone to confront as "aggressive and hostile," and at another as "silly teenyboppers."

Bennett reminded the jury of Wells's earlier statement to police, that he had sat drinking and thinking over ways to deal with the incident.

He also called Wells's former wife to the stand. She said she had been visiting friends nearby that day, and she and her mother had gone for a walk in what was familiar territory to her. The two had met Wells and spoken to him, but he didn't answer, she said, and there was an "intent" look on his face.

Maybury's mother took the stand during the proceedings, and described with composure her son's impending move to Blacksburg to attend Virginia Tech. But she cried steadily after the verdict: life in prison, the most severe of five possible findings. Dulaney asked for a psychiatric report on Wells, but the motion was denied by Judge Berry.

Still, at the first of the year, Wells's sentence was delayed for mental exams. And the story kept getting more disturbing as the defendant's various follow-up appeals continued. The former wife testified that Wells had beaten her, and it turned out that he had once confronted a work supervisor at the naval station in Norfolk with a screwdriver held as a weapon. A victim impact statement was very touching—Joe Maybury's parents spoke movingly of their son, and added that Joe's seventeen-year-old sister wouldn't go to bed in her room for three nights, waiting up for the phone call saying there had been a mistake and her brother was not dead after all.

The conviction was appealed to the Virginia Supreme Court, where the case was dismissed. Wells then petitioned for habeas corpus relief in federal district court. His argument there was based partly on pretrial publicity, and partly on an earlier case in which some of the jurors in his trial were involved. In that instance, the jury found a woman not guilty of embezzlement, and the judge scolded the members, saying he would have found the defendant guilty without difficulty. Counsel for Wells had cleverly dug that up to make the case that the experience might have influenced the jury to be tough in making their decision.

The final decision by the U.S. Court of Appeals for the Fourth Circuit letting the conviction stand did not come until 1987. Shortly after the Culpeper trial, Wells wrote to me as the trial reporter and asked for copies of all the stories that had appeared in the paper. He also made a point of the difficulty that the several writers who worked on the story had in determining his age, and clarified it for me. I was willing to provide the stories, but not tempted to try a jailhouse interview. Not only had I been in court for the arguments about pretrial publicity, I had seen the man in action. I was even familiar with the locale, because I had ridden my horse with friends around the pond a number of times during the period when Wells lived there, and we were all glad we hadn't been tempted to trash anything that seemed like an abandoned car.

There were other memorable criminal trials—one in 1972, when a young mother of five who shot her husband was found guilty of involuntary manslaughter. The entire family, very young children and the dead husband's parents, were obviously very sad but firmly agreed on the details of what had happened. I described them as having "an attitude of dignified unity," and said that the in-laws leaned over the court railing to comfort the obviously sorrowing defendant. The gun had been borrowed from the father-in-law, who testified that the safety didn't work. The young wife was putting the shotgun down on the roof of the car when it discharged, striking the husband.

Unusual cases weren't all murders. A few years later, Edward Allen Strack, thirty-five, of Baltimore was charged with felonious assault on one of twenty-five youths he was directing and theoretically watching over in a military-style summer camp in Culpeper. The camp was later described as having turned into a kind of prison, with authoritarian behavior by its commandant, until two of the boys escaped and made it out to a highway.

Strack made bail, and left the jail hurriedly in the company of his wife. His attorney, S. Page Higginbotham of Orange, known for presenting spirited defenses on behalf of questionable clients, was with him, and I was able to quote a witness to the jail departure. Strack asked the lawyer "What can I do?" and Higginbotham was said to have replied "The first thing you can do is tuck in that shirt." The attorney argued in court that the whole thing was exaggerated, but convinced no one. Strack was sentenced to ninety days in jail after being found guilty of twenty-four counts of contributing to the delinquency of a minor.

A very memorable case, one that created an odd rapport between the defendant and me, was a charge of assault against H. Hamilton Hutcheson, longtime chair of the Culpeper County School Board. Hutcheson was found guilty in district court, but felt unjustly dealt with and waged a successful appeal.

According to the evidence, his indignation was justified; the lower-court judge probably was so taken aback by the accusation of assault against a fourteen-year-old girl that he did what seemed like the reasonable thing. I covered the appeal. Hutcheson's daughter had gone home with another girl after a fight with her mother. Her father went after her, and a "scuffle" ensued between father and teenage friend. The girl said he had struck her with his fist and kicked her. According to the defendant, he had maybe hit her glancingly with the back of his hand.

The jury of six women and one man heard a great deal of detail, but the gist was that Hutcheson had spent a long afternoon searching for his daughter, and when he finally found her he was understandably a bit out of sorts. He grabbed her by the collar, all parties agreed, and at that point the other girl jumped on him to protect her. Judge Berry said in his instructions to the jury that a person had the right to resist any violence to his person. The final wrap-up came quite a while after the incident, and the Hutcheson daughter testified that she in fact loved her father and they were getting along fine.

It was one of the rare instances where someone who had been on trial complimented the accuracy of the paper's coverage. I had put in my years on the school board beat and apparently had made no enemies there, and Hutch and I remained friends from then on. As I said, it was a small community.

Once again the fact that our area counties experienced spillover from the metropolitan Washington area was illustrated, this time in another and very unusual murder. Oddly, I had met the victim, Rance Spellman—my friend Mary and I had once gone to look at a horse he had for sale, a ways from us in Rappahannock County. We didn't buy the horse, but on the drive back we both admitted to some rather strong masculine vibes from the man. He was a big guy, soft-spoken and gentle and knowledgeable with the horse.

A few years later, Spellman was shot to death while working on a bulldozer to widen a disputed right-of-way. It seemed he was farm manager for Patricia Saltonstall, a member of a very old, historically significant, and political Massachusetts family. She described herself as a farmer and writer, working at her Points of View Farm at Flint Hill.

She was prominent enough that an account of what happened made it into the *New Yorker* magazine, and there was considerable coverage by the *Washington Post* in light of the significance of the Saltonstalls. I wasn't sent to Rappahannock for the trial, but the *SE* covered it closely, and it held my interest as it did that of others.

The murder evolved from an argument between neighbors over a right-of-way. The woman charged was Diane Kidwell, who had by then also made the national news independently, having been the prime witness against her employer, Dr. Murdock Head, in his trial for what was a bit of a national scandal. Head, who owned a conference center where Diane Kidwell worked, was convicted of trying to bribe two congressmen.

At any rate, Kidwell and her husband lived next to the Saltonstall estate. There had been a discussion over the right-of-way, and major disagreement. Then early one morning an armed Spellman had driven the bulldozer into the disputed space to clear everything out—including a section of the Kidwells' fence and some shrubs. Diane Kidwell said she had shot the man because she was frightened, and that he had threatened her husband. She said further that he had reached down to his side, where no one denied he had stashed both a pistol and a shotgun.

Saltonstall said there had been a mix-up with her attorney that led to work beginning without an agreement on the right-of-way. The jury was unable to reach a verdict, and a mistrial was declared. A second trial ended in acquittal. In the not-to-be-believed category, the case also stirred up local politics. In sealed documents that were opened by the judge after the first trial, the commonwealth's attorney said Kidwell's original lawyer, David L. Konick, wiped Kidwell's fingerprints from the shotgun when he was summoned to Kidwell's house shortly after the shooting. Konick said in court that he had "freaked out," and made reference to such things being done by Paul Drake and Perry Mason on TV. Truth stranger than fiction here. After this questionable statement, the lawyer ran unsuccessfully for Rappahannock Commonwealth's Attorney and went on to make a name for himself by bringing various suits against county governments.

Even before the second trial, Saltonstall had set up a living memorial for her farm manager—an award for young people who had outstanding farming interest and abilities. The website for the award, which at this writing was still being given, described Spellman as "a man who lived his beliefs in stewardship of the land, preservation of farming, and mastering of its essential skills [and] in the human protection of animals and birds." He was credited with transforming Points of View Farm from "an abandoned apple orchard and cattle farm into a productive and handsome registered cow/calf operation."

I'd have to say that during all these activities I was almost never disappointed in the behavior of judges. From Shackelford to Berry, they were patient, determined, professional, thoughtful, and ethical, as far as the observer could tell. Just before I left the *SE*, I did an interview with retired District Judge Basil Burke, who lived near us. It was illustrated with my photo of him in a checked shirt on his Mountain Prospect Farm. His background was typical of the impressive credentials many of these men (almost never women) had. "From Manhattan Island to Yale University to a prison camp near Frankfurt, back to Yale and then on to law school at U.Va.," I wrote, "the early years of Basil C. Burke Jr. of Leon were as varied as the days he has spent on area judges' benches." He had served for ten years as a district court judge, and had spent one hundred days in the German prison camp in World War II.

I wrote about Judge Berry's using the bench as something of a bully pulpit. He wasn't happy with sentencing a twenty-five-year-old defendant to the prison system. The resources of the system were not adequate to properly treat a prisoner's alcoholism or other serious problem, he declared. "Everyone wants to tell him what his problem is, but no one is willing or able to deal with it on a one-on-one basis."

Most judges were fairly quick to call out attorneys for improper behavior, but almost never did you see one admonish a defendant, or be anything but direct and matter-of-fact in sentencing. The bully pulpit was not used to bully those who were already down and out. The system worked, and it was because of those who carried out the law.

CHAPTER SEVENTEEN
Perhaps Why Courts Are a Branch of Government

W hile criminal court activities provided a lot of front-page copy that was eagerly read in our small community, the civil cases were in many ways more demanding. Often they included actions by or against prominent folk, people with leadership positions in the town and county. Reporters had to remember that they would have to live with what they wrote—I described that reality many times as having to walk up the street on the day the paper came out and face the people I had just written about.

One of the cases with the most reverberations was a malpractice suit brought by the widow after her husband had died after treatment by some of the more revered practitioners in the local medical community. It came just before I left the *SE*, and the paper's coverage showed the change from newspeople with real, daily involvement in the community to those with a more impersonal approach.

There was a fairly new, young managing editor who had come to the *SE* from a larger paper and was eager to impress on his tiny staff how knowledgeable he was. As the court reporter, I was told to produce a "jury to be selected" story at the beginning of the action. I obediently did; it didn't seem worthwhile to protest, even though in most local cases jury selection wasn't time-consuming and the case might be more or less over by the time there was further reporting. It wasn't something that we had done routinely, but it was a pro forma thing to do elsewhere.

The advance story explained that the $2.5 million malpractice suit had been brought by the widow of a man who died of apparent infection. The hospital was named in the suit, as were four Culpeper doctors and a very well-known and popular dentist. The upshot was that the "preview" story was viewed as unnecessary and inflammatory, and there was an immediate eruption of protest, saying we were giving extra exposure to claims against good people.

It was the era of massive malpractice claims, and perhaps discomfort was justified. I actually knew none of the defendants, being young enough not to have to go to doctors much, and not being a frequenter of the Culpeper Country Club. I was of course well acquainted with officials from the hospital, since they were a source of frequent news and press releases.

There were letters to the editor and there was general unhappiness, but without any claim that there were misstatements of fact in the story. The real tipping point came when I was called by a local minister, a man I did know, telling me that the dead man and his family were unworthy of attention in the newspaper, that they were terrible people; he in fact used a particularly unministerial word. I knew nothing of the plaintiffs and would not have let it affect the story if I had, and the man was, after all, dead at fifty-four. But so vocal was the outcry that I was taken off the trial, the only time this ever happened.

Coverage was turned over to a new young reporter. She wrote that the lawsuit was directed toward what was said to be improper treatment, rather than misdiagnosis. The physicians' counsel argued that the patient's alcohol withdrawal and delirium tremens had kept treatment from working, since the man had been on a drinking binge that week before going to the dentist. His wife testified that they had had "a wonderful marriage," and that her husband died because antibiotics were not given soon enough.

The jury cleared the defendants—the story was in the Sept. 14, 1984, paper, only four days after the original headlines. There was little fallout from the rest of the coverage, but the changing approach to news (Bill Diehl wouldn't have asked for a jury selection story, and in any case he would not have taken me off the trial) crystallized for me why I'd only be working there another couple of months.

My up close and personal experience with civil suits began in 1972. Diehl had done an interview with Dr. Donald J. Waldowski, a thirty-two-year-old pediatrician who was leaving Culpeper because, he said, he was unhappy with the medical atmosphere. I had been taking our daughter to Dr. Waldowski, and based on admittedly limited experience, thought well of him. He had hinted a few times about his differences with the hospital and other doctors, but since I was small-daughter-centered when involved with him I hadn't taken much notice. When Bill got the idea to do the interview, he came close to assigning it to me, but happily I was going to be gone for the next few days to my brother's wedding in North Carolina.

The interview came out on Feb. 24, and it said that Dr. Waldowski, in Culpeper only a year or two by then, was opposed to the expansion of Culpeper Memorial Hospital. He said he had resigned from the hospital staff "because I could not condone the quality of gynecological and obstetric medicine I saw there." I wasn't experienced enough then to know what a red flag that was, mostly because the providers of such care in Culpeper were very, very few in number. Waldowski didn't identify any doctors in connection with what he was saying he didn't have to—but he added that it was "not uncommon for him to treat heavily sedated babies." This was a bad thing to say, and to print.

Things went pretty ballistic, immediately. Letters to the editor came, some pro-Waldowski, some con, pretty much all indignant. One writer declared "Someone is finally making a noise about the terrible medical conditions in our community." Then on March 1, the hospital president said that a statement would be issued by the hospital about the resignation of Waldowski and the "exposure given to it by Mr. Bill Diehl." The statement was stiff, correct, and itself quite indignant. There was eventually a long-running court action; Walter Potter apparently and properly stood up for Bill and the paper, and it finally wound down to very little.

As I said earlier, it was a period rife with malpractice suits and other sorts of litigation. A local man sued Massey Ferguson Inc. over a tractor accident, asking for $700,000 because of "defective design." There were civil suits in the deaths of Jack O. Lam and Rance Spellman, following in the wakes of criminal actions. A suit was filed against that well-known Culpeper character and pillar of the community Ruby Beck. She had sold her Boxwood Restaurant to a man who then prepared to sell it to another buyer. But then, he complained, Beck "maliciously" filed a petition for attachment against him, whereupon he sued her. Many such actions were dropped once a judge had looked closely at them.

Perhaps the most convoluted (and painful) case was one that began in 1981, eventually rolling together a malpractice suit with claims of discrimination and other misdoings. Obstetrician Parviz Modaber had been suspended from the hospital; the complication was that Modaber was Iranian, and the country and Culpeper in particular had just been up in arms over the Iranian hostage situation. Phil Ward had only been home about six weeks when Modaber filed suit in the federal court, asking several million in damages from Culpeper Memorial Hospital and people connected with it. He asked for an injunction that would allow him to continue to practice there.

Then, in April of 1981, Modaber's suit was postponed indefinitely, with no cause given. But in May the federal court dismissed it, saying there was no constitutional right to a medical practice. Not one to give up, the physician tried again in October, seeking use of the hospital facilities. It wasn't until December that the paper learned that a $10 million malpractice suit against him had been filed by the parents of a stillborn baby delivered by Modaber at Culpeper Memorial.

The actual trial, which occurred the next year, was very saddening because the loss of the baby seemed to have been caused by thoughtlessness. The mother already had five children, all girls. The infant who was stillborn was a boy. It easily filtered through the legal maneuvering that the patient was a woman with complications such as hypertension, that she was worried about her baby and knew things weren't going well, and that the couple had chosen badly when they needed an obstetrician. The trial lasted several stressful days, with medical experts on hand to testify that proper tests weren't done and that the mother wasn't hospitalized when she should have been.

The final, gripping piece of the story came when Modaber took the stand in his own behalf. According to testimony and nurses' case records, he had been extremely late getting to the hospital, even though he was called by phone repeatedly. He had been home, in bed. Asked for his reaction when hospital personnel called him, he said "I did not panic" because he was waiting for a second blood pressure reading to follow up on one that had disturbed the nurses. According to the written records, however, he had not even asked for the reading.

He said on the witness stand that after the call he "sat up in bed" and began recalling all he could about the patient. When he finally went to the hospital, he said, he soon grasped the severity of the situation, and was changing clothes in order to perform a caesarian when the baby was born. According to the medical witnesses, both nurses and experts, the baby should have had close, informed monitoring by a physician from the time his mother reached the hospital. Chart records showed when the unborn child began to be in serious trouble, and when that happened, delivery should have been within minutes.

Pushed by the plaintiff's attorney, Modaber finally admitted in so many words that during his in-bed mulling he had only "some idea" about exactly who the woman in labor was.

It was all so wrenching that it seemed only fitting when the attorney for the couple wondered in his closing argument if there was anyone in any situation at all who wouldn't "lift a hand" to save a dying child. But, he concluded grimly and a bit mournfully, "There is one among us." The award to the plaintiffs was $750,000, the maximum then allowed by law. In later court action, Judge Berry denied a motion to set aside the $750,000 verdict, but did allow that a lower settlement would be possible. However, he commented in unusual candor that this was "the clearest case I've ever seen on causation." Modaber's hospital privileges remained firmly and permanently revoked.

When the ob-gyn was next heard from, in 1984, he had been indicted in Norfolk through his association with an abortion clinic there, specifically on a charge of performing a second trimester abortion outside of a hospital. The clinic was one of a group, scattered from Washington, D.C., to Hampton Roads, and the owner was charged with, among other things, performing (and charging for) abortion procedures on women who were not actually pregnant. Modaber still listed a practice in Culpeper at that point.

His Norfolk ended in a hung jury, and a judge finally acquitted him. In fact much of what happened to Modaber indicated that indeed there was no real prejudice against him for being Iranian, and that doctors still got a lot of breaks. His defense attorney referred to him as "a country doctor from Culpeper," according to press accounts, and said his client was "a scapegoat" for problems at the by then closed-down clinic.

When the state medical board finally heard Modaber's case, his license was put on probation for five years. Later he got into unknown trouble in Oklahoma, and the license was indefinitely revoked. The obstetrician, a man with a medical degree from a German university, was advised to get more medical education.

In 2005 there appeared a *Washington Post* story about Modaber's further difficulties. It seems that the former doctor, who had given up and allowed his license to expire and was then living outside Charles Town, West Virginia, bore such a deep grudge against Virginia for the wreck of his career that he was littering its highways—and the litter included items with his name on them. He was arrested four times, several of them because a man who lived in the area had developed his own grudge against the litterer and was determined to have him stopped.

Modaber's attorney and therapist both said the former physician dumped his trash in Clarke County because it was near where he lived in the next state. A psychologist had diagnosed an obsessive-compulsive disorder stemming from his Virginia problems with the hospital and the courts. His tendencies were infamous, so police watched for his car, particularly in his favorite dumping spot, the median of U.S. 340 running through Clarke. He was fined and did hundreds of hours of community service picking up other people's trash, the *Post* story said, and even had to pay $2,500 to the local anti-litter organization, but he continued single-mindedly to hurl his trash onto Virginia roads.

After the fourth conviction, General District Judge Norman deVere Morrison banished Modaber from Clarke County, telling him, according to the *Post*, "If you're found in Clarke County, bring your toothbrush." Banishment in lieu of jail time was a legal decision.

While we were dealing locally with murder trials and civil lawsuits, those stories shared space on the front pages with state and national news. That's something that doesn't happen much anymore, in my observation, and it's too bad because it lent a sense of perspective. The results of my time spent listening all agog in the courts usually appeared at the top of the page, because they were after all big local stories, but the reader could drop down and read about other national court activity.

For example, in the '70s, Patty Hearst was charged in the shooting done by the Symbionese Liberation Army. The whole Watergate thing developed, and one story declared with shock after the Nixon tapes were discovered that the tapes contained "some of the most outrageous language you ever heard." Squeaky Fromme, would-be assassin of President Gerald Ford, was pictured being carried into court. John Hinckley Jr. bolted from a courtroom on hearing Jodi Foster's videotape disclaiming any relationship with him. We felt we were part of a whole system of telling readers about the legal activities of the nation.

Longer-running stories developed locally, often of state or even national interest. For some pretty awful reasons, Culpeper was the focus of two ongoing environmental semi-disasters, brought to court by state agencies in the early '80s. Both ended up as Environmental Protection Agency Superfund sites, meaning monitoring was ongoing because of the threat to human health or the environment. One was a spill into a stream from a holding pond at a wood preserving plant, and the other involved a private hazardous-waste storage facility.

The wood preservers incident was a two-hundred-thousand-gallon spill of chromium, copper, arsenic, and other chemical wastes into a tributary of the Rappahannock River. There was immediate outcry over a time gap between the reporting of the spill and notification of local governments.

Fredericksburg, downstream along the Rappahannock, was very unhappy, and closed off its intake from the river to its water supply. Culpeper farmers reported greenish foam in the water of Jonas Run, the waterway that was the immediate recipient of the chemicals, and then dead cattle, chickens, and even pond fish. This went on and on, with the newspaper trying to serve as best it could as the conduit for public information and apparently justified accusations from downstream farmers. This wasn't easy.

Tests were deemed inconclusive, although there was admission that even before the dam breach the pond had not been in compliance with State Water Control Board regulations. A month after the spill was reported, the SWCB sent a letter to John Jones, then chair of the

Culpeper Board of Supervisors, who had demanded to know why the county hadn't been informed. In it, board staff said they had not believed it was a public-health or water-supply problem. "In contacting the county health department we assumed that information on the incident had been relayed," they said, and they therefore had concentrated on getting the word to agricultural officials.

That letter arrived a month after a citizen reported the spill. The wood treatment plant was located on Route 666 on the west side of town. The hazardous waste facility, unhappily, was at Inlet, very close by. In the Inlet case, which occurred somewhat later than the first disaster, the owner of the waste business was charged with improperly storing industrial waste. It was hard to tell for some time, for well owners and farmers downstream and close by, what the source of various pollutants was, but they were there.

The wood preserving plant was and may still be on the National Priorities List because it is considered one of the worst hazardous waste sites that the EPA has listed.

While the state dithered, farmers were required to dump their milk rather than sell it, and to quarantine their cattle. There were technicalities raised in court. While one man ordered his own tests on one of his animals, and his veterinarian found dangerously high levels of chromium and the like in examining a dead calf, the state vet concluded that the cattle had died of common diseases, pneumonia and infections, and even neglect. The Food and Drug Administration was involved. One of our reporters wrote that "answers were hard to get from state officials as each one would transfer" the responsibility for providing public information to yet another department.

Area residents asked that the wood preserving plant be closed down until there was clarity, but that didn't happen. One farmer went all out by drinking the water, with the thought that if anything happened to him it would prove his point. "Maybe it's something you don't know to look for," he said.

The waste treatment story went on for a shorter time and drew less public outcry, but did indicate the growing concern of various state and federal agencies with what people might be doing in rural areas. The company collected, stored, and disposed of sewage and industrial waste.

The industrial waste, much of it from the construction site of the fairly nearby North Anna nuclear power plant, drew the attention of both the SWCB and the state Department of Health. We never heard or printed that there were materials that might be radioactive, but of course that was a local concern.

The owner was charged with improperly storing industrial waste. It was hard to tell for some time, for well owners and farmers downstream and close by, what the source of various pollutants was, but they were there. When samples were taken in 1980, quite a few years after the storage began, some of the compounds found were methyl ethyl ketone, xylene, and toluene. A plan was submitted for reclaiming the land, but something wasn't carried through, and the case ended up in federal court. After more than a month of delay, the judge granted an injunction against the company, and the plaintiffs were given permission to go on the property to look it over.

After the inspection, no further problems were identified, although the remains of the business is an archived Superfund site, since it had been considered to be a risk to the environment. These were not minor problems, and without the local press, most people who stood to be affected might not have known about them.

CHAPTER EIGHTEEN
Local Issues
Covered Locally

As in the environmental-safety cases, many of the stories we covered were the same kinds of things that were written about in larger markets, and we felt the responsibility strongly. Informing a community about threats to its soil and water, trying to keep up with the changes brought about by the very concepts of zoning and controlled land use, and recording and interpreting state and local court activities were certainly journalism.

Still, there was no forgetting that it has also long been a function of newspapers to entertain and to illuminate oddities. For the small-town press, there is also a tendency to spotlight the differences between life as it is lived "down home" and the way things are in metropolitan areas. There is the irresistible temptation, in such cases, to poke around at why some of those differences are there, and to come to the conclusion that the locality is kind of better than the metropolitan areas. In the papers from the early days when I worked in Culpeper, and even as the decades moved forward, there were memorable news items that said a lot about what made the community so strongly itself. Still, for every story about it being small-town, there was another about it moving into the larger world.

An example of how the small town of Culpeper was growing was the pink box of "don'ts" in an article about a new sewer ordinance. Among the things not to do was maintain a privy. No small deal, really, since septic and drain field really wasn't an in-town option and not being allowed to have a privy meant you had to hook into the town sewer system and pay for it.

Fitting the bill for the "things are better here" viewpoint was a nice story in the '70s about the young sheriff, Robert E. Peters. Pete had stopped in the dead of night to help an elderly black man change a tire on Route 29. He was wearing his uniform, but any mark of rank was pretty invisible, and he didn't identify himself as the sheriff. This was only about ten years after school integration in Virginia, and the motorist, who was from New York, was understandably impressed by the big young man and no doubt the manners that were an integral part of Peters's personality. He later sent the sheriff's office a check for $10 in appreciation, and a letter he hoped would get Peters promoted. The letter said his friends in the North were surprised that a white man, much less a white lawman, had stopped in the dark rather than just grudgingly calling a tow truck.

"Pete" Peters served until 1995, and in 2015 a new sheriff's building was dedicated to him and was well-deserved.

Really, the law enforcement in the time of the man I used to call the "high sheriff" (because he kind of liked it) was not as provincial as the New York motorist might have expected. Officers went to state trainings, and they paid attention.

Commonwealth's Attorney Jack Jeffries even took a trip to a prosecutors convention in London. After his travels I did an interview with Jeffries, who had followed in the footsteps not of his father but of his mother, Helen Jeffries, the first woman lawyer I ever knew. On his return, he talked with considerable excitement about the differences in English law. He observed the courts there, saw judges who wielded great power by being able to instruct juries on which witnesses to believe, and had his photo taken with the counsel to the lord mayor of London.

Many disparate things added up to Culpeper. Not odd, but heartwarming and telling, was a big story in 1974: a fire more or less destroyed Rental Uniform Service. RU was a big deal in town, a major employer—it was the supplier of uniform clothing and the like to various businesses and industries for miles around. Scamstresses, laundry operators, and route drivers all claimed some of the more reliable jobs in the area. RU eventually became part of Cintas, a business supply company with a number of locations and a NASDAQ-100 listing, speaking of growing into the larger world.

That fire was during my time working on the women's page, and I didn't get to it. But volunteer companies from Brandy Station, Richardsville, Orange, and Madison joined Culpeper firefighters to battle the blaze. The company's stock in trade, clothing that was presumably flammable, made the fire very difficult to fight. Reporter Tom Osborne wrote in the next day's paper that RU was far from down and out. Routes were being run, picking up uniforms, janitorial materials, towels, and rugs for cleaning, and other similar area plants were offering their services to help with washing and ironing. Customers were calling to say they could manage to get their own laundry done somehow until the facility could be restored, to take part of the pressure off. Lots of community feeling there.

Sometimes there would be a happening that was a tribute to the small-town atmosphere while at the same time gently poking fun at people's acceptance of and even pride in it. For example, downtown lawyer J. Robert Yeaman accepted the delivery of three chickens and two rabbits to his law office. It could only happen in a place like Culpeper, was the feeling. Yeaman declared that he took the animals in payment of legal fees, but finally reluctantly admitted, at the risk of spoiling the tale, that he was just doing a favor for an Arlington client who was sending pets out into the proverbial country to run sort of free.

Small-town pride was on display in a really unique experience, Culpeper's participation in the *Almost Anything Goes* TV show. Imaginative and fun, this early reality-type competition lasted only two seasons; the Culpeper show featured Regis Philbin long before *Live! with Regis and Kathie Lee*. The idea was for communities all across the country to compete with each other in physically challenging contests. Teams mostly from within a given state were pitted against each other, and the triumphant ones then moved on to compete with winners from other states. Teams of pretty able adults were formed, and faced off over tasks that ranked from just difficult to absurd.

It was the regional contest that was held in Culpeper, and the Culpeper Minute Men went into action against two opponents, the Chambersburg, Pennsylvania, Raiders and the Westminster, Maryland, Bullies. It was the ninth show that was being filmed, in early December 1975, and the film company was headed back to California after this final taping of the season. The program was a mid-season replacement for the unsuccessful *Saturday Night with Howard Cosell* on ABC, so it would get some attention in its time slot. The local show wouldn't air until February, but that was okay—it was all as exciting as an opening night.

The paper had a special tabloid-sized section as a prelude to the event, and there were all sorts of ads. "After the Minute Men WIN take the family to Tastee-Freez," one read. Most were just wishes of good luck or support, but the downtown Leggett had an *Almost Anything Goes* special sale.

An elaborate set was constructed at the football stadium, with workmen swarming efficiently over steel scaffolding and erecting an enormous and sparkling scoreboard. Vans pulled up that were practically bulging with costumes and props, and even a swimming pool was miraculously conjured into being. The Holiday Inn on the other side of town was overrun with people wearing red nylon jackets that proclaimed "Almost Anything Goes"; well, maybe not overrun, since there were only about thirty-five in the crew, but it seemed that way. They spoke rapidly on their walkie-talkies, and the light of showtime was in their eyes.

On the team (aside from referee Waugh Crigler, who was then I think a lawyer, later a judge) were court clerk Cindy Sisson, soft-drink truck driver Earnest Dinkins, teacher Ann Boyd, Bill McLain, wine salesman Ron Johnson, and the youngest, sewing-factory seamstress Jeanne Mackison. Alternates were Judy Tolson and Dennis McMullen. The coach was assistant principal John Pegues, and the mascot was Betty Robson. Cindy Sisson was injured before the taping, and Tolson replaced her. Quite a few years later I did an interview with Earnest Dinkins, who was the only black team member, and he recalled the whole thing with great enjoyment. He had been an involved member of the community anyway, with participation in things like coaching Little League, and had been a football player. More than thirty years later, well past the expected retirement age, he continued to be a familiar and well-liked employee of the local Safeway store.

At any rate, tickets sold out, but our family was able to go on the strength of my press credentials, and we had a great time watching people do ridiculous and perhaps dangerous things, like scaling forbidding heights. As on the modern reality shows, contestants were willing to do about anything, and Dinkins had the fondest memories of taking on daunting activities dressed as a big yellow chicken. Unhappily, the Minute Men came in second to Chambersburg, but later did get to make a trip to Las Vegas to compete further. What was Earnest's takeaway about Vegas? "No clocks," he said.

While life went on with weird entertainment, there was a strong interest in maintaining the rural atmosphere. Oddly, both Culpeper and Madison had their activist time during a historical period when activism wasn't happening much. In 1979 I was covering Madison, logically enough because I lived there, and a unique story came up. It seemed that something called the World Plan Executive Council–U.S. was proposing a school for transcendental meditation near tiny Novum, at that point (and still, many years later) mostly the home of a church. When the group came before the county's planning commission early in the year, it was to seek permission for new residential and agricultural uses. Immediately it ran up against the Madison distrust for the outlander, and this got fairly outlandish.

At first the six young people who represented the group came across well. They were articulate and sincere, and displayed no tattoos or nose rings. Of course, these things had not come into vogue then, but one never knew what to expect when the words "transcendental" and "meditation" were being bandied about. The representatives described TM as a "simple, natural, easy process," and the site was to be used to teach teachers—but an immediate alarm was sounded when everyone heard the planned scope of the school. They expected to educate four hundred teachers at a time, with the student body changing frequently and people coming in and out.

The landowners in attendance were impressed with the young people, and they tried not to be rude. It was just that, as one man said, the name struck him as "ominous." World Plan? Executive Council? The reps assured him this was not a cult, but rather a group prepared to pay $350,000 for the fairly remote property, and use it to benefit mankind. Agricultural uses would be carried on to help support the effort financially. Not much specific was brought up in response, because the preparation of the young spokespeople was a bit overwhelming. There was a tentative mention of the almost nonexistent traffic-carrying capacity of gravel Route 604 leading to the proposed site, and the prospect of four-hundred-plus cars trundling along it from time to time.

After a couple of weeks it was announced that the Virginia Department of Transportation had found the road adequate for the number of buildings and dorms planned. When a public meeting was called by the "executive council" itself in late February, two traditionally touchy subjects, religion and money, produced a heated discussion. Eighty or ninety people attended the meeting at the War Memorial Building, a good crowd for Madison, not surprising considering what was proposed. The council had purchased 402 acres, at above market price, land that could be reached only via a series of back roads. It planned a $4 million facility, and confirmed that it planned to have ever-revolving groups of four hundred students at a time.

Two young women and seven men represented the council. They spoke about the question of religion, and probably unwisely described a flowery ceremony, including the speaking of Sanskrit and ritual bowing, that was part of the teaching. But they said that was not really religion but tradition. The TM representatives even described the meditative technique—it was done for fifteen to twenty minutes twice a day, with the practitioner only required to sit quietly and free the mind, thereby allowing the body to experience deep rest while the mind functioned in a "maximally orderly manner."

Hard to object to, but people gave it a shot. One minister at the meeting declared to applause that TM was "man pulling himself up by his bootstraps" while Christianity was "God reaching down and pulling him up." That was actually a good summary of many of the differences in approaches to religion, seeking meaning, and all sorts of other endeavors.

The next public meeting was in March, and by then there were representatives of an organized group, the Concerned Citizens Committee of Madison County, to speak against the plan. Citing an opposition to the mere scope of the project, one resident said, firmly not getting into the many variants of religion, "We'd have been against 1,600 Billy Grahams coming to Madison." Again, a good summarizing argument. There were also more discussions of the sewage and land-use considerations that would be attendant on having so many occupants.

By the time of an April hearing that lasted more than three hours, both sides had come armed with lawyers. The TM group pledged frontage for improving the roads, and the focus changed to water and the probable tax exemption considerations for a $4 million development. One woman with the opposition group had done research, and said that the group's income was down and interest in TM was apparently waning. This was more or less true at the time, but a total fade-out never quite happened, as the group and offshoots have continued in various forms, and millions of people worldwide have been involved in the practice over the years.

But for Novum, the planning commission eventually denied the use permit, approving only placing mobile homes on the property for agricultural uses. Young representatives of the World Plan Executive Council–U.S. said they would have crops and perhaps a small dairy, but whatever the thinking was, not much developed. Eventually the property was sold. During the same time period, the Madison government had expressed interest in a potential state prison to be located in the county, thinking jobs and income. But another uprising put an end to that, even before it became obvious that the lack of a good water supply was kind of a deal-breaker.

There were even greater conflicts of values (and yes, entertainment for reporters) over an issue in the town of Culpeper, an adult bookstore that planned to open in a rather prominent location on Davis Street in 1980. The enterprise was legal under the town code, and owner Deborah Hudnall got a permit for it without rousing objections from anyone in the government, but after a specially called meeting the town council rescinded the permit. Members were responding to publicly voiced objections, including the presentation of a petition with a long list of signatures. Culpeper really didn't want the bookstore, which in a larger town would have come to a back street somewhere and then eventually faded away.

Reporter Edmond Rennolds covered the controversy, and he quoted Hudnall as saying "I did not get a fair shake" in a story that ran with a large photo of the crowd at the hearing. Rennolds followed up with an interview with the would-be bookstore proprietor, who said she planned to open anyway. Then she sued the town for $400,000, having had to look to Greene County for an attorney willing to handle the case.

Since this was a daytime happening, I was eventually assigned to find my way (with some difficulty) to the U.S. district court in Alexandria to hear a federal judge overrule the town and say that Hudnall must be allowed to open her store on what was one of the two main shopping streets in the downtown, as she wanted. The judge agreed that the town had a "legitimate concern," but granted the injunction as a matter of law, leaving the civil suit ongoing. Of course there was local outrage, but the plaintiff was ready to open and said she already had the inventory.

Reporter Kurt Bacci went to the somewhat less than grand opening of the store on Monday, May 19. At 9:15 a.m., he wrote, Hudnall made her first sale. The male buyer declined a bag, saying he wanted to walk out with the book in hand. Bacci wrote that he himself found the inventory somewhat scanty. At the end of the week there was yet another story, saying that thieves had entered the store and taken $1,000 worth of materials. Although police reported that Mrs. Hudnall broke down in tears, needless to say there was little sympathy from the town residents.

Thieves or not, the lawsuit resumed. The breakdown: Hudnall wanted $300,000 in punitive damages against the town, $5,000 from each member of council who had voted to rescind the permit, and $500 from each member for each day she was prevented from opening. The only councilman not involved, perhaps oddly considering the nature of the controversy, was a minister, Rev. Horace Douty. He had missed the meeting and the vote.

There was intense worry among the town leaders. It wasn't until October that the judge granted immunity to the council members, because they had made the decision in their legislative capacity. He did say they had "acted in bad faith," and had denied Hudnall her constitutional rights by using prior restraint. The Rennolds story ran with a photo of the curtained front of the store. As far as I know, no one from the paper went in to peruse the titles after Bacci's original visit the day of the opening, but our little newsroom took some glee in the proceedings simply because people apparently expected it to be the end of small-town innocence and maybe even the world as they knew it.

Hudnall was awarded $25,000 in damages, for violation of her civil rights. She said that she had expected to be upheld, and in court she read from the list of titles, a list that the paper shamelessly quoted. *Swedish Nymphs* was one, *Seduced Wives* another. The town attorney argued that there was nothing malicious about the actions of the town governing body. "Culpeper is a small town" with a conservative nature, he said, and the council simply felt it had to carry out the will of the people.

Reaction to the verdict was mixed, from secret sniggering by reporters born outside the area, to one local woman's stern opinion that this was very wrong because Hudnall "had been rewarded for evil doing," to grudging agreement that the court was probably right. There were motions filed by the town following the decision, and council member Jack Kearns, a man of honesty and directness, remarked that before going too far the council should talk it all over with lawyers in depth. "I went against them last time and look where I ended up," he said wryly, indicating there may have been legal discussions before the council went off the deep end and rescinded the permit. Kearns, quoted earlier in connection with the Phil Ward homecoming, eventually served as mayor, and always took a committed and realistic view of his elected position.

The bookstore eventually failed, closing in early 1982. Hudnall complained of increasing electric bills and unfairly raised rent— although the claim of a rental increase was firmly refuted by the building's owner—and that was the last of legal smut on Davis Street, at least to date.

More worry and indignation arose in late 1980, after Canada-based Marline Uranium Corporation leased thousands of acres in Madison, Culpeper, Fauquier, and Orange in search of uranium. Speakers at a December hearing detailed the dangers associated with the element, and there was a Citizens Concerned About a Safe Environment group from Madison County.

By the next year, despite more opposition expressed in public meetings, energy companies had leased 3,500 acres in the Inlet– Stevensburg–Brandy Station area. Leases on some of the biggest farms, including the Smith dairy operation on Route 3 and the farm owned by the Lenn brothers close to Stevensburg (a future county park, innocent of radiation), were held by Eastern State Exploration. The company was associated with Merrill Natural Resources, which apparently had come into being shortly before.

The *Star-Exponent* circulation area wasn't the only part of the state under such a threat. Visions of radioactive bulldozers and trucks were being raised elsewhere, including in Pittsylvania County. During the 1982 legislative session, the Virginia General Assembly passed laws to govern exploration for uranium. It also imposed a moratorium on actual mining until regulations on any such activity were in place. In July of 1982 the Culpeper supervisors adopted a uranium resolution, telling the General Assembly's uranium subcommittee that it was being watched closely. Or some such threat.

At any rate, even though Marline announced that summer that it had discovered 110 million pounds of uranium on land it had leased in Pittsylvania County, mining never happened because the price of uranium apparently tumbled. Marline let all its leases in the Culpeper-Madison area go, and became just one more in a string of outside groups that from time to time made plans to pounce on the bumpkins, make money, and then let the chips fall, etc.

Economic issues mostly kept such plans from reappearing for quite a while, but if there's money to be made, most rape and pillage schemes come up again. The Pittsylvania property, called Coles Hill, arose again a quarter of a century later. State committees and studies were announced, particularly because of the lack of prosperity in that part of Virginia, but the threat to water in tributaries that went to the populous east coast was the key block. In November 2013, right after being elected governor, Terry McAuliffe announced that he would veto any legislation that authorized uranium mining. A month later, Virginia Uranium Inc., the most recent company involved with Coles Hill, reacted by suspending its efforts—but again probably as much in response to another price drop as to the governor's ultimatum.

But in 2018 it was all back again. The U.S. Supreme Court that year agreed to consider whether Virginia actually has the right to enforce such a ban. The suit is once more centered on Pittsylvania, where the deposits are considered to be the richest source of the form of the mineral used in nuclear reactors in the nation.

The Culpeper area actually seemed a bit ahead of its time in its ability to organize protests and bring people out to meetings, and then even to counter protest. Perhaps practice made perfect. An interesting small example was the plot to do away with the Blue Devil, the Culpeper High School mascot. A petition was sent to the school board, wanting to replace the mascot because of its dire satanic associations. *SE* sports editor Jack Moore, not one to back away from a fight, produced a column on the subject. Titled "Raising heck about that nasty Blue Devil," the screed recalled a team in his native Omaha called the Bunnies. They never had a winning season, he declared, but "Am I suggesting that [the school teams] suffered as a result of the effete mascot?" Certainly he was not, he insisted (and he refused to tell even co-workers whether in fact Bunnies had played football in Omaha).

The final decision? The Blue Devil stayed. People were asked, and 802 wanted to keep it. Ninety-five (74 of them the original petition signers) wanted it to go. 'Nuff said. And through the magic of technology, through which nothing can remain unknown except maybe the meaning of life, it can now be told that there is in fact a Bunnies football team.

A few other articles in the same time period worth noting in the "only in Culpeper" category included one on sunflowers, one on a grocery-store strike, and a review of a book authored by a former *SE* reporter.

The sunflower story was mine. Someone had told us that there was a rather overwhelming stand of the stalwart blooms out on a county farm, and it seemed like something for Piedmont Living. The elderly homeowner and sunflower aficionado welcomed me and my camera. The sunflowers were indeed pretty wonderful, and there was a whole field of them. The owner declined to pose with them, instead sending a neighbor to stand among the towering stalks.

He told me he had planted them for his wife, but she was away right then. I wrote the story accordingly, and was taken aback when the knowledgeable and wry clerk of the court, Dot Faulconer, informed me that was indeed away, but, well, her absence was not limited to "right then." "She done passed," noted Dot, a very bright and responsive elected official who could do the local vernacular quite well. Embarrassingly for me, she was right, and the woman had indeed died about four years earlier. But at least she was remembered with sunflowers. No one else ever commented, probably since the elderly retirees apparently never did a lot of mingling, and I let well enough alone.

The late 1983 strike by workers at the local Safeway was a fine demonstration of excellent local labor relations. Union members obediently carried out the strike, but after a while went back to work. We had an editorial approving the abandonment of the strike. "We work for Safeway, not the union," one of the ex-strikers remarked, and "That is the way it should be," according to the Worrell-special editorial: a brief strike, then negotiation, and finally a business win, with no one going all out to have their demands met.

The book review was written by Edmond Rennolds, and was a review of the third novel by Carolyn Banks, whose reporting career had overlapped with his at the *SE* for a while. I had first contacted Banks about a book she had published about her horse, *The Adventures of Runcible Spoon*. Since we had horses and writing in common, we became friends (and still are, at last count, although she lives in Texas now). Runcible was in fact an interesting horse, given to abrupt behavior and deliberate, faked panics. Carolyn had moved to a few acres in Rappahannock County after she felt her career as a novelist was under way, and lived there with her teenage son Donald, along with Runcible, a couple of cats, a beagle named Rooney, and a goose that periodically flapped its wings and attacked her menacingly.

The book Edmond reviewed was *The Girls on the Row*, which was a rather frightening thriller. It followed on the heels of several other Banks books dealing with mayhem, and they had all done pretty well. But Carolyn was finding out that few novelists actually make a living and can pay a mortgage, and when she needed work she stayed with what she knew how to do and wrote for the *SE*. She was lively fun, from her horrified introduction to local government meetings ("oh-my-god, they go on *forever*") to her citified but mild swearing in a place where such verbalization from women was not looked on kindly. One regular advertiser complained to the publisher that he had been at a restaurant in a booth just back of Carolyn and Eleanor Glattly, an also somewhat urbanized and very talented photographer, and felt forced to depart the establishment because of their language. The rest of the staff loved the story, although the publisher (by then representing advertiser-protecting Worrell Newspapers) was not pleased.

CHAPTER NINETEEN
The Unusual Makes News

T wo of the most engrossing ongoing stories to hit Culpeper during my tenure on the paper were the sagas of Commonwealth Park and the Finders. Commonwealth Park was a horse-showing facility that began with a great deal of vision and went on to attract Olympic riders to Culpeper and entertain the horse-crazy among us with endless variety. The Finders were something else again, something nobody, including reporters from national magazines, ever figured out—a movement, a cult, or simply a strange man with oddly intelligent and committed followers.

The saga of the horse property got under way inauspiciously enough, with a small Page 1 item in March of 1978. "Man throws chair through bank window," the headline read. A man named John Reynolds had in fact done that very thing, and was duly charged with destroying private property. Police said he had "some misunderstanding" with the bank related to the interest to be earned on $50,000 (and who among us has not experienced suspected mishandling of large sums of our money). He withdrew his cash from the downtown Second National Bank, and sure enough followed up by hurling furniture through a glass office partition.

There was a story being bandied about that Reynolds had bought an old farm out on two-lane Route 522, and planned to "move Frying Pan Park" there. Frying Pan Park was a horse show location in Northern Virginia, not far from Dulles airport; still was, at last check, along with being a large-scale Fairfax County park that preserves a picture of farm life from the 1920s to the 1950s.

At any rate, the chair-throwing and horse combination was too much to resist, and after sorting through the rumors as best I could I drove out

Route 522 one day and found Reynolds, known as "Monk" for reasons I never learned but kind of wish I had, out beside the highway bordering his property. He was working hard with a crew building a board fence, the official hallmark of a horse operation. After a bit of hesitation he talked readily enough to me, and from the beginning I liked him. He was funny, self-deprecating, clever, unusual in many ways—and maybe seventy-five percent believable, or possibly that is generous. But sure enough, he was planning a big-time show facility, with rings, a grandstand, and stabling for hundreds of horses. He was investing a lot of money, but as near as I could tell, then and for long afterward, he *had* a lot of money.

He also was quite aware that for the most part any publicity is good publicity, and while he dodged around some of my questions, the story as I understood it was pretty satisfactory. The facility, to be called Showday, appeared likely to be a good thing for Culpeper, offering employment and drawing visitors to spend money, and for those of us residents who couldn't stay away from anything equine, promising hours of prime entertainment. And it did do all of that. Reynolds lived on the place, at least part of the time, with a wife and a very attractive young daughter, and was as hands-on with the whole operation as he was with the fence building. I can't tell you now how tall he was, but he seemed to me from the beginning to be a big guy, with a fierce head of curly hair, quite a bit of physical strength, and lots of determination.

The daughter had been interested in horses, and that's how he came upon the idea of a show facility. Frying Pan Park was, to his mind, in a bad location, hard to get horse trailers to because of traffic, as well as being overcrowded and generally to the north of Virginia horse country. Why Culpeper County, he never really said, but presumably the site was chosen because it was inexpensive real estate not very far from Route 29. He did tell me—as an aside that kind of endeared him to me, because he trusted me to keep the off-the-record secret but wanted me to know a bit more about his background, plus he was secretly a bit proud of it—that he had pretty much made his money with topless restaurants in Northern Virginia. I always prided myself on remaining impassive during interviews, but I think I may have slipped that time. Uh, what kind of restaurants? I believe I may have asked.

But no matter his other endeavors, the horse facility was ready to open in the spring of 1979. The first big rated show, the Showday National, was set for June 8–12, fencing was mostly in place and painted white, the administration building was complete, there was seating and there were stalls. I wrote the story on the premiere for the June 7 paper, and on June 9 there was a splendid photo page of pictures I took of the healthy turnout of competitors, since the *SE* really had no photographer then. The rest of the season continued to draw a good number of competitors, the hotels were full, and restaurants had extra patrons. But plans to charge onlookers for admission never gained much traction because there weren't that many spectators. The population to pull from wasn't exactly that of Fairfax County.

An attention-getting feature was his "Kong Wall," a huge jump with the movie ape King Kong painted on it. There was a sizable prize for anyone who cleared the intimidating thing, and there were horses and riders who managed the scramble. This is something I wouldn't think of going near now, and it probably should have been stopped by some humane organization, but it wasn't stopped, and it was thrilling. That did get crowds, and no one was killed and no horses were injured.

That first winter, Monk began to branch out some. There was an ad for a turkey shoot at the Mitchells Ruritan Club, with a Reynolds touch visible in the offering of a powder-puff class. The next year a highlight was the big Central Atlantic Appaloosa Show, and the year after that the Budweiser Clydesdales came for the Winston National show. By then Ray K. Saunders was the paper's official photographer, and he took the photos, but I did get to rhapsodize in print about the Clydesdales.

Things stayed pretty busy on the grounds, with income from the rented portable stalls, a Monk specialty, as I recall. My friends and family and I went out to Showday from time to time, and my daughter even rode in a local show that made use of the facility. There was obviously some good marketing going on, because Mitchells and environs wasn't the first place to spring to mind when you thought "event to gather crowds of people."

But by the end of summer in 1983, there were plans for a big change at Showday. I have to assume it just wasn't making enough money to justify the cost for its entrepreneurial owner. A Texas real estate developer, originally a lawyer from New Jersey, was set to buy the place. Charles and Cece Ziff of Dallas had gotten a pony for their son and become involved in showing in a big way, eventually running the Dallas Fall Charity Horse Show. The Ziffs apparently also had lots of money and at least one other home, although his business and/or legal interests apparently allowed them to live on the farm through much of the show season.

At about the time of the changeover I went out for an interview with Glen Randall, the seventy-four-year-old trainer of Cass Ole, the black Arabian that starred in the movie *The Black Stallion*, featuring Mickey Rooney as the trainer Henry Dailey, from the Walter Farley series of books. Randall had trained Roy Rogers's Trigger for twenty-three years, and had gone to Italy to teach Charlton Heston to drive chariot horses for *Ben Hur*. I had seen *The Black Stallion* and liked it, but when I heard the Roy Rogers connection I practically swooned, what with my reverence for old Roy.

Anyway, the trainer was a great interview, and was perfectly willing to talk more about the palomino star of old than about the current movie. He told me there were three main Triggers, and that the best one, the "trick Trigger," could do about anything. That was the wonderful horse in *Son of Paleface* with Bob Hope, and some of the things he did were so good, Randall declared, that Hope jealously didn't want them kept in the film. The scene where the star and the trick Trigger share a bed, and the horse keeps swiping the bedclothes, may be the best example of animal scene-stealing ever.

Before going on to the wonders of the new, bigger-money-backed Showday, renamed Commonwealth Park, I have to mention the next adventure of Monk Reynolds. He established a restaurant in Culpeper, although clothing was not optional. The building was the former Wiener King, home of hot dogs in many forms, and Reynolds said he had gone to the auction of the failed place to buy a hot-chocolate machine for the show grounds. Then the restaurant went so cheap, he explained, that he bought it.

My first story on the restaurant quoted Monk and manager Brigid Corrigan (who had a college degree and experience with the Marriott chain) as saying it would be a "nice place for nice people." Besides the dining room, there would be a lounge, and it would have an equestrian theme. The name, in fact, was Stallion Station. It sounded cool, sort of, if you weren't thinking about bar denizens. The article was a nicely displayed feature with a photo of Monk, Paul Bates of Culpeper—a partner in some way—and Corrigan, who was rarely seen after that, at least by me.

The next Stallion Station story I wrote, though, after about six months of apparently unsatisfactory operation, had a headline announcing "Restaurant may go topless." Oh, right, he had experience with this. The restaurant was closed for renovations, I was told for the story, and if it wasn't sold in the next few weeks (for more than $500,000) he planned to lease it to a woman who would have topless entertainment there. Monk, who had a vengeful side, said he had received a property assessment from the county that he felt was unacceptable, because it valued his real estate way above what he thought it should be for tax purposes. He had gotten mad, he admitted, but apparently hadn't thrown any chairs—yet. "If I don't sell it, there'll be topless dancers there in three weeks," he declared, adding, interestingly, that on Wednesdays the dancers would be male. Stallion Station indeed.

From there the plot got even better. The sign outside read "Closed for Remodeling—reopening approximately three weeks. WELL [all caps, no apostrophe, indicating that the declaration of what 'we' would be doing had been hastily written] have the Beef." There was nothing in the town code regulating such a use, Reynolds said, because he had asked the town offices earlier, when he bought the property. By then town officials had learned by experience with the adult bookstore.

The topless dancers and presumably waitresses never materialized, raising suspicions that the woman who was going to run the unsavory operation had never existed, and the restaurant sank quietly. The real estate was finally sold and a CVS pharmacy was built there. No topless waitresses and no beef had ever appeared.

At some point Monk went into court as a witness in a case charging that his life had been threatened by an employee. I was there, and was unable to resist writing about it simply for the joy of one line from the defendant. Guns were involved and there was an altercation, and the employee had emotionally declared to Monk that he was "a dead man." On the stand, the defendant said earnestly that he did not mean the statement as a threat to kill his employer, but instead was simply stating his opinion of the restaurant owner's character, that his "soul and conscience" were already dead. Because I was so taken with that great explanation and it has stayed with me so strongly, I have no memory of whether the man was convicted of the threat. I have to kind of doubt it. Monk had whispered to me in court not to write about the proceedings, and when I did he was gravely disappointed and, sadly, it was the end of what had been a fun relationship.

Returning to what was now Commonwealth Park under Ziff's ownership: The infusion of new money provided better and better entertainment as well as sports-page fodder. Olympic riders and horses competed for big prize money, and there were constant thrills. I was in the stands for much of this high-flying competition, and got to interview Dickie Smothers, then living in Northern Virginia and apparently a horse-showing fan.

But in 1984 there was a push from Ziff to get Culpeper County to buy the place, since it was of course losing money because of the huge prizes needed to attract the likes of those Olympians. The county was not interested, and it turned out neither was the state of Virginia, although it was actively in search of a place to build a horse center. By then there were a number of show rings, several restaurants, covered stands, an air-conditioned pavilion, and hundreds of permanent horse stalls on the Commonwealth Park grounds out on Route 522.

But the state preferred to build from scratch, and chose land in Rockbridge County, just outside Lexington. Rockbridge had pledged to contribute both cash and the land, and was happy to get the facility. Adding insult to injury, the state group making the choice actually met for their vote at the Holiday Inn in Culpeper; the decision took a half hour, and no second choice was mentioned. Rockbridge was praised as having unlimited potential for future development, and the site was extensive enough and hilly enough for a good event course, which Commonwealth Park was not. The Shenandoah Valley county had also not dropped any hints of a desire for an element of local government participation in the operation of the horse park, which had been mentioned in Culpeper.

But Ziff didn't just throw up his hands, and during that summer Commonwealth Park was still going strong. I was enchanted with the chance to interview Harry de Leyer, who had horses stabled there for an event. De Leyer, owner and trainer of the famous jumper Snowman, was from Holland and had an accent. Late in his career he moved to a stable he bought at nearby Earlysville in Albemarle County, where he stayed in the horse business for many years. He was totally charming, and very disarming in his acceptance of his horse-world fame; in 1984 he told me he didn't mind being called "the galloping grandpa," and more than likely he went on to be the galloping great-great-grandpa.

The story, and the horse, that really put de Leyer on the equine world's radar go back to 1956. De Leyer arrived late to a horse auction in Pennsylvania on a cold day, and when he drove up he saw an almost emaciated, dirty whitish plow horse that had been loaded onto a truck full of slaughter animals. Snowman had not drawn bidders at the auction, so he was headed the way such equines end up. But de Leyer saw something about the big horse that drew him. He handed over $80—or maybe $60 plus $20 hauling, the stories differ—and took Snowman home to a place he then owned on Long Island. It turned out that what looked like a draft horse was a jumping sensation.

He didn't look like a jumper, with a long body and a somewhat clumsy way of moving. But de Leyer kept him for a while and then sold him to a man who lived nearby. Snowman returned, having jumped the doctor's fence. The new owner came to get the big animal, and presumably raised the fence, but he returned to de Leyer—the last time dragging a log that he had been tied to with the thought that that would stop him from soaring over the fence. So Snowman stayed.

They were a team from then on, and won the National Horse Show open jumper championship at Madison Square Garden a couple of years later. Snowman was particularly famous for being willing to jump a row of other horses; apparently he was ready to do anything that was asked of him, and if it involved jumping, even better. There are thrilling photos of the two soaring over fences, de Leyer clinging to his back and demonstrating incredible balance.

De Leyer had come to the U.S. in 1950 and was a great immigrant story, ecstatically happy with his adopted country. He could have followed his father into the brewing business at home, but had realized "I hate breweries." On his arrival in the U.S. he was surprised he could make a living riding horses. In our interview he talked about the trademark move he was known for, tossing his hunt cap into the air after a victory. He praised the facilities at Commonwealth Park, and said that in his American life he was grateful not only for good horses but for "a good country."

Shortly after, I got to see and write about Olympian Katie Monahan, who won the Commonwealth Grand Prix on a horse named Jethro. She also rode to third place on The Governor, named for New York governor, ambassador, and Cabinet member Averill Harriman, then still living. The horse was owned by Harriman's wife, Pamela. Another very famous rider, Orange County's Rodney Jenkins, was the local favorite, but had a rare off day when I saw him in action.

Later a local estate broker was out on his morning run when the idea came to him that he should buy Commonwealth Park. He did, but it didn't go well. Years later Monk bought the place back, and sold it again—always coming out all right, I suspect.

Kind of at the opposite end of the spectrum from the horse-sports version of a feel-good story (and I mean that as a good thing, a great thing—some people, like Randall and de Leyer, just make you happy to talk to them and try to get into writing what they are about) were the Finders. Much of the narrative of the Finders has to come from memory or the Internet, rather than the newspaper morgue of stories I wrote, since I left the *Star-Exponent* before they really made the big headlines.

My first experience with them was an *SE* interview with a young woman named Diane Cox, in a small office on West Davis Street. According to my Dec. 5, 1981, story, she told me that she and her husband were starting a business in Culpeper, called The Finders. They would be finding people, places, information, organizations, and anything else someone wanted, by request and for small fees. Vacation-home trades would be arranged, and people seeking financial investments or loans would be gotten together with those with available money.

The photo I took for the story was of a pretty woman, and I remember liking her. No alarms went off. She said her husband was the manager of his own computer-systems company and that she had been in emergency services. Spinning off from the computer systems, they were going to have a network of people and data.

It wasn't until quite a few years later that I learned the Finders were a genuine cult, decades old, organized and headed by one Marion Pettie, who was (astoundingly, once you heard the whole narrative) a Culpeper native. No one was ever quite sure how many members there were or what their ultimate aim was, but the best guess seemed to be that their goal was to behave weirdly and keep everyone guessing. And also, to judge by later legal activities, to stockpile quite a lot of money and other assets from various technology-related enterprises.

The group had begun in the Washington, D.C., area, possibly even before World War II. Pettie apparently drew people fairly effortlessly, and many of them seemed to be very bright. The Finders were somewhat involved with the government in the '80s, possibly as a contractor for computer work, since members were an advanced lot when it came to computers. Again, best guess, they were perhaps a utopian commune of sorts, with at one time a duplex in Glover Park in Washington, a warehouse in the northeast part of the city, and other properties. Often they had business listings in the National Press Club building. I don't have any firsthand knowledge of their past, and never did a direct interview with any of them after Diane Cox. (Lists of the Finders that turned up later did not show Diane as having even been a member.)

Pettie had retired from U.S. Air Force intelligence way back in 1956, and had had no known employment since. He had had a wife (herself apparently a CIA employee) and two sons, one of them a member of the cult. At least one granddaughter lived in Madison and went to school there.

It wasn't until 1987, when I had moved on to another paper, the weekly *Culpeper News*, that the Finders jumped into national notoriety in a way that belied the general acceptance in Culpeper that they were harmless kooks. In February two men were arrested traveling with six children in Florida. They were living out of a van in a park. Telling the police that they were taking the children to school in Mexico, the men also indicated at some point that both they and the mothers of the children were members of the Finders.

While the children were ragged, dirty, and, most compellingly for law enforcement, confused, the men were well-dressed and neatly groomed. Authorities reacted, not surprisingly, by taking the children into state custody and charging the men with misdemeanor child abuse.

Finders properties in Washington were raided and piles of documents were seized, but there was nothing subversive. A very impressive array of computer equipment and software was also found. But the discovery that really set things off was a photo album titled *The Execution of Henrietta and Igor.* The amateurish snapshots showed robe-wearing adults and milling children slaughtering goats in an outdoor setting, and included one shot of a goat's head being presented to a child, who seemed taken aback. In general, the pictures were grisly and the activity looked ritualistic.

The local media gathered for a court hearing in Madison, since the goat slaughter was believed to have occurred up near the mountains there. The event depicted in the photos was thought to be some kind of awful devil worship as well as a bizarre form of child abuse. However, little came of the court appearances except huge amounts of media attention and stories describing the group as a free-form family, dancing about the fringes of society, making a living in some way and pooling their resources. Marion Pettie was referenced, but did not come out of the woodwork for the court proceedings.

There was never any proof of child abuse; the Finders explained the goat episode as simply a way of introducing the children to the facts of a self-sustaining lifestyle that including growing (and killing) food. Sure, wearing robes for the occasion was off-putting, not done in 4-H, but it wasn't actually a crime, so charges were dropped.

One of the theories was that the Finders were a CIA front, with top clearance and protection in whatever it was they were doing. Research from various sources since then indicates that they were a very loosely organized society held together by Pettie, taking assignments from him and traveling extensively to look for information on a variety of subjects, some of which paid well and some perhaps not so much. Pettie seemed to be a gatherer of data for its own sake.

We poked about the edges of all this, without having a lot of success since we had few resources, but certainly getting a great deal of entertainment. A new employee on the *Culpeper News* lived in Madison and had worked for a "natural" food company in Rappahannock that at one point was thought to have some Finders connections. I made a field trip to the Madison clerk's office to check the employee's home loan to see if there were Finders names involved, since we were wondering if he was a plant in the enemy press stronghold to see what we were up to. Well, yes, it was rather an overestimation of our own importance, but those were suspicious times.

The deed check was, disappointingly, negative. I also went up to Macoy Avenue, where the house that Pettie owned in Culpeper (it had been in his family) was located, and knocked on its doors and peered into windows—nothing. But the next day we received a note of unknown origin threatening me with court action for trespassing. Thinking back on my window-to-window snooping, and the idea that I was being watched, it was pretty creepy.

Apparently the Florida incident involving the Finders was the beginning of the end, unless of course they are still out there lurking and recruiting younger folk. The mothers of the children reacted a bit belatedly and not surprisingly left the group, taking their offspring with them. Other longtime followers departed, and then eventually Pettie and the Finders were sued by nine former members who wanted their part of those mysterious shared assets. The plaintiffs estimated the value of the assets at $2 million, which seemed like a lot of computer contracting work and perhaps should have been enough to make goat-raising and goat-slaughtering unnecessary.

After that, Pettie sort of came out of hiding and began wandering around Culpeper, eagerly questioning people about all sorts of things and then buying the very old theater on Main Street and allowing it to continue to fall into disrepair. Pettie, or presumably a younger and more agile leftover confederate capable of climbing a tall ladder, used the marquee to post cryptic messages. They advertised a "School for Akters," and "free money." There was an interesting display in the front window: an unstaffed office was set up there, with computers and, oddly, a typewriter. There was even talk of a Justice Department investigation, not unusual with the many cults that arise here and there in American society, but apparently nothing really illegal turned up.

There was still a ninety-six-year-old Marion Pettie listed at 409 Macoy Avenue in 2017, but my personal suspicion was that Pettie had somehow programmed himself to be listed forever in various internet search engines.

Pettie was a frequent visitor to the local library in his later years, I've been told, after I had ended my newspaper career and was no longer paying much attention to what was happening in Culpeper. When I am getting books there now I am sometimes asked if I know anything further, or someone who had been an employee of the library for a while will recall for me a bizarre Pettie conversation from the years when he called himself "the Stroller" and walked every street around. Surely not all small-town newspapers have quite this sort of thing going on.

CHAPTER TWENTY
Where I Was Heading All Along

W hen I first thought, well, maybe a book, my initial idea was to write about a central theme of my working life and how it echoed the changes in society and business in general: the disappearance of privately owned community newspapers. Small papers had been devoured in one merger after another, leading to huge media conglomerates and the loss of competitiveness, all this abetted by advances in technology. I was right there, observing up close and personal (and with a constant sinking feeling) as the business of informing people moved from the glacial pace of the cold-type era into the uncontrollable rush of technology-driven instant news—and lost that thrilling rumble of the press just feet away from the news desks.

I was in the mostly deserted old Safeway-*Star-Exponent* building on March 4, 2016, going through old papers, when I read the news of the closing of on-site production at the building in that day's paper. The *SE* was by then owned by BH Media (and you don't get much more conglomerate-sized than Berkshire Hathaway) and BH Media had bought a large recently constructed production center when it acquired the Fredericksburg *Free Lance–Star*, one of the last independents.

Production Manager Jack Griffin was philosophical that day, and not surprised, but we mulled over the changes together, more than a little sobered. Jack had spent almost all of his working career there, and had scheduled his retirement for that summer. A major concern for him was the future of the few remaining pressmen, and he was glad some of them would be able to work in the new production plant. The news people had for several years been located out of the center of downtown in rented space, and they would be moving back to the old Safeway store. That seemed like a good thing, too. But you could tell Jack really didn't want the press to fall silent, much less be cannibalized for parts, which I suppose is what happened.

But as I've been struggling to get this down on paper I've come to realize that really the sea change doesn't have to live up to the sinking feeling, that the potential power of the free press still lives, although it may sometimes struggle to compete with the need for profit at all costs. In the age of Donald Trump, I have been feeling more hopeful about the value and staying power of the First Amendment and those who guard it.

One reason for the switch from my habitual gloom about such things is this quote in the *Washington Post* from the *New Yorker*'s David Remnick, in January of 2017. Remnick said that more journalism, "rigorous, deep, tireless and fearless," is the answer. "If that sounds righteous," he wrote, "so be it. The job, done at its best, has not changed. And when a lie is a lie—when you can discern willful inaccuracy, when you can discern deception and not merely error—we should call it what it is."

This is one answer to the age of "fake news" and social media. As soon as the cyber world shakes itself down enough to distinguish real journalism from the confusion of enormous amounts of blather, we'll be back to having a handle on the truth, and if people think along those lines, we will absolutely get there.

This is by no means the first panic about the fourth estate. In January 1971, syndicated columnist James J. Kilpatrick, who has appeared elsewhere in this account, because by God the man could write, noted that there was a strike by garage mechanics at the Washington *Evening Star*. "This afternoon my newspaper is closed by a picket line and I am miserable," he said. Newspaper folk "surrendered like sheep to a handful of auto mechanics" and he was in despair. "I am no part of these times. They have passed me by." Just wait, Kilpo.

In the spring of 1971, the Virginia Press Women, which I was automatically a member of by virtue of being a female news employee, held its annual awards program at the Holiday Inn in Culpeper. The speaker that year was, not very surprisingly for the time, a man. He was Joe McCaffrey, a television newsman from WTOP in Washington, and he came to Culpeper often because he owned a farm in the county. His subject that day was the intimidation of reporters, set in the context of the Vietnam War. The war may not be reported entirely right, he said, but "the truth has always managed to filter through" where there is a free press. More on Joe later, and more on threats to the truth's ability to filter through.

Culpeper press women winning awards that year were Mary Stevens Jones, columnist Anna Townsend Willis, and Kay Potter, wife of the *SE*'s owner. Although I was billed as one of the organizers of the lunch, which I really wasn't, I didn't win anything, since I had taken the last two years off with my new baby. The big step the *SE* had taken in my absence was to add a Saturday paper (although for quite a while the masthead continued to say, rather carelessly, "published every weekday morning," next to the listed subscription rate of $16 a year by mail). And there was still no photographer and no darkroom; photos were a mix of shots by Alan's Studio, the successor to Goad Studio, and Polaroids.

If we at the Holiday Inn were taking ourselves seriously as journalists who were helping truth to filter through, perhaps others were not. Locally, I think women paid a lot more attention to good recipes than to good writing. A big deal that spring was a special section, with many ads, on the paper's cooking contest. Recipes were printed, along with the names of the submitters, and winners were chosen to considerable acclaim in the community.

While the paper was making money in its independent way that summer, through recipe contests as well as less exciting government coverage, there was a harbinger of something wicked our way coming. Walter Potter, or theoretically his company, purchased a daily newspaper in New Jersey, the seventy-year-old *Long Branch Daily Record*, to add to his collection of small Virginia operations. I never heard even a theory about why he did it; perhaps it was the early rumbling of media consolidation as the way to go if you wanted to stay in the game, or maybe the paper just sold too cheaply to pass up, but from the beginning the venture didn't go well.

The *SE* itself continued moving right along. In June there was another special section, a salute to the dairy industry. This was a big thing in Culpeper County, where there were seventy-five grade-A dairy farms, shipping sixty-two million pounds of milk a year, according to Extension Agent Mason Hutcheson. In fact, a cow was now appearing every day on the front page, providing what Bill Diehl hoped was a gentle daily chuckle. The cow, named Freda, was prone to relating stories and little jokes. Freda noted, for example, that some local folk had had a little girl come to see them with her parents. The child had looked around the family's well-stocked library, in which they took great pride. "We get books from the library too, but we take ours back," Freda quoted the little girl.

Potter, even though he permitted a bovine to speak on the front page of his paper, apparently felt the stirrings of further ambition aside from, or perhaps connected with, the acquisition of more papers. In August of 1971 he announced his candidacy for the Republican nomination in Virginia's 26th Senate District. But he didn't win, possibly because of stronger country roots on the part of the successful candidate, possibly because he seemed to be by nature a reserved, even standoffish kind of man spectacularly unsuited for campaigning.

Ambitions aside, change seemed to be pending on all fronts. Of course, in readership as well as politics, there was always a back-and-forth between rural traditions and what passed in Culpeper as urbanization. We were busily covering shopping-center rezonings and house-trailer restrictions, the town's fierce opposition to the proposed Salem Church Dam—considered an interference with public waterways—and a successful protest to the town council that blocked some street widenings.

In the intermixed state and national stories there were some events that had a bearing on newspapers: Vice President Spiro T. Agnew "scolded" the media, a headline said, over publication of the Pentagon Papers. But the courts were upholding the newspapers, their publication was approved fairly quickly, and "rigorous, deep" journalism continued despite such distractions as Freda at the bottom of the page. (The locally generated cow pronouncements were, unhappily, replaced with the prepackaged Small Fry Diary in early 1972.)

Around then all things gave way for the big story of that year, Hurricane Agnes. It was my first real disaster story, and again, I admit freely, I remember only the excitement as I got the immediate story together. I drove around in our almost-new Ford Torino, a car that always had a tendency to cut off abruptly when it got wet; it was a testament to the story's importance that I ignored this—successfully, for that day. I was even able to listen to Sammy Davis Jr. sing "Candy Man" on the radio while I drove from danger spot to danger spot. Good times.

The Sleepy Hollow Trailer Court had to be evacuated; fields were underwater; the normally quiet and meandering stream called Mountain Run inside the town went wild. Culpeper was declared a disaster area, and there was much criticism of the Army Corps of Engineers and even some of local efforts. The story went on for days.

The town-county strain showed clearly as our coverage efforts veered from storms to local politics. A hearing was held on a western bypass to loop around the town, going from Rt. 229 heading north to Warrenton to tie in with the bigger and busier Rt. 29 on the south end. Two hundred people came out, a sizeable group considering the population. Many said they objected because other needs would not be met if funds went for the bypass, while others said the road should go farther out. I have always marveled that thirty-five years later Culpeper finally got half of that bypass, from Route 229 to Route 522, but not the half on to Route 29.

The two political subdivisions did join together in resisting a state effort to divide counties into planning districts, and there was also agreement when the then joint Town and County Planning Commission dropped a proposal to forbid keeping large animals on less than two acres. But a new sewer ordinance did pass a bit later, one of the earlier steps toward government control of things that hadn't had any such meddling before. Growth was under way by then, and the population of Culpeper County was forecast to reach 22,500 by 1980. There remained a strong community feeling, echoed by Freda in Mary Stevens's annual Christmas poem headline: "Freda says it's lots more fun to live in Culpeper-on-Mountain-Run."

The breadth of what a local paper covered back then, before local and national news became so constantly available, was illustrated on a day in July of 1973. There were stories on the gas shortage, high food prices, and standoffs on meat marketing because of a customer boycott and a delay by farmers in selling cattle. These were all things that were happening, and affected everyone, and we were taking a look at it at home.

A month later, the story for the day was headlined "Standing room only seen on school buses Monday," and our coverage detailed the growing school-age population in Culpeper and how far behind the county was in providing facilities, buses, gasoline, and even food. This was very local, and had nothing corresponding to it happening elsewhere; had we not done it, no one would have known about the school difficulties following on population grown.

Shortly after, we had the prescience to note that "A very large, probably irretraceable step for Culpeper" was occurring with its new subdivision ordinance. There was a hearing on the ordinance, which would replace the "grow-at-will" approach. Government was going places it hadn't been before, and there was a reason. The state had come down hard on the town and county for its sewage handling, and while there was some argument about both the ordinance and the spending for infrastructure upgrades, the future was pretty plain. If decisions about schools were made at home, other issues reflected bigger developments.

So change was in the air, and the newspaper that reported it pretty much exclusively was thriving. By this time, in the mid-'70s, the paper was up to at least twelve pages and often fourteen. The advertising was adequate not only to justify the sizable news hole but to support extras like the Washington's Birthday Sale special, which ran to sixteen pages all by itself and had ads for just about anywhere in Culpeper that sold things. Those were times when fortunes were being made in newspaper groups, as the huge media empires were getting started. And while the news signaled by the front-page eight-column head on Nixon's pronouncement about the need for conservation in the energy crisis— "President's speech inspires little zeal"—was shared nationwide, the interviews I did with local government and business leaders about their reactions were probably of more interest to our readers.

Speaking of national news and local handling, a look back at old papers reveals that there was a headline machine problem in the spring of 1974, with odd spaces appearing in such heads as "Nixon to make public transcripts of tapes." (Just a typesetting machine that wasn't working right—no comment on the 18-minute gaps in the tapes themselves, although it would have made for good commentary.) Following a few months later was the head "Nixon out, Ford in." As a head, I still like it. The story was accompanied by a sidebar on how some Culpeper people still supported Nixon.

But a bigger upheaval for the *SE* was signaled on Sept. 6 of that year, when the paper announced "Diehl named *Record* editor," and detailed a Potter statement to that effect. The Long Branch paper was apparently in a nosedive, and Diehl was being sent into the breach. Reporter Sean Kilpatrick became the *SE* editor. The article reported that Diehl had been in Culpeper for ten years as managing editor, and would be general manager and editor in New Jersey.

Sean, as the son of James J., had of course had quite an immersion in newspapers all his life. His reporting job at the *SE* in 1968 and 1969 was the beginning of his career. After he left Culpeper he worked with papers in Fredericksburg, Newport News, and Annapolis, Maryland, before returning to the *SE*. At that point he and his wife, Sharon, were living at Hawthorn Farm in Rappahannock. Only thirty then, he was congenial to the rest of us, and we all pulled together pretty well. But with Bill went my lodestar in the search for a "hell of a story," first and foremost, as well as an unquestioned standard of ethics. From then on, I felt kind of on my own and free to follow my own conscience, although it was his, transplanted.

The good news was that Sean lent me his very impressive Nikon SLR camera so I could take a brief photography course that included darkroom work. It opened another phase of newspaper work for me and helped advance the *SE*'s offerings, since I took the plunge and bought my own Nikon SLR and often served as the darkroom tech. I think maybe the darkroom had been added for sometime sports editor Donnie Johnston, who made a living for many years afterward as a photographer. The days of predominantly wire-service or local studio pictures were going away, with only a brief interim period of Polaroids.

Darkroom work was engrossing, even thrilling. While I can't now imagine abandoning the ease and many joys of digital pictures, the magic of watching a black-and-white photo that I had taken emerge in a pan of chemicals lit only by a safelight is a powerful memory. As an art form, I guess it's over, but a part of me regrets it.

But I digress. During this period of *SE* history, most of the front page contained state and national news; interesting, looking back, since at that point the paper was trying to be all things to all people, etc., but more recent developments in community newspapers in competition with the internet have tended to be in the direction of local news in a local paper. Back then, while stress was being put on stories like "Ford pardons Nixon," the inside pages dealt with Culpeper much more fully. When teachers sought a 13.48 percent pay raise, it did make the front, and when the publisher spoke at Memorial Day ceremonies at Culpeper National Cemetery, urging national dedication, that of course got well-positioned coverage.

The news was produced by a constant stream of young reporters, since once someone got a bit of experience he or she immediately began the search for a job on a larger paper. The bottom line was, well, the bottom line, and no one was paid more than a pittance. Sometimes a new young writer came on staff who was obviously going places. One, a relaxed but excellent reporter named Estes Thompson, wound up going to the Associated Press and making us all proud. Most political events both day and evening had shifted to Sean, since it was the established prerogative of the editor and this one had politics in his blood.

A couple of only-in-Culpeper stories got good attention. One was the "Name the lake contest." I wrote that a visitor might ask a local person about the name of the rather scenic new lake that went under Route 29 south of town, and the local would have to answer "Dam Number Fifty." Perhaps not a good thing. A name was also being sought for a smaller lake.

At any rate, there were an astounding 175 names submitted. The winners were both women, with Mrs. Paul Hounshell suggesting Lake Pelham for the bigger one on Mountain Run, and Mrs. Frances Brown coming up with Lake Catalpa for the impoundment on another small stream, Ball's Run. A Confederate artillery officer who was born not locally but in Alabama, "The Gallant Pelham" died in Culpeper of a head wound received in battle at Kelly's Ford, and the county was rather proud of him. Generating more pride in our own front yard, Governor Godwin came at about the same time to lead the celebration of the two-hundredth anniversary of the Culpeper Minute Men, the Revolutionary War group that formed to fight the redcoats.

Stories were featured on the first use of voting machines, the closing of a second downtown business, and the much-heralded last-minute rescue of a historic downtown building: co-owners Charles Browning and Angus Green were beginning the renovation of the A. P. Hill Building at the corner of Main and Davis (Hill, also a Confederate general, had lived in the structure as a boy), a fine counter to the loss of businesses and a precursor to the town's eventually successful Main Street Program.

But the blockbuster story that year, in midsummer, was the canning-lid shortage, locally and nationally. Culpeper was a gardening community, and those with tomatoes ripening became restive when canning couldn't be done. People (mostly women, of course—I myself was a prolific canner) became so testy that one local merchant begged people to quit calling his store, and offered to have his premises searched to prove that he had no canning lids hidden in order to jack up the price. Rep. J. Kenneth Robinson got involved. Extension Agent Brenda B. Olafsen used her Homemakers' Column to explain "Why canning problems?" A crowd gathered in early August outside the Western Auto store, waiting for it to open and sell its new shipment of lids.

This got attention, as did another story that I wrote, about the retirement of a mailman who was finishing fifty-two years of delivering the mail to Elkwood. Broadus Maddox, who was seventy, found himself forced to leave because of mandatory retirement. It was a story of great local appeal. Maddox, whose father, Felix Maddox, had the route before him beginning in 1914, had been a medic in the army, and for three years he stopped every day to give an insulin shot to a diabetic storekeeper on his route. He also helped out in other ways. A woman on his route had raised a piglet on a bottle, and it had to be fed every four hours. If she was going to be away for the day, she would leave a note, "Please feed the pig," and the mailman would oblige.

The *New York Times* would find it hard to beat that. And speaking of big papers, the press at the *Washington Post* was wrecked by vandals while yet another strike was ongoing. The *SE* ran a photo of a helicopter lifting off from the roof of the *Post* building to take its prepared print materials to other plants nearby. In fact, the Culpeper pressroom was excited to print some of those papers, since the plant was an easy helicopter hop from Washington.

People felt strongly vested in the paper. When Sean began writing a column of mostly corrections, ME's Notebook (the ME stood for managing editor), he mentioned a reader who dropped his or her subscription because of the astrology column—they thought it was promoting something a bit irreligious. And I felt pretty vested too, when I was among the VPA winners that year and really felt like a journalist.

CHAPTER TWENTY-ONE
Ripple Effects

On Dec. 24, 1975, Mary Stevens Jones's Christmas poem included the couplet

"To all officials reelected—

"A fine performance is expected."

And she did expect that; I think we all did. I came to think very well of the people who ran the government. A few were in it for the attention, but mostly they did feel called to public service—either that or the local and state jobs were pretty good ones. They worked hard, they were for the most part open with what they were doing, and there was no sense of scheming. A bit of an antagonistic relationship between the town and county governments and the press did simmer occasionally or even boil for a week or so, despite the *SE*'s local ownership. I think this was inevitable because even the young newcomers on the staff displayed real journalistic integrity about telling the facts, and sometimes the facts could be a bit embarrassing, but mostly there was a peaceful give and take between the paper and those who made the news.

The elected town council and county board of supervisors were good folk, although very conservative. Of course, there were more worldly people like Capt. Jack Kearns, who spoke up during a hearing on rezoning land for a Mormon church. There was strong opposition, but the councilman said firmly "This is unspeakable bigotry and I will have none of it." Where is the captain when he's needed?

I also wrote that year about D. French Slaughter, who had spent twenty years in the Virginia General Assembly. A local aristocratic type by background, the attorney chose to run for election and be answerable to constituents even though he was not fond of the spotlight and didn't do a lot of mingling with those in his district. He later became the area congressman, and did a good job of that too.

Another telling article on a public servant was about Hult Wilson, another lawyer with an amazing background in the D.C. orbit who came to Culpeper to retire and then signed on as executive director of the chamber of commerce. I wrote that he was a genial, witty man, who used those qualities to push his ideas—ideas that unfortunately were ahead of their time. He tried for a senior center, a downtown mall, even a minibus system. My feature story on his retirement, I noted, was "the only downhearted interview I ever had with him." He explained sadly that "You can't be full of projects, and have none of them succeed, and keep on."

So it was a community of well-intentioned folk who at bottom had mostly the same interests, in spite of the occasional tension between reporters and the people they wrote about. It was a different era, but that purchase of the New Jersey paper was going to have a ripple effect.

I seem to recall that there was no public announcement, but sometime in 1976 Bill Diehl returned; the Long Branch paper had gone under, and there was no job there any more for Bill. Sean Kilpatrick stayed in place as the editor. At once Bill's column, Dealing It Out, reappeared. One on the growing pace of bank computerization ran the same day as Sean's ME's Notebook. The rest of the news staff at that point were Estes Thompson, a young woman named Pat Wilens, and me—oh, and of course a sports editor.

In April 1977, Sean went off to a new job and Bill took over again, but very temporarily. After a time, sports editor Tom Osborne was named the ME. Tom was from Maryland, and was bright and hardworking. He began immediately returning the paper to more of a local slant. Shortly afterward a new sports man arrived, Michael "Kip" Coons, who as it turned out was to stay in the business a long time, moving on from sports and retiring as the editor at the Raleigh, North Carolina, *News & Observer*.

It was the end of August 1978 when the ripple effect slammed into us. Looking back at the direction newspaper ownership was taking, it was of course inevitable, but we were all a bit flustered as Potter became a statistic by going into a "merger" with Carter Glass Newspapers of

Lynchburg. On Aug. 29 the masthead still listed Potter as president and publisher, but the Aug. 30 paper saw the first appearance of the Glass name. As time went on, the ownership appeared above the editorial: "Published by Newspaper Publishing Corporation, Thomas R. Glass, chairman of the board." Potter remained president and publisher.

Somewhere along in there the Diehls had moved to Lynchburg, where Bill began working for the *Daily Advance* and Dorothy finally got some overdue recognition when she was named a "merit mother" for the state.

I don't have a clear mental timeline on this, but I don't think it was long before we had the first of what would be a series of "Nothing is going to change, just keep doing your job" talks. That's the part when the new ownership comes to reassure the staff, taking care not to really give any information. I think I endured those talks four times, and I could have given one myself, except I would have expected lightning to strike me and would have felt I deserved it.

And really, that first time, things seemed like they improved for a while. The Christmas special section was bigger than ever that year, possibly reflecting more ad salespeople, I'm not sure. Somewhere along the way, as the staff expanded (actually by a very limited number), the car dealership on the east side of the old Safeway building was added to the paper's real estate; the news staff moved there, leaving the ad people in the original building. The press, as always, was back in a cavernous space that seemed built for a press rather than for the display of groceries.

The *SE* had always had special sections, although not a great many, but around this time such add-ons began to be a major consideration in the bottom line as newspapering became more corporate. Special sections like the ones for Dairy Month or for home improvement consisted of assorted display ads on a theme, heavy on clip art, with the news holes devoted for the most part to appropriate filler from various national services. A local story or two could be highlighted, but writers didn't need to be diverted from their daily beats or from whatever timely features came up.

But on January 30 of 1979 a hefty sixteen-page section, the Progress Edition, was published. It had a theme: "It's a whole new world . . .

brighter, richer and more abundant with dreams to be fulfilled." I never had a clue as to whose idea the theme was, or indeed what it was supposed to be about, but local copy had to be generated on whatever could be made to echo the "brighter" or "more abundant" thing. This, obviously, did take away time from our real purpose—covering the news.

Less than three weeks after the creation of this paean to progress, Stanley Bates, an assistant vice president of Carter Glass Newspapers, was named co-publisher of the paper. The announcement was made with some fanfare, jointly by Thomas R. Glass, president of Carter Glass, and Potter, as president and publisher of the *SE*. The front-page story said that Newspaper Publishing Corporation had merged with Glass the previous year, and that the Lynchburg company had also acquired all the stock of the Southwest Virginia Newspaper Corporation. The new masthead listing, which soon followed, said the paper was published by Newspaper Publishing Corporation, a subsidiary of Carter Glass Newspapers. Things in the office still didn't actually change much. Presumably there was another soothing talk to the staff, but I couldn't say for sure.

Bates wasn't around for long, although it was during his tenure that a huge computer system, running the length of the wall in the typesetting room next to the newsroom, was installed. Jack Griffin, deservedly promoted to management, took to the huge relic willed to us by the Lynchburg paper with ease, and made it operate—sort of. It was already antique, but it did the job for a while.

And then the bell did toll. The Glasses had, from my limited viewpoint, been a gentlemanly lot, (and the organization had seemed to be all men) allowing Potter to remain at the helm at least in theory and taking a news-first approach for the most part. But in July 1979 an awful announcement appeared in print in our paper and no doubt in the others involved: Charlottesville-based Worrell Newspapers had purchased a "controlling interest" in dailies in Culpeper and Lynchburg, and in Southwest Virginia weeklies. Worrell, the story said, owned and operated twenty-nine newspapers and two television stations in sixteen states, including the widely circulated Charlottesville *Daily Progress* and the Northern Virginia *Potomac News*. That announcement was made by Thomas E. Worrell Jr. and Thomas R. Glass, the presidents of the two corporations, and both said they were "pleased with the new association."

The staff wasn't pleased. Again we were told nothing would change, keep doing your jobs, etc. This time, things started to change immediately. A week or two later, John Fitzwater was named publisher and president. He had studied journalism at the University of Kentucky and had been an associate publisher at the *Daily Progress* for a couple of years. His ascendancy was made known immediately on the masthead.

Fitzwater went on to retire in 2007 as publisher of the Polk County, Florida, *Ledger*, after what sounds like a creditable career—he was quoted in a glowing retirement story as saying "I'm very proud of all our staff has done. The way the business has grown had been very gratifying. The publisher doesn't do that himself." Apparently he had gone from one growing conglomerate to another: Steve Ainsley, publisher of the *Boston Globe*, was quoted in the retirement story as saying that Fitzwater was a vital component in the success of the Times Company's regional media group.

I say this in Fitzwater's defense even though he didn't do much for the *SE*, from my viewpoint. When the official changeover came, I went my way that first day, busily covering the annual farm show—something I could have done in my sleep but always enjoyed. My plan was to "keep doing my job." The holdover managing editor, Tom Osborne, lasted only a few weeks before going off to his dream destination paper, the *Baltimore Sun*, a move I'm sure had been in the works long before Worrell happened to us.

New trends manifested themselves in the paper. There was a spell without much local coverage on the front, along with a flurry of Fitzwater editorials—things like "The System Works" about Congress, and much ado about the good news that the state budget was on the positive side for the year.

The new publisher was a devoted Kiwanian, and a speech he made at an installation of officers got coverage that struck me as a bit overdone. And then he named women's-page editor Becky Clayton to replace Tom as managing editor.

It was new-regime time with a vengeance with the October inclusion of the brand-new Women on the Go section, twelve pages with a great many business ads by people who didn't want to offend women, often introducing the women on their staffs. I wrote about Dorothy "Dot" Faulconer, the elected county clerk, noting that the atmosphere in the office was all hers—friendly, breezy, relaxed, and efficient. Dot was a pretty wonderful woman, plain-spoken (she was the person who had told me that the sunflower woman "done passed"), and beloved by her staff, with the proverbial steel-trap mind on all subjects local. I also did a story on town councilwoman Margaret Smith, even though councilwomen were no longer a freak occurrence. An article about Becky Clayton was featured in the section, noting that she was one of fewer than a half dozen female managing editors of dailies in Virginia.

Since I was pleased with my day-shift job, deeming it appropriate for a woman with a husband and a ten-year-old child, I had never expressed any interest in being the ME. Both Becky and I were early feminists, in our different ways, and she was proud of being the editor. We had always been casual friends, with lots of jokes based on the fact that she was about eight inches taller than I was.

No denying it, though, as the new regime got into operation I was pesky for a mere underling, possibly even more than a little self-righteous. My column, Wandering Mind, won a first place at the Virginia Press Association that year, and there was nice coverage with a photo of me and the declaration that I was "one of the reasons the *SE* is more than just the news." I guess I felt that a somewhat successful veteran had some grounds to resist. And there were things to resist, so I did. Self-righteously.

We had begun running a series of photos of local people at the top of the front page, with their answers to the question of the day. I mentioned this earlier when I recalled the question on the Iranian hostages, but another example was "How did serving as Jaycee president benefit you?" To Fitzwater's credit, neither he nor Becky ever sent me out to conduct this exercise, but it still seemed worth being snarky about.

Other changes were better, and the new operation began to find its footing. We started running state stories bylined from the "*Star-Exponent* Richmond Bureau," done by a Worrell writer who supplied a number of papers. Local coverage again began to proliferate, done by Edmond Rennolds and Carolyn Banks, who as a novelist wrote quickly and easily. There were plenty of my bylines as well. And somewhere in there came the happy addition of editorial cartoons by Jeff MacNelly, the very successful cartoonist who began in Richmond and went on to big-time fame, not only on the editorial page but on the comics page with *Shoe*, before his untimely death.

The end of February Progress Edition was the largest published in Culpeper since the *Exponent*, the older of the combined weeklies, celebrated its seventy-fifth anniversary in 1956. The publisher wrote "Hope you enjoy it," explaining that it was about Culpeper's people and places. It was very ambitious, featuring good quality photos of community leaders gathered on the courthouse lawn, with two sections about Culpeper and one on Fauquier. It was all a tremendous amount of work, and news coverage, as I had expected, was hard to keep up concurrently and adequately.

For that edition I wrote about a small rural community called Eggbornsville, and particularly about Bill Eggborn, the cattleman who bought his bulls from Brandy Rock Farm. Bill had grown up there and remembered how things had been in the area as far back as the '30s. My friend Mary and I had rented pasture room for our horses from him for a while, and were well acquainted with the area as seen from horseback. Mostly there were cows there. But Bill had a sense of people living on the land for a long, long time. "At one time I think there was a Chief Eggborneagle, who wore feathers and leather pants," he once said, looking out at a sunset from his side yard. He wasn't totally kidding.

And I wasn't kidding either when I thought back to the people who had devoted themselves to Culpeper newspapers. Even if corporate greed provided a reason to write about Eggbornsville, I wasn't pleased (see self-righteous, above) with the tendency to offer content designed to draw ads and more ads. True, I wasn't pleased with actual stories about men's clubs, either. A rewrite of a paragraph or two of a handout was enough for the Kiwanis or Lions, I figured, unless they had someone as a speaker who had something to say.

This minor sense of rebellion finally came out in a bit of a contretemps involving my reaction to an employee evaluation (possibly generated in part because the words "employee evaluation" were just about enough to incite me to join Chief Eggborn on the warpath). Then, suddenly, Fitzwater was gone.

On Saturday, June 21, 1980, Fitzwater was president and publisher. On June 23, Gary M. Greene was listed as president and publisher. A major addition Greene made to the paper was the syndicated column of Paul Harvey, which drew a letter to the editor objecting to the substitution of editorials by Harvey "for those of Fitzwater and Clayton." Letter writer Jack Kearns declared that the change did not "represent any advance in local journalism," but that was the rare comment on the many continuing changes in the paper.

Soon Gary Greene was gone too, and on Sept. 10 Stan Wade became the publisher. He was the former head of the *Smyth County News* in Marion, Virginia. Mostly he had been an ad man, joining the *Daily Progress* as a classified-ad account executive in 1976. He was only thirty.

Stan lacked experience, but didn't interfere much with day-to-day operations, although he carried on with the irritating Women on the Go section. We all wrote on women who held various prominent positions around town, and I got to know Ann Browning, who was on the board of supervisors and the county welfare board and loved horses. Still, there was that bothersome illustration on the front, the woman running, hair tossing, and nevertheless looking quite glamorous. Stan was happy with the ads, so all was okay.

The times they were a-changing, and I knew I had to accept the repercussions, even as Walter Cronkite was making his low-key last broadcast as anchorman for CBS television. TV newsmen were authoritative and gentlemanly, but their on-air time was limited—"News at 11" rather than around the clock. Print was winning, really thriving, but news media in general were about to come a long way down. A woman jogging with tossing hair to denote being on the go and making moves on that glass ceiling was nothing to agitate about when the future included Sean Hannity and Bill O'Reilly, had I but known it.

Another successful special issue, this one in the spring of 1981, was something I felt better about. It was all about "our first 100 years." I did the story on the front (for some reason printed in somewhat illegible orange ink—possibly an orange ad somewhere) for the paper's centenary, and there was a reproduction of the *Exponent* front page for April 15, 1881. It said, proudly, "Number 1. $1.50 a year." The first issue was put into the press by the founder, Angus McDonald Green, the reproduced page noted.

Another page included was of a 1926 issue, with more Green names. Raleigh T. Green had run the *Exponent* since 1897, that issue said, and that issue featured a story about "[Richard E.] Byrd's thrilling story of return trip from N. Pole," saying that the Virginian had brought honor to his native state. That reproduction was from Vol. 46, No. 6.

The 1941 paper that was included in the special issue proclaimed at the top that the paper was the "publishers of *Green's Notes on Culpeper*," the only history of Culpeper that had been done by then, a book that had 320 pages and could be ordered by mail for $10. The news that day included observations on the attack on Pearl Harbor, and it faithfully gave the local side of this huge story. Banker and town councilman Giles H. Miller—who was still active in the community at the time of the anniversary—was the chair of the 1941 effort to collect salvage material, and local draftees were now in the army. "Culpeper men in warring area," the headline said, and they were listed by name and location. One was said to be at Wheeler Air Base in Hawaii, and one on "Wakefield" (presumably Wake) Island. It must have been chilling.

For 1953 there was a front page of the *Star*: "*Virginia Star, Culpeper Exponent* to merge April 1 into *Culpeper Star-Exponent*." The announcement was by Potter, and it included the startling claim that the combined paper would have the largest circulation in Northern Virginia. Just what would have been considered Northern Virginia at that time I don't know, but Manassas must have had a paper with a bigger circulation.

President Ronald Reagan sent a congratulatory telegram to the paper on that one-hundredth milestone, even though he was still recovering from the assassination attempt that wounded James Brady. The telegram said "The *Star-Exponent* has, during the course of the past century, acquired a well-deserved reputation for responsible reporting and for serving the needs and interests of your local community." Reagan, who was then and always had been hugely popular in the county, obviously could write a good mission statement, and we were pleased.

Just a week later a serious managing editor, Larry Giesting, joined the paper. He was from Indiana, and had been editor of the Rushville, Indiana, *Daily Republican*. Becky Clayton stayed on as a reporter. The *Daily Republican* was another Worrell paper, and it was sobering to think that the group covered that much ground; easier to just think Charlottesville and Lynchburg. And if anyone had any doubts about the importance of news staff in the pecking order, when the *SE* won awards at the annual Worrell Management Conference in Jackson Hole, Wyoming, only Stan attended.

The publishing world in the area was shaken when the afternoon *Washington Star* went out of business that August. The final issue was snapped up in Culpeper as a keepsake, and Mrs. Thomas O'Halloran compared the event to losing the Washington Monument. Service station owner R. L. "Wussy" Gilmore declared "I'm crazy about that paper." But after existing under various names from 1852 to 1981, most of that time as the paper of record for the nation's capital, the *Star* ceased publication and filed for bankruptcy. Its final banner head read "128 years of service ending." Wasting little time on sentiment, the *Washington Post* bought the *Star*'s buildings and even its printing press.

Larry Giesting did not prove to be a very apt choice, although he was a hardworking and gentlemanly boss. His stories were few and scattered, but he managed to produce special sections as required, including Pigskin Preview 1981 with area high school districts covered in one section and pro football in the second. At some point the paper had acquired its first female sports editor, a young woman named Sue Freakley. Also added to the staff was Howell Posner, one of a long list of in-and-out writers, but one who frustrated me particularly because of his inability to grasp that many of the people he considered down-home locals and quoted accordingly were actually transplants from elsewhere. Well, he was young, not-from-here himself, and took my objections quietly.

Then in December of 1981, Bev Winston was promoted from Fauquier bureau chief to *SE* editor. Lorraine B. Keenan was promoted in Fauquier, making things pretty female among the writers. This was probably because women worked for less money but the paper was really a revolving door for both writers and ad reps; people got a little experience and they moved on. There were lots of Howell Posners, and for several years there seemed to be a profusion of short-term MEs. One was Dave Autry, who said he was kin somehow to the famous cowboy. Dave was a reporter one day when I went out on my afternoon rounds, and when I came back he was the editor and the man who preceded him was gone.

It was a bit sobering to realize how much the people part of the paper's equation had changed. In early 1982 a story ran saying "Potter to seek Republican nod." It declared that the former *SE* publisher, "now of Lynchburg" and a "consultant" in the news biz, would be seeking the 8th District seat in the Virginia Senate. I'm not sure just when he decamped to Lynchburg. As it turned out, his political ambitions were again thwarted.

The corporate ownership seized as an opportunity what I always recall as the dread Family Y episode. For some reason Stan Wade was a booster of the YMCA, and the paper set out to be sure Culpeper got such a recreational facility. Frequent support for the organization appeared, things that I had been taught by Bill Diehl were improper—advocating like mad, and not reporting the story dispassionately. In midsummer there were daily headlines that pushed the Y, and frequent urgings of support, not only in editorials. July 31 brought a story that the Family Y was short of its goal, but very, very close. "Let's make today a day to be proud of!" was the pronouncement.

I have to admit that I obediently, if grudgingly, produced the next story, announcing that "The YMCA Is Here to Stay." During the effort, names of donors had been listed in the paper daily. There was not exactly an outpouring, but there was a determined board that ignored a shortfall and voted to "roll up our sleeves and reorganize." The next head said "You did it PD [Planning District] 9! You Saved Our Y." I didn't write that.

Then reality began to intrude. A week later, the town turned down a request for free office space for the "troubled Y," according to a story by Gary Close, who turned out to have one of the more prolonged and varied Culpeper careers of an *SE* reporter (he left to go to law school at William & Mary, then returned and became commonwealth's attorney, and later wrote for a weekly paper while turning science fiction novelist). A bit later, Culpeper Travel offered to donate space for the Y, but the board of supervisors turned that down, and instead named a new recreation council. Meanwhile yet another editor, John Howland Jr., came from the editorial staff in Charlottesville, and was described by Wade as "just the shot in the arm the paper needs." Perhaps he was figuring Howland would make the Y a go; it had hired a new director, Desy Campbell, who also had a seat on the recreation council.

The finale to that saga: Toward the end of the next year I put together a story that proclaimed "Northern Piedmont Family Y calls it quits." Clark "Bud" Glass, then the head of the group, cited lack of participation as well as funds. Alternative programs were already being offered, he explained, by "many capable organizations." Campbell had resigned, saying she was frustrated. Culpeper simply wasn't ready to support a Y yet, she had concluded. The funds never went up any more after the drive, which the *SE* called a "well-supported fund campaign."

The Fauquier bureau continued regular contributions, making the push into Warrenton the most sustained attempt to broaden circulation up to that point. There was a story about the storied horse-sports and horse-society photographer Marshall Hawkins, the guy who had gotten the famous shot of Jackie Kennedy taking a spill over a fence. That picture was in *Life* magazine, and I would guess it was the highlight of Hawkins's professional life. He was a competent and friendly man, who had been around the race courses in the area enough to know where falls were apt to occur. That, rather than what was thought to be a sixth sense for mishaps, had helped him gain a reputation as being the cameraman likely to be there for the best shots. He helpfully conducted me to such a spot on the Montpelier course at one meet, and sure enough, a horse and rider took a tumble.

The 1982 Women on the Go section was something I had come to accept as inevitable, and in the one for that year I wrote about a potter, Ann Friend Clark, and about Madison Mayor Sarah Frances Johnston. She was one of those people who would be interesting in any setting, and was also an example of someone who had ended up in the area because of the proximity of the capital. A native of Cheyenne, Wyoming, she came to Washington during the New Deal, taking a job with what eventually became the Farmers Home Administration. She worked with the "resettlement" people who had been ousted, sometimes forcibly, from land that was to become Shenandoah National Park. Many of them were settled in Madison, so Johnston was introduced to the area and took a liking to it. She ended up as a management analyst with the State Department, and after retirement she moved to Madison, first with plans to live more or less as a hermit, and then, when she realized she needed involvement, being absorbed into the community. Culpeper and Madison willingly accepted good people, so she was eventually elected mayor.

The news kept happening despite new attitudes from the paper's management, and we were able to find time to write about it even working around special sections. There was the blizzard of '83, called the worst storm since 1940. Businesses closed as snow piled up to fifteen to twenty-four inches. I wrote in Piedmont Living about "how to cope in a blizzard." It was heartfelt when I noted that "those of us in outlying areas discover how cut off one can feel after only a few days." Never one to let a photo opportunity go by, I illustrated my account with a shot I took of Jack's wonderful farmer cousin Clay Penn clearing our driveway with a front-end loader. Stan Wade submitted a picture he took, tellingly of the deserted country club.

We got a new ad director in April, but the big change came in July, when Robert Childress was made publisher. Stan was to go off and take Childress's job as president and publisher of the *News Messenger* in Christiansburg, a weekly. We assumed Childress, forty-two, was getting the promotion within the Worrell group with the transfer to a bigger paper, and he set out to earn it with local editorials, heavy on tourism boosting. It was all confusing, and it seemed like a good idea to take notes to remind yourself who was in charge.

A good-sized redesigned editorial box beginning that fall proclaimed that the paper was a publication of Carter Glass Newspapers, and it listed the ad manager, business manager, and production manager—all before the news staff. As listed, they were at that point president and publisher, Childress; managing editor, Paul Homberg; Fauquier bureau chief, Lorraine Keenan; city editor, Becky Clayton; and reporter, me.

Actually, there were other reporters, and Caroline Kane (later Kenna after she married Mike) and who was to be a mainstay for some years, arrived around then. But I recall being told I was considered the "senior reporter" to justify my slightly more than subsistence but still paltry salary. I even took a turn writing an editorial or two, one remembering the Kennedy years for the twentieth anniversary of the assassination. As I recalled the day, it was a shock not only because the death of the vibrant young president was hard to accept, but because things like that didn't happen to presidents in the United States. That, of course, was before the assassinations of Bobby Kennedy and Martin Luther King, events that seemed less surprising after Lee Harvey Oswald received his death wound on television, live.

For me, 1984 began well, with three awards from the Virginia Press Association, although no firsts. It was an interesting time for the staff, my last year. Gary Close was still writing, and the byline of Sheri Stanley appeared. There was a review of former *SE* reporter Carolyn Banks's third novel; she was doing well, and while I was glad for her I was sorry that she probably wouldn't be back to report for us anymore. We added an additional sportswriter in March, a real sign of prosperity.

Signs of prosperity were all around, in fact, in an era when media fortunes were being made by ever-bigger companies. The June graduation issue had photos of grads in Madison and Fauquier, and even Rappahannock. The Dairy Month section noted that Fauquier had fifty-six dairy farms with 6,500 cows, and Culpeper had 4,429 cows. An extension agent warned that the government was trying to cut down on surplus milk, but at that point the dairy buyout was safely in the future and the revenue was there. There was a thriving big Community Life section on Wednesdays, and the well-funded Entertainer tabloid on Fridays. Advertising was coming from national agencies, and it was obvious that mergers meant profits. The *SE* was named the top small daily in the Worrell Newspapers group, with the fastest-growing circulation; the second-place paper was located in San Marcos, Texas.

As a means of measuring how healthy our small-town paper was, consider the bound volumes in the old *SE* building where I did much of my research for this book: For most of its time as a daily, the papers were bound into big books with two years to a huge, heavy volume. But beginning in 1984, only one year's issues were collected together, because there so many pages. Quantifiable progress.

CHAPTER TWENTY-TWO
Who's Got the Dome?

I 'd have to admit that the highlight of my last year at the *Star-Exponent* came courtesy of the sports page. It remains one of my favorite stories of all time, although a serious newspaper person (which I was, but not to the exclusion of all else, mainly gallows humor) should have been horrified.

Fairly late in my tenure, a new and perhaps more intellectual than usual sports writer came along. He was one in a long line of sports people, and it was pretty much a principle of mine to ignore sports guys. But he was hard to ignore, because he was a tiny bit arrogant about being fifteen years younger than I was, as well as unusually intelligent. And not just for a sports guy.

Also, unfortunately, we shared a computer terminal. We each had a desk, but they were side by side, and ownership of the computer switched depending on who was at their desk. Since I was on the day shift, it was mine by rights until 5 p.m. After that it belonged to the night shift, for better or worse.

He was in his very early 20s when he started, presumably right out of college. If I ever asked him which school he went to, I don't remember it. He was bearded, smoked like mad, and was incredibly—and it seemed deliberately—messy. And of course I wasn't necessarily finished with my day when he showed up, and there was some tension, which I dealt with by pretending his bearded self was not there glowering at me. He, in turn, consistently left our mutual premises littered with cigarette butts, ashes, and food wrappers when he went home at night.

Somewhere along the way I realized he wasn't the sports editor/writer that Culpeper readers might have wanted, since they had long been captivated by homeboy Donnie Johnston. But people didn't spend a lot of energy "taking agin'" *SE* staffers, because they knew they were mostly temporary. This one may have written a bit above the head of the average Culpeper sports fan, but he covered sports locally as well as nationally. He was perfectly willing to follow the local team, and write knowledgeably about exactly how come the "Devil bid falls short," but when he wrote columns, they were mostly about bigger concerns, and they relied heavily on sarcasm.

When basketball playoff season began, the sports page declared that the NCAA college basketball tournament "is about to make a forced entry into our living rooms," but that at least the occupation would be brief. Suggestions for improvements were offered, like eliminating the celebratory cutting down of opponents' nets, and instead perhaps torching them. Another recurring theme of this writer was a dislike of the pro sports powers that be, as when he put a head on the story about the Baltimore Colts moving to Indianapolis that said "Let's face it: owners can do what they please."

Another of his columns commented on the incentive bonus, and he mused about transferring the concept from games involving inflated spheres and such to other fields: "Like I always say, there isn't a problem in the world that can't be solved by a bunch of jocks."

Then there was the time that he won a first-place award in that big annual marker, the VPA contest. I had scored in a couple of the contests that year, although no firsts, and we went down to Richmond to the convention and awards banquet. A couple of other people went, including my husband, and we all gathered for the dinner. Sports guy hadn't been there for the afternoon session as was expected, and we wondered vaguely where he was. At the last instant he did wander in, looking a bit worse for wear and gazing at us thoughtfully from some other place that he seemed to have gone to during his period of tardiness.

Anyway, he did his two-year stint at the *SE*, proving very reliable about coming to work and very unforthcoming about what he did with the rest of his life. Eventually it apparently occurred to him it was time to head off into the sunset, and he duly handed in his resignation with no indication of where he was headed next. I looked forward to fewer ashes on my desk and didn't think much about it—the revolving door had claimed him, and there would be a new sports guy just like there was always a new editor.

But *then* came his last night on the job, a Friday evening. As the daytime staffer I was never clear about the details, about who noticed what or what was said. Everyone who was around the evening shift kind of developed amnesia about that night. But the Saturday morning paper had a very impressive photo of the Astrodome, the actual domed stadium, superimposed over the track behind Culpeper's very own junior high school, and a headline that said "Stadium nears completion." The story reported that the long-awaited completion of Culpeper's new, giant stadium was indeed near, and quoted the contractor for Largemen (get it?) Construction Co. as saying that they were proud to be finishing ahead of schedule.

Since I skipped the sports page as usual on Saturday, I didn't even see it until I went in to work on Monday and found not a kerfuffle but an uproar. The corporate owners, actually rather conscientious newsmen, were infuriated. One member of the board of supervisors was irate because he hadn't been informed of the "multi-million-dollar facility." The source of that much money would in fact have been a mystery.

The dome story had noted that Culpeper Town Council had a terrible problem with the stadium, because here it was almost done and there was no name for it yet. Names like Devil Dome and Satan Stadium had been rejected, he wrote, never being one to let something like the Blue Devil petition rest. He said a local church group had come up with another petition, this one to name the facility The Holy Sepulcher, but that didn't fly either.

The story explained that there was also considerable turmoil over events that might be held there. The bond proposal to raise the needed money had putatively stipulated that the stadium would be used for non-athletic events in order to raise funds for another project, this one near and dear to local hearts: the four-laning of Main Street, something that was apt to be pretty costly because the downtown, so old it really and truly had been surveyed by George Washington, was pretty much filled with large masonry buildings that would have to go.

Mixed in was a sensible, low-key discussion of the types of sports that would claim space in the dome during various seasons, and then the story added that such cultural events as Mormon Tabernacle Choir concerts and an ice revue, Smurfs on Drugs, were tentatively scheduled. There were operational details about covering the turf for basketball and bringing in "a lot of ice" for the Smurfs. Real concern was said to be coming from the council about the rumors that Michael Jackson and the Sex Pistols (who had regrouped especially to play in Culpeper) would appear. There was a quote from the owner of the Redneck Bar & Grill, which may have been a bit heavy-handed, but then there was a conclusion that was hard to beat.

A last, minor problem remained, he wrote. The domed stadium had forty thousand seats, and there were maybe fifteen hundred available parking spaces. The fact that there was only one entrance also apparently had people worried.

Still, there was a bright side. When it was pointed out that "You could put everyone within a thirty-five-mile radius of Culpeper in that domed stadium," a town policeman thought that was pretty useful: "Well, at least we'd know where everyone was."

So it was pretty funny, and it was surprising that anyone would take it seriously, Largemen Construction and all. But they did, as demonstrated by the stream of traffic that weekend looking for the Astrodome suddenly transplanted to Virginia. Staffers who came in on Sunday night said they were kept busy fielding calls from indignant readers who wanted to cancel their subscriptions; they also found that the news editor, a young woman who had only been on the job a short while, wasn't there on Sunday night as expected. Instead, the bureau guy from Fauquier, Frank Edens, was editing, and he explained briefly that the woman had been fired.

Observing from the sidelines as the week went on, most of us who worked there found it fairly entertaining that such a fuss was being made, but needless to say we didn't feel it was a good thing to mention. We all shared the noble and genuine thought that the first rough draft of history was perhaps no place to make jokes, but still there were hidden smirks all over the place.

Misdemeanor legal charges were brought against the ex-employee rather quickly, for transmitting false information to a newspaper, obviously something we could support since we were constantly on the lookout for people lying to us, or at least omitting to tell the truth. We did wonder whether it would have been all right if a disclaimer had been added in parentheses at the bottom of the story; something along the lines of "joke, it's a joke, honest, joke."

No one laid eyes on the offender in the ensuing weeks, not surprisingly because he had worked out his two weeks' notice and wasn't exactly buddies with anyone on staff. It was not until July 19 that the rest of the story played out in court. Since I was the court reporter, I was dispatched to cover the event, and went prepared to be entertained. And I was.

Note here that no one told me what to write, or cautioned me about presenting the owners' viewpoints, or touched the article after I finished it. Publishers in my experience had some of the important basics of journalism pretty much at heart.

Not that I would in any way have gone off the rails in reporting the resolution of the dome scandal. I wrote that it turned out the charges were dropped in district court "with the agreement of the ownership of the paper." Commonwealth's Attorney John Bennett, probably pretty entertained himself to be on the scene because he knew most of the newspaper people, made the motion to dismiss the charge. This was in response to a letter from representatives of said ownership saying they were willing to not proceed, accepting the public statement from the accused that there was "no malicious intent" and that he hadn't meant to "hurt anybody." Ownership was listed as Carter Glass Newspapers, a creditable group with a long and fine history in Virginia, although of course by then Worrell Enterprises was the owner. The official statement from the paper was that the charge had "served its purpose."

There were quite a few reporters in and around the courtroom, since other papers were drawn to the legal action against someone in their ranks, and they were told for purposes of quotes that "our main concern was our readers." Some people had thought the prank was funny, he said, but others did not. A bit sanctimoniously, but probably sincerely since he had always seemed a rather committed man, he added that "Any false story in any newspaper hurts the industry."

Sports guy stayed in character, replying to the reporters' questions with his usual reserve and restraint but with hints that at any moment he might give way to manic giggling. He wisely said he "wouldn't venture to speculate" on the ramifications for the industry. He explained that his quoted statement, that he didn't intend to be malicious, had appeared in an AP wire story, and this was "crucial to the case." My interpretation, which of course did not appear in print, was that he had found a congenial reporter to tell all this to, with the added bonus of maybe getting himself off the hook.

The reaction from the community was decidedly mixed—in general the public got that the prank was a bit outrageous simply because it was so convincing, although some felt the charge shouldn't have been placed. The youthful writer said he resigned because after two years he had "accomplished everything I wanted at the *Star-Exponent*." He said he wouldn't have done it if he had known someone would be fired. "I'm sorry people didn't see it for what it was," he added piously. I didn't buy it, but you do what you gotta do.

CHAPTER TWENTY-THREE
Departure and Aftermath

During the final two years of my time at the *SE*, I had sporadically looked around for another job. As I was going about my daily routine in maybe 1982 or '83, the publisher called me aside to assure me that, rumors perhaps to the contrary, I was not about to be fired and that I was in fact a valued employee. Huh? Such a thing had never occurred to me, nor had I heard of any rumors. In retrospect, I remembered a few doubtful glances directed at me in the newsroom, but I hadn't paid any attention. I knew I was earning more than other reporters, but it was still such a pittance that it seemed unlikely that even a greedy corporation would worry about it. It didn't seem like a matter of overconfidence that after about fifteen years I would assume I was worth more than a twenty-three-year-old who knew nothing about the business or the area. But it undeniably rattled me, and the job search seemed more urgent.

Not being willing to move made it more difficult for me than for the unattached, rootless young folk that generally filled the newspaper's positions. A possibility was a public relations job at the University of Virginia, then well within comfortable commuting distance from our house in Madison. I interviewed, but didn't get hired. Ditto with a communications job at Germanna Community College, although I felt afterward that I would have done better and lasted longer than the person they hired. That woman was more qualified, since she had worked for various big companies, but she left Germanna pretty quickly, so there.

Then, shortly after the dome debacle in 1984, an ad appeared seeking an editor for an agricultural weekly. Called *Virginia's Farm & Country,* the paper had been begun by a Culpeper couple who were divorcing. Feeling the need for some financial settlement, they had sold the tabloid-size paper to—you guessed it, a newspaper group. This one published a pretty prosperous weekly called the *Delmarva Farmer* and a couple of other industry papers. Headquarters was on the Eastern Shore, in Easton, Maryland, but the Virginia paper was based in Culpeper. I went to talk to the publisher of the *Delmarva Farmer*, who had been made the publisher of *Farm & Country* as well, Bruce Hotchkiss. We liked each other, he felt my credentials were appropriate, and he saved me from the *Star-Exponent*.

Well, I felt pretty much hyped up as I prepared to give Paul Homberg notice. My only previous resignation had been eighteen years earlier, from the federal government, and I had really had no other practice. When Paul came in as usual at 3 p.m., I was lurking, ready to make my announcement to him. But he insisted on talking to other staff, chattering on, until finally I interrupted, saying quickly "I'm leaving, this is two weeks' notice" and went off on my rounds. It felt good.

On Dec. 1, 1984, I got a front page story about my departure: "Hoffman has new position." There was a nice photo, along with some complimentary quotes from Homberg and Childress. I said in the article that I must have done a hundred retirement stories over the years, and people always said it was the people they would miss, and I figured it was something you'd say to a reporter. But it was true. I had had what I have always described as a "horrible job" in my first full-time employment, working for the defense supply center in Richmond, and coming to Culpeper was an abrupt switch to something pleasantly challenging and engrossing. There were no unhappy federal bureaucrats at the adjoining desks.

Sadly, now there were unhappy young reporters at the next desks, and it was all a long ways from the days of Bill Diehl and Walter Potter.

In the farewell story, which I guess functioned as an exit interview, I not only mentioned the pull of the local people I saw almost daily, but also confessed to a thrill when I head the press running. "There's something very vital about all that noise, all that speed, directed toward communicating on a large scale, telling someone something they want to know or need to know."

The *SE* had become burdensome, though. The switch to working for the farm paper, as I perhaps unwisely told a writer from the *SE*'s rival, the weekly *Culpeper News*—I had never really been interviewed before, and I pretty much said what came to mind—was like dying and going to heaven. And that was an apt description, although I kind of wished I hadn't said it, because I really liked working for a daily paper for most of the years I spent there.

But the agricultural paper was new and different, and there was less pressure about what came out in print; I didn't meet the people I wrote about while headed downtown the next morning. I went all over Virginia in search of interesting agriculture-related features, covered pork, beef, and dairy banquets and annual meetings, and went to the land-grant agricultural school Virginia Tech in far-off Blacksburg for events. I was on the road so much I had to get an actual new car, a red Ford Escort that soon displayed a license plate reading "Farm & C."

Farm, orchard, and hobby niche product operators welcomed me, and it was charming to find both them and the business-conscious established beef, grain, and dairy farmers so ready to share anything that worked for them with other Virginians involved in the same businesses. People, mostly men, happily discussed their ideas about crop rotation, sparkling-cider creation and marketing, and even horse breeding. Standing around in barnyards, going to Chippokes Plantation Park near Williamsburg for a big crop day even in pouring rain, driving to Richmond to find out that there really was an annual recognition by the hog industry of a young woman to be Miss Porkette; it all meant life was busy but entertaining.

After a couple of months the new owners and Hotchkiss decided the office would be moving to Fredericksburg, thirty-five miles away. Chesapeake Publishing, the parent company, was based on the Eastern Shore, where it created its agricultural publications like the *Delmarva Farmer*. The *Farmer* was directed toward agriculture as practiced in Delaware, Maryland, and Virginia, and Chesapeake liked as much of its staff as possible to be within reasonable driving distance of its location in Easton. *Farm & Country* had been printed at a very small operation in King George County, Virginia, but it was fairly rapidly switched to a much bigger plant in La Plata, Maryland.

So my routine became working on the paper Monday through Wednesday at the office in Fredericksburg, then driving all the materials to La Plata on Thursday to be pasted up and printed, and spending Friday going somewhere for the next week's big feature. This went on for nearly two years.

There was lots to learn. Because I had taken the photography course that included darkroom instruction years before, I developed and printed my pictures myself in Culpeper and then in Fredericksburg until I could hire a darkroom guy for a couple of hours a week. Type was set on disks on the "Trash-80," an early Tandy Radio Shack word processor that would happily dump everything you had done on a story if you didn't save it promptly. Then the articles were printed out in the usual way and pasted in, with the production process going on off-site.

Once things were moving along pretty well, I was allowed to hire an assistant editor, a woman named Annette Wisniewski. We were an excellent combination, me low-key and unexcitable, her overflowing with enthusiasm for whatever she was doing.

We had quite a few stringers, and we ran a *Delmarva Farmer* columnist's dairy industry analysis that got, as they say, pretty deep into the weeds. At Virginia Tech I met a candidate for governor, Wyatt Durrette (who was not successful), and I went to see the farm in Raphine, Virginia, where Cyrus McCormick invented his reaper. Things were good, until . . .

It happened again. Just before the end of 1986, Chesapeake Publishing sold *Farm & Country* to Lee Publications. First, Hotchkiss came down to tell us that Chesapeake was giving up on the paper. It took us all by surprise—I'm not sure why, since I at least might have seen in coming, since I had been caught up in the merger phenomenon firsthand. He brought along copies of a letter on Chesapeake Publishing letterhead, signed by Chuck Lyons, the head man. Lyons wrote that they had "decided that our organization can no longer afford to continue publication" of *Farm & Country*. He added that operating losses for the paper for 1986 were in the neighborhood of $100,000.

Apparently to make us feel better, he wrote that the organization felt the paper was "an outstanding publication," and that its excellence was a tribute to the work done by the staff. Further, he explained that

Chesapeake was trying to find a buyer, because they preferred to "give it an opportunity to go on publishing" rather than close it down. If they couldn't, he said, they would stop publishing at the end of the year, and every staff member would be given six weeks of severance pay.

So I was thinking, that's enough time to hunt up another job, not bad, and this time I'll look to some other field, perhaps. There was the problem of the Farm & C license plate, but still . . . then Lee Publications stepped into the picture, thinking there were financial possibilities. The company, then only about twenty years old, was on its way to doing a good-sized business handling trade publications for any number of industries. It seems to have done pretty well for itself. The tabloid first changed its name to *Farm Chronicle*, moving back to Culpeper, and then became or was included in the *Mid-Atlantic Country Folks Farm Chronicle,* I'm not sure which. That magazine-format publication seems to be ongoing.

Anyway, no six weeks' severance for us. As we continued to get out the paper, the new owner showed up, and instead of the nothing-is-going-to-change talk, he quickly made it clear that advertising was to come first. "When you girls are out in the field doing stories," he instructed Annette and me, "if somebody wants to pay a bill, you take it." It was probably out of line for me to take umbrage, but take umbrage I did. Advertising and news were separate, right? All right, I was having trouble making the transition to an industry publication. Also, I hadn't been a girl in a while.

The new publisher who was sent into the office with little introduction offered no hope of anything different, so I quit in early 1987, thinking that I would take my time finding another job and that the idea of another direction for employment was maybe a good one. But before I finished working out my notice, I got a call from the weekly *Culpeper News*. Mike McCaffrey, the editor—and son of publisher Joe McCaffrey (remember him, the distinguished Washington TV commentator who lived part-time in Culpeper and spoke at the Virginia Press Women meeting?)—asked if I'd want to work for him. Doing what? I asked. "Oh, news and features, whatever," he said.

For some years, *Culpeper News* reporters and I had rubbed elbows in our little community. Joe McCaffrey had always wanted to own a small-town paper, so he started one as he faced retirement from television. Mostly for the entertainment value, we at the *SE* had a bit of a rivalry going with the *"Snooze,"* as we referred to it. But it was a weekly with less circulation than the daily, and I didn't think so. I said thank you, but no.

A week or so later he called back, and wanted to know if I would like to be the editor. By then I had interviewed a time or two for public-relations-type jobs, and neither I nor the interviewers were thrilled. And of course, there was going to be no six-week severance. The *News* had always had good people working for it, so why not, I thought. I knew how to be an editor by then.

So I had my third newspaper job, if you count *Farm & Country*, and I did in fact count it because it had found a readership even while advertising lagged. Even though I came back to work in Culpeper with the actual title of news editor rather than managing editor, it was okay, partly because the paper was a good one and really was a throwback to the old local-owner days. The *News* had a board, but mostly it was run by Mike, who despite his youth juggled a small staff and the often insistent demands of his dad rather gracefully. The paper was located in an old two-story frame house on South Main Street, a building that also housed a copy center, providing copies and sending faxes for whoever happened in.

As I always found in the newspaper business, daily or weekly, everyone who worked there tried with every issue to make it the best it could be, to have the paper tell the truth and give readers information that would entertain and inform them. Joe had known a lot of people in the metro area, and he brought an old-line ad man with him, as well as a columnist who had retired to the mountains nearby. He also had various contacts that meant he could get good reporters, so the paper wasn't an amateur effort, as so many local start-ups are. Once when the nearby *Fauquier Democrat* was boasting of its staff's nineteen years or some such of news experience, we totaled ours, coming up with close to one hundred. This included Joe, of course, and by then I was up to more than twenty years on my own.

Joe McCaffrey was a good example of the kind of people who have made news reporting great, important to democracy, and certainly something that should be above hurled accusations decrying "fake news." When he died in 1995, after he had sold the little paper and it had been swallowed whole by corporate takeover-itis, the *Post* ran a substantial obit. According to Martin Weil, writer of the obituary, one of McCaffrey's first assignments once he was in the nation's capital was contributing to broadcasting about the D-Day landing on June 6, 1944. Weil had researched the obit thoroughly, and gave me all sorts of new knowledge about my former employer. He had joined the Army Air Corps when the U.S. entered World War II, and was flying to Europe when his plane went down near Newfoundland. The crash killed twelve people, and his injuries resulted in a discharge for McCaffrey just in time for him to help cover D-Day back home.

He worked for WMAL radio in Washington and was a newscaster for WMAL-TV in the city during the '60s and '70s. But his main gig was *Today in Congress*, a ten-minute daily commentary on whatever had happened that day on Capitol Hill. "Mr. McCaffrey knew the halls of Congress particularly well and was highly regarded there, among both his colleagues and those he covered," Weil wrote. He also served as host of a Sunday afternoon interview show, *Celebrity Parade*, that ran until 1956 and won an Emmy. Senate Democratic Whip Mike Mansfield of Montana, not a man given to hyperbole, described McCaffrey as "one of the national's finest and most impartial men in the news and public service fields."

The newsman may have been the only broadcast reporter in the House of Representatives on March 1, 1954, when four Puerto Rican nationalists entered the gallery and began firing with handguns, wounding five people (but failing to decimate the legislative body because they had no assault rifles). McCaffrey calmly went into action with his microphone and did a major exclusive for the Mutual radio network, then his employer.

After a judge was shot in 1970, a man who said he had done the shooting called McCaffrey in the House radio-television gallery to confess, saying he was an admirer and wanted to give him an exclusive. Fellow reporters elected him in 1956 as president of the Radio-Television Correspondents' Association. In his later years he worried that politics was being trivialized by television, and that thoughtful government would increasingly be weakened by electronic journalism. As Weil wrote in the now more than twenty-year-old obituary, Mansfield had much earlier remarked that electronic media were "already putting forth a surfeit of bombastic, biased newscasts," and "We can ill afford not to use to the fullest the talents of a Joe McCaffrey."

In a word, Joe was the real thing. He was admired for non-intrusive interviewing and his ability to never hog the show and to get it right as well as fast. He also thought a great deal about journalism, both when he was in the thick of it with Congress and later. Print journalism appealed to him a great deal.

As he grew older, the attractions of his farm in Culpeper County seemed more welcoming, and he moved there full-time in the '80s. He had founded the *News* in 1975, and wrote a regular opinion column called without fanfare A Column. When I started work there in 1987, I found that one of the hazards of being the editor in name was a Wednesday afternoon or early evening call from the charged-up publisher to inform me of what had gone right and what was wrong with that week's issue. We would have done last-minute stories Wednesday morning while pasteup was going on, argued about what would fit and what would have to be held over, gotten the photos chosen and sized, and watched Mike drive off in the van to get the whole works printed in Fredericksburg.

Needless to say, by the time he had gotten it all done, loaded up, and returned to Culpeper, Mike was not very receptive to his father's calls. Nor was I—by then I had a daughter graduating from high school and a busy life. When I got off on Wednesday afternoon, it meant a couple of hours of alone time to ride my horse out with our dogs and leave the week and the latest issue behind. Phone calls that would delay getting saddled and out of the yard weren't good, and there was no caller ID in general use yet; hence the acquisition of the Joseph McCaffrey Memorial Answering Machine.

By the time I got to the *News* I had adjusted to the weekly timetable, but it never seemed as comfortable and inevitable as the daily setup. On a daily, you had the day itself to report on what had happened, there came a deadline, what could go into the pages went in, and the next day we did it again. At the *News*, there were off days and somewhat frantic on-deadline days. Besides, we were always thinking we should do more in-depth, thoughtful pieces; but we were an experienced staff, and we were good, and we couldn't help competing with the daily to get things first. By then the cost-conscious *SE* was operating with mostly people right out of school, and with management often drawn from Worrell Newspapers' advertising staff, so time and again we were able to stay ahead of them even with the weekly time lag.

We wrote about a controversial effort to preserve historic Civil War locations in the town and county, about the continuing effort to expand oversight of growth and development, and about the usual high crimes and misdemeanors. There was creeping up on me the realization that I was no longer the detached "conduit" I had once been. Developers became the bad guys, and I began to compile an enemies list of sorts. Not that I ever did anything improper, because the influence of Bill Diehl was too strong. But I wanted to, and I knew it wasn't right to want to.

Having good fellow employees was certainly a plus. There was no longer a constant stream of the young and untried, since Mike had been at this for a while, and eventually we added another *SE* refugee, Caroline Kane, who had not yet married Mike Kenna. She had begun work in her mid-teens on her father's paper in Southwest Virginia, and had assumed not only the work ethic but the moral stance he passed along. And Joe, of course, had seen the business from his lofty and varied perches, and knew the ins and outs.

He also knew famous people, and a highlight of my time at the weekly was when Walter Cronkite came to town. Cronkite had by then left his anchorman position, but still kept his hand in by doing whatever projects were offered to him that he found interesting.

Some years before, dinosaur tracks had been discovered after blasting was done to get to a new level in a local quarry. The veteran newsman was to narrate some kind of film special aimed at children, clarifying what kind of beasts might have made the tracks, and for how long they had been preserved beneath layers of rock. The deeply imprinted marks weren't going to last indefinitely once they had been exposed to the weather, and they were the object of quite a lot of attention and school field trips.

McCaffrey and Cronkite had known each other in a previous life, of course, and Joe invited me to go with him when the "most trusted man in America" came visiting. I was to do an interview and get a photo when Cronkite was at Farmington Elementary School doing a few scenes with eager children, and then the three of us were going to lunch. I was somewhat atwitter; the CBS newsman was the real thing—he was the man who noted that "Freedom of the press is not just important to democracy, it is democracy." I associated him with space shots and, most indelibly, with the assassination of John Kennedy. There had been that moment when he was about to cry, and took off his glasses . . .

I got my chance at him in the gym at the school. I had come up with a question about the effects of the growing cult of personality in television's own rough draft, which was of necessity a bit less carefully weighed than the one being compiled in print journalism. I got it out with some hesitation, and with the hovering worry that he got asked some form of this question all the time but I hadn't seen any comment he may have had about it on TV. The great man looked at me, and then in that thoughtful, considering voice, the inflections just right and making me catch my breath, he gave me a lengthy, somewhat worried answer. We had a fairly long discussion, and it was one of the highlights of my life.

Finally, with the young female director of the dinosaur project pushing him to hurry, because time was short, we wound up, and he insisted to the whole crew that he was going to take time for lunch, because he and Joe had planned it. What could have been more thrilling? To me, honestly, not much.

Not that it was a luxurious, dazzling lunch. Cronkite, true to his reputation, heeded the agitation of the young director, and said regretfully that he would be limited to fast food. We went a couple of blocks away to the Roy Rogers. There Joe and I insisted that he order first, to give him a few extra minutes of downtime. I watched from just behind the famous man as he placed his order. In the sonorous tones familiar to anyone who had been alive more than six years, he asked for "A roast beef, please," and a drink that I don't remember. I was waiting for the middle-aged woman behind the cash register to swoon or at least comp the lunch. Nope.

"You want fries with that?" was the only thing she said, aside from the amount due. Probably wouldn't have bothered to go see dinosaur tracks, either.

In spite of the satisfaction that working with a good staff at a well-run paper brought, I only lasted five years at the *News*. In early 1992 there were a number of reasons to think that my newspaper career might be waning. I began to see my objectivity becoming hard to maintain, particularly on the issues of preservation versus development, and it was more difficult to do the job right. But worse was the sensation that my personal history was about to repeat itself.

The *News* was a strong little family, but Joe had rounded up investors to help get it under way, and they grew restive in light of the money being made in merger-mad media. At some point the worst happened—Worrell made an offer and it was accepted. Before the probably inevitable sale occurred, though, I had departed without really planning it at all.

The paper limped along for a while before being subsumed into the *Star-Exponent*, and survives many years later only as an occasional publication that's really just an ad vehicle. When I think of what it meant to us all at one time, and how much we cared about what went into it, I try to think about something else.

CHAPTER TWENTY-FOUR
Life After Newspapers

T here was a life after newspapers.
I had done some freelance things on the side while I was with the *News*, including writing and designing a newsletter for a regulatory association. The American Association of State Social Work Boards was a national organization of the boards that regulate social work; its name was later shortened to Association of Social Work Boards when the Canadian provinces and others had begun to join. It had wound up in Culpeper in its very early years because an early executive director, Frances Goddard, lived there.

A nonprofit, only a few years old then, the AASSWB was run with funds that it took in via the complicated task of developing and maintaining the social work licensing exam. It needed a writer, and Goddard was familiar with me from my newspaper interviews with her when she worked at the department of social services, and with my writing in general. After I had done the every-other-month newsletter for a while, she asked me if I was interested in working part-time. I wasn't; the *News* would have tolerated it, but the inevitable result would have been my working about thirty hours a week in each of two jobs. Then she asked me to come and talk with her. I went, thinking no, I wasn't ready to surrender as a journalist quite yet, even though all media had become terribly corporatized and conscious of profit above all.

But I was forty-nine years old and married to a man more than eight years older than I was. We were friends with another couple with a similar age difference, and both husbands were talking about retirement. Both had jobs with the government, and both had good pensions that would reward them after years of working with transportation departments, Jack with the state of Virginia and John, our friend, with Fairfax County.

The other wife, a teacher, also had a pretty good retirement plan going. I, on the other hand, had really nothing to show for my years in the trenches (although to my surprise, when I neared sixty-five I got a letter from a company representing Carter Glass Newspapers, informing me that I was due a pension of about $27 a month).

I was making in the neighborhood of $23,000 a year at that point, and when Frances said $25,000 to start, probably a nice raise after the first year, and a darn good retirement, I consulted briefly with my feelings of unease about the future of the paper and said sure, and two weeks later there I was.

For a time, I continued my custom of getting the nuts-and-bolts work of producing the six-times-a-year AASSWB newsletter into print at the *News* office; I brought them the articles and headlines, as well as old-fashioned dummy sheets with the articles and photos penciled in, and the typesetters and print manager did the rest. But at the end of 1992 the sale to Worrell went through, and I found another printer.

I was pretty nervous about what amounted to changing my profession, although writing was writing. One worry was spending my days at a desk, when I was accustomed to being out and about. When I reported for my first day I was shown to what was essentially a cubicle, although it had high walls and was fairly private. The first shock was that I would be using an actual computer, not a Trash-80 but something with full-color graphics and infinite possibilities. The SE had limped along with a hand-me-down system that was already outmoded when it was installed, and at the *News* we handed pages done on manual typewriters to the typesetters.

The next unexpected development was that I would be traveling all around the country for meetings and conferences. Life opened up and I didn't look back much at all, thrilled when I caught sight of Mount Hood from a trolley in Portland, Oregon, or climbed to the cliff dwellings near Santa Fe, New Mexico. There was a world out there. Wherever I went, I saw the local papers, and found they were concerned and writing about the same issues as everyone else.

Not looking back included giving up a freelancing connection with another local publication, *Culpeper, the Magazine*. It was the brainchild of Donnie Johnston, the one-time sports editor and popular columnist who had worked for both newspapers. Once the *News* was sold, Donnie promoted his slick-cover magazine as the only locally owned and produced publication in Culpeper, and I was happy to be a contributor.

But in 1994 a headline in the still family-owned and high-quality Fredericksburg *Free Lance–Star* proclaimed "In Culpeper, chain makes another grab." The story noted that Worrell Enterprises was now part owner of the magazine. Donnie had told the *Free Lance–Star* only a few weeks earlier that an offer had been made, but he hadn't taken it. In the agreement he quickly reached, he said, Worrell would only sell advertising space and share in any profits. It wouldn't have a controlling interest, he declared firmly.

The Fredericksburg reporter, Amy Satterthwaite, got in touch with me and another former newspaper writer, Troy Elliott, who by then worked for the AASSWB and contributed to the magazine. Both of us had felt burned by Worrell and figured we were landing a blow for something or other by not working for a publication owned by what was becoming a major media conglomerate. I even had some regrettable cross words with Donnie when we ran into each other at the post office and he assured me that he would absolutely still be in charge. Not likely, I said, firm in my experience with media takeovers.

Well, I guess we showed them. Worrell went on to take over more papers, including the venerable *Richmond Times-Dispatch*, and eventually sold out for what no doubt amounted to a fortune. All the papers are now owned by Berkshire Hathaway, a part of the Warren Buffett empire, although their value in the changing world of media is debatable. There aren't many papers who haven't been touched by consolidation, and the end result is often closing down. That is what happened to the Manassas *Journal-Messenger,* in 2012. Digital news sources often step into the breach, but because they are on a suspect platform, I despair of them being able to be THE trusted news source.

As I was winding up this account, articles appeared in both the print papers we subscribe to announcing that BH Media Group had hired an organization called Lee Enterprises to manage Berkshire Hathaway's newspaper and digital operations in 30 markets, beginning pretty much immediately.

Lee (no connection I can find to the buyer of *Farm & Country*) was quoted in the news item as saying it would collect at least $25 million in fees over the five years of the contracted work, aimed at reducing costs for BH Media Group's papers.

It went on to note the benefit of "deploying Lee's successful strategies" at BH Media, and implementing "revenue initiatives." BH would continue to own the papers, and Warren Buffett himself said "I love our newspapers and am passionate about the vital role they serve in our communities." He also spoke of Lee's success in "faithfully fulfilling its public trust" as a source for information. Others involved in either BH Media or Lee spoke of combined efforts, markets and savings, and of the help that would be provided to the papers to "keep up with technology needs and centralize operations."

That may be the final chapter, or there may someday be a state media. At any rate, I hope the employees at these papers are prepared for the "nothing is going to change, keep doing your job" talk. It saddens me to even connect the words "successful strategies" and "revenue initiatives" to newspapers. All right, Women on the Go was a successful revenue initiative, so the ideas conveyed by the corporate speak weren't anything new.

All things considered, my career change was a good thing. I became communications director at ASWB as we added another writer, and then deputy executive director. My retirement account grew, and I enjoyed the work and the travel. It seemed fine and inevitable that I had moved on and abandoned journalism . . . until oh, say, 2016, when politics in my country went mad, and sometimes it seemed the only thing holding the democracy of the founding fathers together was journalism.

I grew up about four miles from Monticello, and along with most of Charlottesville I revered Thomas Jefferson, James Madison, and the rest. They pushed political thought past any known bounds and created something wonderful. I hadn't known how important the American experiment was to me until 2016.

Well, really, 2017. Of course, as a journalist I had been very firmly an uninvolved onlooker, and really had few opinions about party politics. I had always voted, though, and I had been concerned enough to join the Madison Democrats' phone-bank efforts in the Trump-Clinton election.

But I went to the Women's March in Washington the day after Trump was sworn in, although I am not by nature a joiner, and I felt it was right. I am also not by nature or habit a proponent of political argument, but the day before the march I heard Trump's inaugural speech on my car radio while I was driving my dog to the veterinarian. When I got there I immediately informed the somewhat bemused vet about what was wrong with Trump's horrible vision of America, and I was sorry I couldn't tell a bigger audience.

Our democracy was threatened, the legislative branch and now the executive branch were in chaos, and the judicial segment was barely holding the line. But the fourth estate was in there pitching, and I was so proud. Okay, by then I was seventy-three, and as a community journalist perhaps would not have been involved in the intrepid reporting that was being done. But other women were in there pitching—it wasn't being left to the male Woodwards and Bernsteins.

These people were, and are, engaging in David Remnick's "rigorous, deep, tireless and fearless" journalism, and Thomas Jefferson, despite his contradictions and his own elite background, had known clearly what was at stake. He knew good, unfettered reporting was the key to the survival of the marvelous thing that the colonies and a few brilliant men had created.

Not unlike Trump's tweets, there is a Jefferson quote for most any occasion. But unlike the tweets, there is wisdom in what TJ said. One such thought could be a mantra for our troubled times: "No experiment can be more interesting than that we are now trying, and which we trust will end in establishing the fact, that man may be governed by reason and truth. Our first object should therefore be, to leave open to him all the avenues to truth. The most effectual hitherto found, is the freedom of the press. It is therefore, the first shut up by those who fear the investigation of their actions."

The man could come up with a quote, and certainly he foresaw and expected the attempts to discredit the truth by calling it fake news. Mainstream journalism is not fake. People work very hard to see that it isn't, and if the people writing for the *Washington Post* and *New York Times* and *Roll Call* and *Madison Eagle* and *Culpeper Star-Exponent* and most television networks don't see conveying the news as a calling, my aging world view does indeed betray me—and is being betrayed.

Index

O

O'Bannon, Mrs. Maurice, 20
O'Halloran, Mrs. Thomas, 200
Olafsen, Brenda B., 91, 189
Orlando Sentinel, 6
Osborne, Tom, 158, 192, 195

P

Payne, Mary, 6
Pegues, John, 159
Penn, Clay, 203
Peters, Robert E., 21, 51, 127, 135, 157
Peterson, Joseph N., III, 98–99
Pettie, Marion, 177–80
Pettus, Pekay, 88
Phillips, Margaret, 84
Pink Ladies Follies, 48
Plevakis, Liz, 19
Posner, Howell, 200
Potomac News, 194
Potter, A. M., 8
Potter, Kay, 7–8, 87, 90, 183
Potter, Robert, 7
Potter, Walter B., 7, 61, 149, 183–84,
     187, 192–94, 199, 201
Potter, Walter B., Jr., 7–8
Presbyterian Church, Culpeper, 72
Prewoznik, Marge, 56
Pullen, Roxanne, 128
Purcell, Harold H., 17, 51, 123–24,
     126–27

R

Randall, Glen, 172
Rappahannock Electric
     Cooperative, 71
Rappahannock News, 14, 82
Rappahannock River, 153
Reams, W. D., Jr., 50, 58, 69
Reasoner, Harry, 98

Remnick, David, 182
Rennolds, Edmond, 162–63, 167, 197
Rental Uniform Service, 67, 157–58
Reynolds, John "Monk," 169–74, 176
Rhoades, Gary, 129
Richlands News-Press, 7
Richmond News Leader, 12, 66
Richmond Times-Dispatch, 27,
     52, 224
Ritz-Hi Hat Restaurant, 19
Robinson, J. Kenneth, 87, 189
Robinson, "Kit," 87
Robson, Betty, 159
Robson, Bev, 89
Rochester Ropes, 20
Rockwell, George Lincoln, 33–35,
     37–39
Roll Call, 118
Roper, Billy, 64
Rose, Lucy, 54
Ross, Martha, 79, 86
Runcible Spoon, 167

S

Safeway strike, 167
Salem Church Dam, 184
Saltonstall, Patricia, 144–45
Salubria, 102
Sandidge, Mrs. Brent, 12
Satterthwaite, Amy, 224
Saunders, Ray K., 99, 116, 171
Scott, John W., Jr., 136–38
Second National Bank, 169
Sehring, Adolf, 106–7
Seneff, Ed, 127
Shackelford, Carroll Kem, 86, 121–22
Shaw, Russell, 129–30
Shifflette, Samantha, 95
Showday, 170–72
Simms, Eckis, 83
Simpson, James, 129–30

Printed in the United States
By Bookmasters